GEOLOGIC TRIPS
Sierra Nevada

Please note these updates for the 2011 reprint:

pages 150 and 152: New phone number for both Emerald Bay State Park and D.L. Bliss State Park is 530-525-3345.

page 274: Current phone number for Lodgepole Visitor Center is 559-565-4436.
Current phone number for Kings Canyon Visitor Center is 559-565-3782.
Current phone number for Lodgepole Visitor Center is 559-565-4436.
Current phone number for Foothills Visitor Center is 559-565-4212.

page 278: Correct phone number for Boyden Cavern is 559-338-0959.

El Capitan, Yosemite Valley.

GEOLOGIC TRIPS
Sierra Nevada

Ted Konigsmark

GeoPress

Geologic Trips, Sierra Nevada

© 2002, 2007, 2011 by Ted Konigsmark
Second printing, January 2007
Third printing, June 2011

All photographs and illustrations are by the author unless otherwise credited.

The cover photograph is Upper Yosemite Fall, Yosemite Valley. (Photo by Marilyn Konigsmark.)

Use caution and common sense while on the geologic trips. Drive, park and hike safely. Do not go anywhere that you feel may be unsafe. The information contained in this book is correct to the best of the author's knowledge at the date of publication. Changes by man or nature can occur along any of the roads and hiking trails. The author and publisher assume no liability for accidents, injury, or any losses by individuals or groups using this publication.

Library of Congress Control Number: 2002094169

ISBN 0-9661316-5-7
ISBN-13: 978-0-9661316-5-9

Printed in the United States of America

GeoPress

Distributed by Bored Feet Press
Post Office Box 1832
Mendocino, CA 95460
(707) 964-6629, (888) 336-6199
www.boredfeet.com

To the many geologists and naturalists who have contributed to the geology of the Sierra Nevada. Without their work, this book would not have been possible.

CONTENTS

The scenic landscape of Yosemite Valley was sculptured out of hard granite by rivers and glaciers over the last five million years.

INTRODUCTION

The Sierra Nevada has had a profound influence on California. To thousands of pioneers, the mountains were viewed as the final barrier on their westward journey. To the forty-niners, the Sierra was envisioned as a source of gold and prosperity. Farmers saw the Sierra as the source of the water that made the Great Valley one of the most productive agricultural regions in the nation. The cities of Los Angeles and San Francisco coveted the Sierran water that would allow their populations to grow. The skier, hiker, fisherman, boater, rock climber, naturalist, caver, and tourist have all looked upon the Sierra as a convenient and scenic recreational opportunity.

To the geologist, the Sierra Nevada is a superlative outdoor geological laboratory. The well-exposed, easily accessible rocks have been studied by generations of geologists since the early days of the gold rush. Petrologists have analyzed the many varieties of granitic rocks that make up the core of the mountains. Mineralogists and structural geologists have worked on the bewildering and complex metamorphic rocks of the Sierra foothills. Seismologists, volcanologists, geophysicists, and hydrologists have investigated the rocks, faults and volcanic activity of the mountains. Economic geologists have examined the origin and distribution of the gold deposits. Stratigraphers have studied the Tertiary sedimentary and volcanic rocks that cover much of the northern Sierra. Geomorphologists have considered how the rivers and glaciers have shaped the valleys and mountains of the Sierra landscape. Through all of this work a geologic story has emerged that describes how and why the mountains were formed. The story is written in the rock, and is there to be seen – if you know what to look for. The story shows that these beautiful mountains had a surprisingly violent and complex early life - but more about that later.

Without the work of the hundreds of geologists who have studied the Sierra Nevada, this book would not have been possible. I have drawn freely on their work in preparing the book. If you are interested in more detail on the geology of the Sierra Nevada or the geology of any particular part of the Sierra Nevada, see the sections in the back of this book on Information Sources and References Cited.

Most everyone who has visited the Sierra has had questions about how the mountains, domes, lakes, and valleys were formed, and how the rocks were made. This book was written to help answer many of these questions and to provide the reader with a better appreciation of the geologic processes that have shaped the mountains.

The book is divided into three parts. Part I provides some basic geologic concepts that will be helpful to the nongeologist. Part II summarizes the geology of the Sierra Nevada and describes many geologic terms that help communicate the geologic story in a reasonably efficient manner. Part III describes the geologic trips. Each trip covers a different part of the Sierra Nevada and emphasizes a different aspect of the geology—the faults, volcanic rocks, granitic rocks, metamorphic rocks, gold, glaciers, rivers, and lakes. The nine trips together offer a good sample of the wide variety of geologic processes that have produced the mountain range.

All of the geologic sites described on the nine trips are on land that is open to the public. Most of the sites involve short, easy walks, although a few sites have short hikes. Most of the geologic sites are in scenic areas and have other attractions as well as the rocks. Allow time to enjoy the scenery and visit these other attractions.

Most of the geologic trips can be made by car and you will need at least a day or two for each trip, depending on your pace. The trips may be done in any order, but many areas are not accessible in winter. Check the weather and the road conditions before going.

PART I

GEOLOGIC BACKGROUND

GEOLOGIC TIME SCALE				
Era	**Period**	**Epoch**	**MY***	**Event** (Age, 100 yr man)
Cenozoic	Quaternary	Holocene	0.01	
		Pleistocene	2	
	Tertiary	Pliocene	5	Sierra uplifted (99.9)
		Miocene	24	
		Oligocene	36	
		Eocene	54	
		Paleocene	65	
Mesozoic	Cretaceous		144	Last dinosaurs (98.5)
	Jurassic		208	
	Triassic		245	First dinosaurs (95)
Paleozoic	Permian		286	
	Pennsylvanian		330	First amphibians (94)
	Mississippian		360	First jawed fish (93)
	Devonian		408	
	Silurian		438	
	Ordovician		505	
	Cambrian		570	First trilobites (88)
Pre-Cambrian			4600	

* **MY**, millions of years to beginning

THINKING LIKE A GEOLOGIST

Most of us deal with common objects that we can see, measure, feel, and count. We think in terms of inches, feet and miles. We think in terms of seconds, minutes, hours, days, weeks, years, and centuries. We think in terms of ounces, pounds and tons, and in terms of hard and soft, hot and cold. However, to understand the geologic processes that have formed the Sierra Nevada, you need to think like a geologist. This thinking is not difficult - just different. Here are some guidelines.

Geologic Time
A century may seem like a long time. However, geologists think in terms of millions and hundreds of millions of years. When you think in millions of years, enormous changes can take place even with very slow geologic processes. If you compare the 4.6-billion-year age of the earth to the age of a 100-year-old man, the oldest rocks in the Sierra Nevada were formed when he was 90 years old, the granite was intruded into the core of the mountains when he was 98 years old, and uplift of the Sierra block occurred about a month before his 100th birthday. A geologist must think in years the way an economist thinks in dollars—millions and billions.

Thinking Big
A mountain range such as the Sierra Nevada may seem large, and the rocks that make up the mountains may appear hard and brittle. Indeed, granite, limestone, and many of the other rocks of the Sierra are used as building stones. However, at a scale of miles rather that inches and feet, these seemingly strong and brittle rocks can easily bend and break. One must think big, and recognize that the rocks that make up the earth behave in a different manner when viewed on a large scale.

Although upward and downward movements of the earth's surface of 30 or more miles may seem large, these movements are not large when compared to the size of the earth. If the earth were the size of a basketball, an uplift of 30,000 feet on the earth's surface would be equivalent to the thickness of a sheet of paper on the surface of the basketball, a slight imperfection on the basketball.

Living on a Dynamic Earth

Although the earth may seem like a large chunk of hard rock, it is quite different. The earth is dynamic. The rocks that make up the earth are constantly moving. Parts of the earth's crust are being uplifted and other parts are subsiding. Some continents are being torn apart and others are colliding. The movement of the continents is caused by heat that is churning and moving the rocks deep within the earth. But why are these rocks so hot?

The only cool rocks on earth are those within a few miles of the surface. From the surface, the rocks get hotter with depth. At a depth of about 60 miles, the rocks are so hot that they behave like warm plastic and flow at very slow rates. This heat is generated by decay of radioactive elements within the rocks. Since rocks are not good conductors of heat, the heat builds up deep in the earth. The inner solid core and outer fluid core of the earth consist of iron and nickel and are extremely hot. The inner core and outer core are in motion, and rotate at a slightly different rate from the overlying mantle. The plastic-like rocks in the mantle are also in motion, and circulate in huge convection cells that reach from the core of the earth to the crust. These convection cells move the overlying brittle crust, tearing the crust apart over rising currents and carrying the crust downward into the mantle along descending currents. As the crust moves, new mountain ranges are formed in some places, and new ocean basins in other places. The geologist sees the oceans and mountains as temporary. Fortunately, these changes take place slowly. If you watched the surface of the earth in fast-forward on a VCR, you would need a seat belt, and you would be in for a wild and unexpected ride.

Erosion and Deposition

Most rocks are formed deep within the earth where the temperature and pressure is very high. When these rocks are uplifted and exposed at the earths surface, they are suddenly attacked by rivers, waves, plants, animals, ice, wind, and rain. The rocks are also altered chemically. Some minerals combine with the oxygen and hydrogen at the surface to form new minerals. Other minerals simply do not like the low temperatures and pressures at the surface, and change into minerals that are stable at surface conditions. Although humans like the surface of the earth, most rocks are uncomfortable at the surface and rapidly break down in this harsh environment.

When rocks break down by mechanical and chemical processes at the earth's surface, they form smaller clastic fragments – boulders, pebbles, sand, silt, and clay. Rivers carry these *sediments* to low spots on the earth's surface and deposit the sediments in *sedimentary basins*. Over millions of years, entire mountain ranges can be worn down by weathering and erosion, until the mountain range is worn to a flat surface near sea level. The sediments that were eroded from the mountains accumulate in sedimentary basins. Sedimentary basins tend to subside as the sediments accumulate, and each new layer of sediment is piled on top of the previous layer of sediment. Over time, piles of sedimentary rocks can accumulate in these basins to thicknesses of tens of thousands of feet. The Great Valley is a large sedimentary basin that has accumulated thousands of feet of sediments that have been eroded from the Sierra Nevada.

Reconstructing the Past

When looking at the rocks exposed in a roadcut, on a mountainside, or along a river, try to erase, in your mind, the present landscape. When the rocks were formed, the landscape was completely different. Look at the rocks and let them tell you what the landscape was like when the rocks were formed. If you are looking at limestone formed in some tropical sea, imagine yourself floating in the warm water of that ocean. If there are several different types of rocks in an outcrop, each type of rock may tell a different story. The rocks changed as the landscape changed. To understand the geologic history of the area, the geologist must piece these stories together, like reading an old tattered book with many missing pages.

The Evolving Landscape

The landscape that we see today - the hills, peaks, lakes, sea cliffs, and valleys - are formed from rocks. These rocks are being attacked by various erosional and weathering processes. The shape of the landform depends on the type of rock that is exposed and on how the present weathering and erosion processes are working on the rock. When you look at a mountain, lake, or valley, ask yourself several questions. What kind of rock is responsible for the feature? Are the rocks hard or soft? Are they fractured or massive? Are they being attacked by ice, rain, wind, or by chemical weathering? How is the landform changing? What will it look like in a short time - say a few thousand years? See, now you are thinking like a geologist.

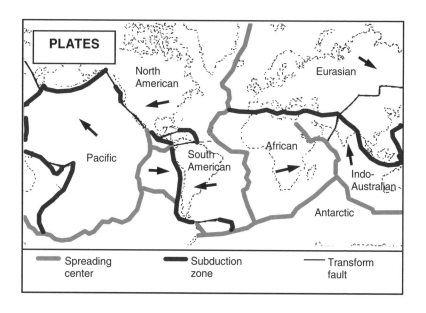

PLATES

North American
Eurasian
Pacific
South American
African
Indo-Australian
Antarctic

| Spreading center | Subduction zone | Transform fault |

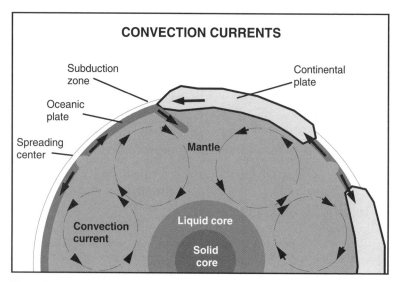

CONVECTION CURRENTS

Subduction zone

Continental plate

Oceanic plate

Spreading center

Mantle

Convection current

Liquid core

Solid core

The surface of the earth is covered by a dozen or so large rigid plates. These plates are carried in different directions by convection currents within the earth's mantle. The movement of the plates and the deformation of the rocks along the plate boundaries are referred to as plate tectonics.

PLATE TECTONICS

For many decades prior to the 1970's, the granitic and metamorphic rocks of the Sierra Nevada had been mapped and described by generations of geologists. Despite all this work, there was no good unified explanation as to how these rocks were formed. There were also many unanswered questions about how and why the mountains were uplifted, and how the gold got into the Mother Lode. In the late 1960's and early 1970's the theory of plate tectonics began to evolve. This theory provided a very welcome basis for understanding the rocks, structure, and mineral deposits of the Sierra Nevada. The plate tectonic theory is relatively simple, although there are many complexities in the details. However, before getting into the theory, let's briefly review the composition of the earth. The composition of the earth provides the driving mechanism for plate tectonics.

The earth is composed of three major units: the *core, mantle* and *lithosphere*. If the earth were an egg, the core would be the yoke, the mantle would be the white of the egg, and the lithosphere would be the thin, hard, brittle shell. The core is mainly an alloy of iron and nickel. The inner part is solid and the outer part liquid. The solid inner core is about the size of the moon, and forms about 15% of the earth's volume.

The mantle consists of heavy dark *ultramafic* rocks that are rich in iron, magnesium, silicon and oxygen. These rocks make up about 84% of the earth's volume. The rocks of the mantle are hot and behave like warm plastic that moves very slowly. The heat is generated by decay of radioactive elements within the rocks. Rocks are not good conductors of heat, so the heat builds up deep within the earth. This excess heat causes the heavy plastic-like rocks of the mantle to slowly circulate in huge convection cells that reach from the core of the earth to the lithosphere. This convection helps move the heat from the interior of the earth to the exterior. The hot parts of the mantle rise and the cool parts descend. The convecting mantle tries to drag the overlying lithosphere in the direction of the current, like the scum on the surface of hot tea. The convection currents of the mantle are the driving force for plate tectonics. These currents act on the overlying lithosphere in some surprising ways.

The earth's lithosphere is about 50 miles thick. These rocks are cool and rigid. Like the shell of an egg, these rocks tend to break rather than flow. The lower part of the lithosphere is the same composition as the mantle. The upper part consists of *oceanic crust* under the oceans and *continental crust* under the continents. Between the lithosphere and the mantle is a zone of hot rock called the *asthenosphere*. The asthenosphere forms a thin mobile lubricating layer upon which the rigid rocks of the lithosphere float and move.

According to the theory of plate tectonics, the earth's lithosphere is broken into about a dozen major plates. Each plate is independent from the other plates, and moves in response to the convection currents in the mantle. The convecting mantle pulls the overlying plate in the direction that the current is moving. Where rising convection currents diverge under the lithosphere, they pull the overlying plates apart. Where descending currents converge, they cause the overlying plates to collide. Convection currents may also move past one another horizontally and drag adjacent plates in opposite directions. The plates act somewhat like huge icebergs carried by the underlying water currents, bumping and scraping and splitting apart.

The rocks in the edges of the plates take most of the abuse while the plates are moving, and these rocks are deformed in different ways depending on whether the plates are being pulled apart, are colliding, or are slipping by one another. *Spreading centers* form where plates pull apart, *subduction zones* form where plates collide, and *transform faults* form where plates slip by one another horizontally. The plate movements take place at a slow rate. Most of the plates move at about two inches per year. Although this rate sounds slow, over time, plates can travel thousands of miles.

Spreading Centers

Spreading centers form where rising convection cells spread out horizontally and pull the overlying plates in opposite directions. The hot rocks in the earth's mantle move upward into the area between the spreading plates and these rocks melt due to the lower pressure near the surface. The molten rock forms a magma chamber along the spreading center a mile or so below the earth's surface. From time to time the magma flows out from the magma chamber onto the sea floor and solidifies as basalt. As the plates continue to move apart, new basalt flows out at the spreading center and the older basalt moves away from the spreading center in opposite directions, as if the basalt were on diverging conveyer belts. The ocean floor thus becomes larger and

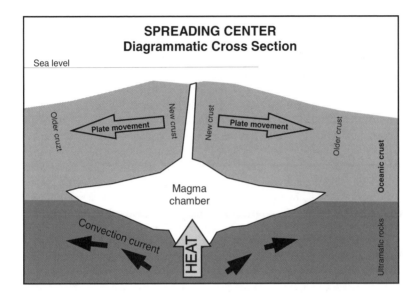

larger as spreading continues. The newer basalt forms at the spreading center, and the older basalt is carried away from the spreading center.

This process of manufacturing ocean floor at spreading centers has been going on for hundreds of millions of years and is still in progress. The rift valleys of Africa represent an early phase of spreading. The African continent is now being torn apart along these rift valleys. If this spreading continues, the African rift valleys will soon become a small ocean basin, similar to the Red Sea. With further spreading, this small ocean basin will become larger, like the Atlantic Ocean, perhaps eventually as large as the Pacific. All of the world's major ocean basins have been formed by sea floor spreading. The oceanic crust that is formed in this manner is typically about five miles thick and forms the upper part of the lithosphere under the oceans.

New ocean floor is typically formed along spreading centers at rates of from one to five inches per year. If you translate these spreading rates into geologic time, it is obvious that enormous areas of sea floor have been manufactured in relatively short periods of time. At an average spreading rate of two inches per year, a spreading center would manufacture 32 miles of ocean floor in one million years or 3,200 miles of ocean floor in 100 million years. An entire ocean basin as large as the Pacific could easily be formed within 200 million years.

Subduction Zones

Most of the metamorphic and granitic rocks that make up the core of the Sierra Nevada were formed in a series of subduction zones. Subduction zones occur where convection currents in the earth's mantle cause the overlying plates to collide and one plate is carried beneath the other plate. What happens during this collision depends on whether the colliding plates consist of oceanic crust or continental crust. Plates with continental crust are relatively light, whereas plates with oceanic crust are relatively heavy. In a collision between continental and oceanic plates, the lighter continental plate tends to override the heavier oceanic plate. The continental plates are light because the rocks that make up the continental crust are rich in the lighter elements - silicon, aluminum, sodium and potassium. The oceanic plates are heavy because they are rich in the heavier elements, mainly iron and magnesium. The continents rise above the oceans because they are made up of lighter rocks and float on the earth's mantle, as marshmallows float on a cup of cocoa. Oceanic crust also floats on the mantle rocks, but since the oceanic rocks are relatively heavy, the oceanic crust floats at a lower level.

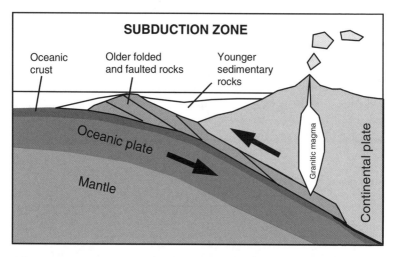

Subduction zones are formed along the collision zones between plates. In this subduction zone an oceanic plate is being subducted below a continental plate. Granitic magma is being formed by melting of the rocks in the subduction zone. Some of the granitic magma is making its way to the surface to form a volcano, and some will cool more slowly below the surface to become granite.

There are three major types of subduction zones: a continental plate may collide with an oceanic plate; two oceanic plates may collide; or two continental plates may collide. Each type generates different rocks and has a different expression on the surface of the earth. This is what happens in each case:

1) Where an oceanic plate collides with a continental plate, the heavier oceanic plate is *subducted* under the lighter continental plate. This subduction process thickens the lithosphere in the subduction zone. The thickened lithosphere rises isostatically and forms a chain of mountains. Most of the world's major mountain ranges, such as the Alps, Andes, and Cascades, have been formed in this manner. Earthquakes also occur along the subduction zones, caused by the rubbing of the plates as one plate is carried beneath the other. When the subducted oceanic plate reaches a depth of 50 miles, the serpentine in the lower part of the plate loses its water and reverts to peridotite. The water, in the form of an extremely hot supercritical fluid, rises into the mantle and melts the mantle to make basalt magma. The basalt magma rises into the overlying crustal rocks and partially melts them to form granitic magma. The granitic magma is lighter than the surrounding rocks and continues to rise into the upper plate as a bulbous mass. If the magma reaches the surface, it erupts as a volcano, like Mt. Rainier and Lassen Peak. The magma that doesn't reach the surface forms large magma chambers in the continental plate several miles below the surface. This magma cools slowly and crystallizes into granite. The granite of the Sierra Nevada batholith was formed in this manner. Over time, this process has formed the light granitic rocks that make up the world's continents.

2) Where two oceanic plates collide, one plate is subducted below the other, the lithosphere is thickened, and an island arc is formed. Most of the rocks in oceanic plates are heavy, so the mountains formed along the island arcs are not high. The earthquakes are of moderate size, and the igneous rocks that are formed are intermediate in composition. The Caribbean Islands and Aleutian Islands are examples of island arcs formed along collision zones between oceanic plates.

3) Where two continental plates collide, one continental plate is forced below the other. Since both plates consist of thick and light rocks, the crust is abnormally thick along these subduction zones, resulting in very high mountains. The Himalayan Mountain range was formed in this manner.

Transform Faults

Where convection currents cause one plate to slip by another plate horizontally, the zone along which this movement takes place is called a *transform fault*. These faults transform plate movement from one spreading center to another. A spreading center such as the East Pacific Rise is not a single continuous break in the earth's surface, but instead, consists of a number of spreading segments connected by transform faults. Since each side of the transform fault is on a different plate, each side moves in an opposite direction. At an average rate of a couple of inches per year, the total amount of lateral movement can be large, as much as 300 miles in 10 million years.

Most transform faults are on oceanic plates and therefore not easily seen. However, some transform faults cut across continents. The San Andreas fault is a large transform fault that cuts across south and central California. Although there are no transform faults in the Sierra Nevada today, there may have been a number of these faults in the past. Many of the terranes within the Western Metamorphic Belt may have come to the Sierra Nevada courtesy of one or another of these old transform faults.

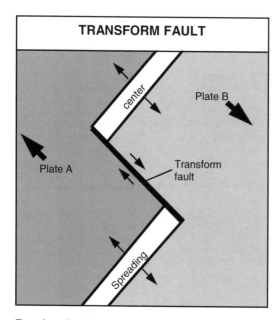

Transform faults form the connecting links between spreading centers and transform plate movement from one spreading center to another. Plates move past each other horizontally along transform faults.

Terranes

Continental plates are constantly being torn apart and moved by convection cells. Broken pieces of the continents may be carried hundreds or even thousands of miles. Eventually, these pieces are swept into a subduction zone somewhere and plastered onto the margin of a larger plate. These broken pieces of continents are called *terranes*. All of our continents are made up of numerous terranes that have been patched together like a crazy quilt. The continents are being recycled.

California is made up of a number of terranes that have been accreted to the western margin of North America over the last several hundred million years. Sonomia was added about 375 million years ago and Smartville about 225 million years ago. The Franciscan rocks were added to North America about 175 million years ago. These terranes were carried northward and eastward to North America by plate movement and then left at the western doorstep of North America like a heap of discarded mice. Some of these terranes are separated by *suture zones* that consist of pieces of oceanic crust that were squeezed between the larger terranes.

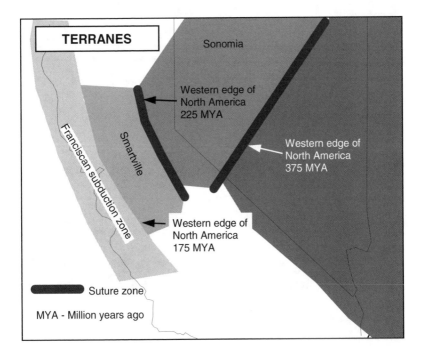

TERRANES

Sonomia

Western edge of North America 225 MYA

Western edge of North America 375 MYA

Franciscan subduction zone

Smartville

Western edge of North America 175 MYA

Suture zone

MYA - Million years ago

At Buckeye Flat, in Sequoia National Park, the South Fork of the Kaweah River flows across steep-dipping, contorted, dark gray metamorphic rocks. At the top of the cascade, the river follows a bend in these folded rocks.

PART II

GEOLOGY

of the

SIERRA NEVADA

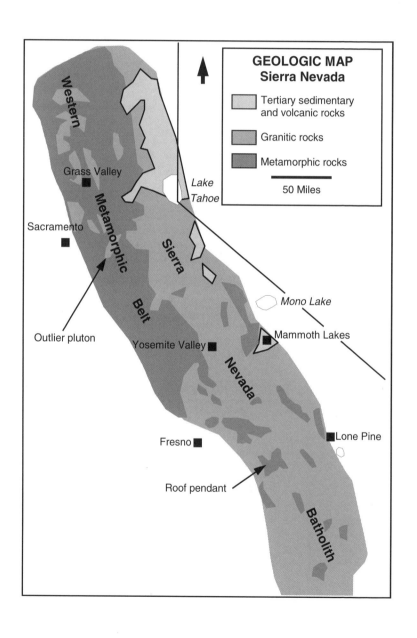

GEOLOGIC MAP
Sierra Nevada

Tertiary sedimentary and volcanic rocks

Granitic rocks

Metamorphic rocks

50 Miles

Western

Metamorphic

Sierra

Belt

Nevada

Batholith

Grass Valley

Sacramento

Outlier pluton

Yosemite Valley

Fresno

Lake Tahoe

Mono Lake

Mammoth Lakes

Lone Pine

Roof pendant

GEOLOGIC MAP

If you were to remove all of the vegetation and soil from the Sierra Nevada, you would get a clear look at the rocks that make up the mountains. Of course, that's a bit drastic, so the geologist must try to "see" below the soil and vegetation, and picture what rocks are present. In doing this, geologists have prepared maps that show the different types of rocks that occur in the Sierra Nevada. The accompanying simplified geologic map shows the distribution of these rocks.

The granitic rocks of the Sierra Nevada batholith form the core of the mountain range. The most extensive exposures are in the southern and central Sierra, and the outcrop belt narrows to the north. A number of outlier plutons of granitic rocks also intrude the rocks of the Western Metamorphic Belt.

Most of the metamorphic rocks of the Sierra Nevada occur in the northern and central foothills in a wide northwest-trending band of rocks commonly referred to as the Western Metamorphic Belt. These rocks are mainly metamorphosed sedimentary and volcanic rocks of Paleozoic and Mesozoic age. Large patches of metamorphic rocks also occur as roof pendants within the granitic rocks of the Sierra Nevada batholith.

In the northern Sierra, the granitic rocks of the Sierra Nevada batholith and the rocks of the Western Metamorphic Belt are covered in many areas by sedimentary and volcanic rocks of Tertiary age. These Tertiary rocks include river gravels of Eocene age and sedimentary and volcanic rocks of Oligocene and Miocene age. These Tertiary rocks once covered most of the Sierra Nevada, but most were removed during the Plio-Pleistocene uplift of the mountains. During this uplift, there was also a large amount of volcanic activity along the eastern slope of the range. Volcanic rocks that were formed at that time cover much of the area around Mammoth Lakes.

Now that you know the distribution of the Sierran rocks, we'll next take a more detailed look at how these rocks were made.

ROCKS OF THE SIERRA NEVADA

Type		Name	Locality
Granitic		Granite Granodiorite Quartz monzonite	Yosemite Tuolumne Meadows Southern Sierra Tahoe Area
Mafic		Diorite Diabase Gabbro	Mother Lode Northern Sierra
Ultramafic		Peridotite Serpentine	Mother Lode Northern Sierra
Volcanic	Lava flows	Rhyolite Andesite Basalt	Mammoth Area Mono Lake
	Volcaniclastic	Tuff Lahar	Northern Sierra
Sedimentary	Clastic	Sandstone Gravel Conglomerate Shale Limestone	Northern Sierra
	Chemical precipitate	Chert Tufa	Mother Lode Mono Lake
Metamorphic		Slate Phyllite Schist Greenstone Marble Hornfels	Mother Lode Northern Sierra Roof Pendants

Composition of the Earth

Element (Percent)	Element (Percent)
Iron (34.6)	Nickel (2.4)
Oxygen (29.5)	Aluminum (1.9)
Silicon (15.2)	Titanium (0.05)
Magnesium (12.7)	Other (3.65)

ROCKS OF THE SIERRA NEVADA

The geologic map shows that most of the Sierra is made up of four main types of rocks - granitic, volcanic, sedimentary, and metamorphic. Each of these can be further broken down into many different specific rocks. A basic understanding of these rocks is necessary for understanding the geology of the range. The rocks tell us how and when the mountains were formed. They also determine the shape and color of the mountains and valleys. Some of the rocks even carry valuable minerals like silver and gold. And some rocks are decorative and just nice to look at.

Fortunately, out of the dozens of different rocks that make up the Sierra, just a few are really common. These rocks are described in more detail in the following pages. Each of these rocks was formed in a different manner and has its own characteristics of color, hardness, grain size, and mineral content. When you become familiar with these rocks, you'll do just fine during your geologic trips in the Sierra Nevada. But don't necessarily try to learn all of the rocks now. With the accompanying table you can easily look up and identify the rocks during your geologic trips.

Granite is one of the most common rocks in the Sierra Nevada. The white grains with sharp edges are feldspar. Irregular patches of light gray quartz fill spaces between the feldspar crystals. The dark grains are biotite and hornblende.

Rock-forming Minerals

All of the granitic, volcanic, sedimentary and metamorphic rocks that you will see in the Sierra are formed from minerals. The minerals are the building blocks of the rocks, and usually appear as grains in the rock, giving the rock a granular texture. Some rocks consist of grains of a single mineral, whereas other rocks are composed of grains of several different minerals. Like pieces of fruit in a fruit cocktail, the minerals in each of these rocks can be distinguished by their color, shape, hardness, and other physical and chemical characteristics. But what are minerals?

Minerals are composed of elements that are combined in a regular crystalline structure. The elements in the mineral behave like soldiers standing in formation. Each soldier stands in a specific spot relative to the other soldiers, based on rank, file and organization. Similarly, each element in a crystal has a specific spot where it stands relative to the other elements, and has closer ties to some elements than to others.

As you know, there are about 100 elements on earth. These elements can combine in many different ways to form hundreds and hundreds of different minerals. However, of all these hundreds of minerals, there are only a dozen or so that are common rock-forming minerals. These are briefly described on the accompanying table. Most of these minerals are silicates that contain various proportions of sodium, potassium, aluminum, calcium, iron, and/or magnesium. The few minerals listed in this table are the major components of most all of the granitic, volcanic, sedimentary, and metamorphic rocks that you will see in the Sierra. If you can recognize these few minerals, you will be well on your way toward identifying and understanding most all of the rocks you will see in the Sierra.

By knowing what minerals are in a rock, the composition of the minerals, and the size and shape of the mineral grains, it is possible to tell much about how the rock was formed. Each mineral forms only under very specific conditions of temperature, pressure, and chemical composition. Minerals with a high content of iron, magnesium, and/or calcium generally form at high temperatures, whereas minerals with high content of silica, sodium, potassium, and aluminum crystallize at relatively low temperatures. Large crystals take a long time to develop, usually from magma that cools slowly deep in the earth. Small crystals form more rapidly, usually from magma that chills rapidly on or near the earth's surface. Some minerals even tell us how old they are. If the mineral contains radioactive elements, the age of the mineral can be determined based on the known rate of radioactive decay. It seems that

COMMON ROCK-FORMING MINERALS	
Quartz	Glassy; hard; conchoidal fracture; common in sedimentary, igneous and metamorphic rocks; usually granular when constituent of rocks, but may form clear six-sided crystals; SiO_2.
Plagioclase feldspar	Light to dark gray; hard; flat cleavage; very common in igneous rocks; (Na,Ca)Al silicate.
Potassium feldspar	White, pink; hard; flat cleavage; commonly twinned, prism-shaped crystals or granular; common in igneous rocks with high silica content; KAl silicate.
Muscovite	White mica; highly perfect cleavage; breaks into thin elastic plates; common in granite and many metamorphic rocks; water-bearing KAl silicate.
Biotite	Black mica; also brown or dark green; flat flakes, single perfect cleavage; common in many metamorphic and igneous rocks; water-bearing K(Mg,Fe) Al silicate.
Hornblende	Dark greenish-black elongated and striated crystals; occurs in many igneous and metamorphic rocks; water-bearing (Ca,Na) (Mg,Fe) (OH_2) Al silicate.
Pyroxene	Black, green, brown; short eight-sided crystals or granular masses; occurs mainly in diorite, gabbro, basalt, andesite; (Mg,Fe) (Ca,Na) Al silicate.
Olivine	Yellowish green to olive green; glassy rounded grains; no cleavage; occurs in gabbro, peridotite and basalt; crystallizes at high temperature; (Mg,Fe) silicate.
Clay	Fine-grained; feldspar typically alters to clay when exposed to weathering; water-bearing Al silicate.
Calcite	White; soft; occurs in many sedimentary and metamorphic rocks; $CaCO_3$.
Common accessory minerals	Sphene: yellow or brown crystals in granite; CaTi silicate. Garnet: red crystals in metamorphic rocks; Ca,Mg,Fe,Al silicate. Pyrite: yellow crystal; all types of rock; FeS_2. Zircon: crystallizes as tetragonal prisms; various colors; $ZiSiO_4$.

we know more about some rocks than we do about many of our closest friends. We know what temperatures they like, how much pressure they can stand, how long it takes them to cool off, and we even know how old they are.

Now that you're familiar with these common rock-forming minerals, let's take a more detailed look at the rocks that you will see during your trips to the Sierra. As you will see, most of these rocks are identified by the types and proportions of their component minerals.

Granitic Rocks

As seen on the geologic map, granitic rocks are widely exposed in the core of the Sierra Nevada. These rocks are typically light-colored, granular, and coarse-grained. They consist of a mixture of quartz, plagioclase feldspar, and potassium feldspar, with lesser amounts of biotite, hornblende, and other minerals. These minerals crystallized from magma that cooled deep within the earth's crust, generally at depths of from three to six miles. At these depths, the magma cooled slowly, so there was sufficient time for large crystals to form. If you look at a granitic rock with a magnifying glass, you can see the sharp edges and flat surfaces of many of these crystals.

Prior to crystallization, the molten rock in the magma chamber was a mixture of ions of silicon, oxygen, aluminum, calcium, sodium, potassium, iron, and magnesium. These ions moved around in the magma in a disorganized manner, like soldiers circulating in the gathering area for a parade. As the magma cooled, the parade began, with iron and magnesium in the lead. The iron and magnesium quickly found some calcium and aluminum and grabbed all the silicon and oxygen that they needed. Having formed their unit, they left the gathering area as crystals of pyroxene and hornblende. After their departure, the magma was richer in the remaining elements and continued to cool. Next, plagioclase feldspar and potassium feldspar formed their units. They used up most of the remaining calcium, sodium, potassium and aluminum, and took as much silicon and oxygen as they wanted. After a while, only silicon and oxygen remained. Finally, at relatively low temperatures, the silicon and oxygen joined to form quartz. Since quartz was the last mineral to crystallize, the quartz had to squeeze between the earlier crystals.

As shown below, there are several types of granitic rocks, depending on the relative proportions of quartz, plagioclase, and potassium feldspar. Although the term *granite* technically refers to a specific rock, as indicated in the table, geologists also use the term to loosely refer to all of these related granitic rocks.

GRANITIC ROCKS		
Granite	Light gray, coarse grained; equal proportions of quartz, plagioclase and potassium feldspar.	Yosemite
Granodiorite	Similar to granite, but less potassium feldspar and more plagioclase feldspar.	Yosemite Tuolumne M. Sequoia
Quartz monzonite	Similar to granite, but less quartz.	Lake Tahoe Alabama Hills

Mafic and Ultramafic Rocks

Ultramafic rocks are dark and heavy because they are rich in iron and magnesium-bearing minerals such as pyroxene, olivine, and serpentine. These rocks form most of the earth's mantle and the lower part of the earth's oceanic crust. In the Sierra Nevada, most of the ultramafic rocks occur as irregular bands and layers of pyroxenite and serpentine in the metamorphic rocks of the Western Metamorphic Belt. The Feather River Belt and the Smartville Complex have extensive exposures of these heavy dark rocks.

The ultramafic rocks of the Western Metamorphic Belt represent slices of the earth's mantle and oceanic crust that were caught up in one or another of the subduction zones that bordered North America during much of Paleozoic and Mesozoic time. In subduction zones, most of the heavy ultramafic rocks are subducted and carried below the continental crust. However, in the Western Metamorphic Belt, some of these rocks were tacked onto the edge of the continent rather than being subducted.

Mafic rocks differ from ultramafic rocks mainly in that they contain plagioclase feldspar in addition to pyroxene and olivine. The most common mafic rocks in the Sierra Nevada are gabbro and diabase. These rocks are the same composition as basalt, but differ in that gabbro is coarse-grained and crystallized at depths of several miles in the earth's crust, diabase is fine-grained and crystallized at shallow depths, and basalt is a very fine-grained and solidified from a lava flow.

MAFIC AND ULTRAMAFIC ROCKS		
Mafic: dark colored; typically contain plagioclase feldspar and pyroxene.		
Diorite	Medium gray; composition between granite and gabbro.	North American Wall of El Capitan
Diabase	Dark gray; fine grained; same composition as gabbro, but crystallized at shallow depth in earth's crust.	Western Metamorphic Belt
Gabbro	Dark gray; coarse grained; large crystals; crystallized at great depth in the earth's crust.	Western Metamorphic Belt
Ultramafic: very dark colored; consist mainly of pyroxene and olivine.		
Peridotite	Heavy; dark; coarse-grained; little or no feldspar.	Western Metamorphic Belt
Serpentine	Green; breaks along shiny, smooth, curved surfaces; slippery; waxy.	Melones fault Goodyear Bar

Volcanic Rocks

Volcanic rocks are formed when magma erupts from a vent on the surface of the earth. Since volcanic rocks cool rapidly, they are mostly fine grained. Some volcanic rocks also contain a few large crystals of feldspar, hornblende, or other minerals. These *phenocrysts* represent crystals that began to form early in the magma.

Most volcanic rocks occur as *lava flows* or as *volcaniclastic* rocks. Lava flows are formed when magma is extruded from the vent as a flow of molten rock. In contrast, volcaniclastic rocks are formed when particles of solid volcanic rock are expelled from the vent. Although there are many different types of volcanic rocks, virtually all of these rocks were formed from basaltic, andesitic, or rhyolitic magma. Each type of magma results in a different type of volcanic rock.

Basalt magma is very fluid and typically forms widespread flows of black fine-grained lava. Basalt is rich in iron and magnesium, and has the same composition as gabbro. On land, lava flows often develop columnar jointing as they cool. When extruded under water, basalt magma typically forms pillow basalt.

Andesite has the same composition as diorite, intermediate between basalt and rhyolite. Andesite is fairly viscous and typically occurs as short flows of volcanic rubble. Many volcanoes are composed of layers of andesite rubble and tuff. Latite is intermediate between andesite and rhyolite, and has phenocrysts of plagioclase and potassium feldspar.

Rhyolite is the same composition as granite, and is found only in continental areas. Rhyolite magma is very viscous and typically oozes from a vent like toothpaste. Most rhyolite is light-colored and fine-grained. If the rhyolite magma has no water content and chills very rapidly, the rhyolite may solidify as dark glassy obsidian. If there is sufficient gas in the magma, the rhyolite can form frothy layers of white pumice. Rhyolite magma typically forms plugs, short steep-sided flows, and volcanic domes.

In many volcanic eruptions, volcanic rocks are thrown from the vent into the air as a shower of volcanic ash. The ash is usually rhyolitic in composition. When volcanic ash falls to the ground and becomes consolidated into a rock, the rock is referred to as tuff. Coarse tuff is usually deposited near the volcano, often forming a rim around the vent. Tuff can also be deposited in water, where it may be stratified and form various slumping features. Very fine volcanic ash may be carried by the wind and deposited as a thin layer that can extend hundreds of miles

VOLCANIC ROCKS		
Lava flows: formed when magma flows from a vent at the earth's surface.		
Rhyolite	Light colored, fine-grained; occurs as volcanic plugs, domes, and short steep-sided flows. May also occur as dark glassy obsidian or white frothy pumice.	Panum Crater North Coulée Obsidian Dome Big Pumice Cut
Andesite	Red, brown, and yellow volcanic rubble; fine-grained; often has phenocrysts of plagioclase and dark minerals.	Mammoth Mtn.
Basalt	Occurs as flows of black fine-grained lava. Forms columnar jointing on land and pillow basalt under water.	Devils Postpile
Volcaniclastic rocks: clastic rocks composed of volcanic material of any volcanic origin.		
Ash	Volcanic ash is composed of particles of solid volcanic rock ejected into the air from a volcano. Air-fall ash refers to ash deposited from the air. An ash flow is formed from a hot gaseous glowing cloud of volcanic material extruded from a volcano. A welded tuff is formed if the hot fragments of an ash flow weld together.	Big Pumice Cut Owens Gorge Soda Springs Chile Gulch Panum Crater Big Bear Lake
Tuff	Tuff is a general term that includes all consolidated pyroclastic rocks.	As above
Lahar	A mudflow of volcanic ash and other volcanic debris; can cover hundreds of square miles.	Mokelumne Hill (Mehrten Fm.)

from the vent. Eruptions of ash are formed when a volcanic vent is plugged by viscous rhyolitic magma and steam builds up under the plug until the volcano explodes.

In some eruptions, volcanic ash flows from the vent as an incandescent cloud of hot gaseous particles. The particles in these ash flows are kept in suspension by gas expelled from the fragments. If the ash flow is thick and cools slowly, the fragments can weld together, forming a welded tuff.

Volcanic ash from a new eruption is sometimes mixed with rainwater and forms mud flows, called lahars. Lahars can travel tens of miles.

Sedimentary Rocks

There are two main types of sedimentary rocks: clastic and chemical precipitate. Clastic sedimentary rocks are composed of particles of preexisting rocks. Typical clastic sedimentary rocks include sandstone, conglomerate, gravel, shale, and limestone. These rocks contain clastic fragments of various sizes and compositions. The clastic fragments were carried by streams and rivers, and deposited in river channels, lakes, and in the ocean. Thousands of feet of sedimentary rock can accumulate in active subsiding sedimentary basins such as the Great Valley. When the deeper layers of sediment are subjected to high heat and pressure, they become consolidated. Sand becomes sandstone and mud becomes shale. When sedimentary rocks accumulate in a sedimentary basin, the oldest sedimentary layers are at the base of the stack, since they were deposited first, and the youngest layers are at the top.

Sedimentary rocks may also form by precipitation of chemicals from supersaturated water. Salt precipitates from sea water, chert from water saturated with SiO_2, and tufa from water saturated with $CaCO_3$.

Metamorphic Rocks

Most of the metamorphic rocks in the Sierra Nevada occur in the Western Metamorphic Belt. Some metamorphic rocks also occur as roof pendants within the Sierra Nevada batholith. Metamorphic rocks are formed when pre-existing rocks are subjected to high heat and/or pressure. At high temperatures and/or pressures new minerals are formed from the previous minerals in the rocks. At low grades of metamorphism, only some minerals are altered, and the identity of the original rock is still apparent. At very high grades of metamorphism, all traces of the original rock may be obliterated. At very high temperatures, the original rock may be remelted and become an igneous rock. Nature thus has its own way of recycling rocks.

Most metamorphism occurs in subduction zones, where sedimentary and volcanic rocks are carried to depths of up to 30 miles. Rocks at these great depths are subjected to very high pressures and temperatures, and many of the minerals in the rocks are altered under these conditions. Sandstone may be changed into quartzite, shale into phyllite and schist, and limestone into marble. Fine-grained rocks altered mainly by high temperatures, usually near granitic intrusions, are referred to as *hornfels*. Metamorphosed sedimentary rocks are often referred to as *metasedimentary rocks* and metamorphosed volcanic rocks are commonly referred to as *metavolcanic rocks*.

SEDIMENTARY ROCKS

Clastic: composed of particles of preexisting rocks.

Sandstone	Yellow or gray; hard; feels sandy and rough. Consists of sand grains cemented to a hard rock.	Gold Run Malakoff D.
Gravel	Similar to sandstone, but clastic fragments are gravel-sized. Fragments mainly consist of quartz or various types of granitic, volcanic, or metamorphic rocks.	Gold Run, Malakoff D.
Conglomerate	Similar to gravel, but fragments are larger, about the size of walnuts and oranges.	Gold Run Malakoff D.
Shale	Dark gray; soft; smooth; breaks into platy fragments. Composed of mud or clay cemented into rock by burial.	
Limestone	Gray; most limestone is composed of fragments of sea shells cemented together; fragments may be fine or coarse; $CaCO_3$.	Crystal Cave

Chemical precipitate: composed of minerals precipitated from supersaturated water.

Chert	Red, black; hard; smooth. Composed of silica precipitated from water. Most red chert was precipitated from silica-rich sea water in the vicinity of spreading centers. Other colors of chert precipitated from silica-rich ocean water or silica-rich groundwater.	Western Metamorphic Belt
Tufa	White; chemical precipitate of $CaCO_3$ from hot volcanic water.	Mono Lake

METAMORPHIC ROCKS

Slate	Dark gray; platy; very fine-grained. Metamorphosed mudstone.	Mariposa Slate
Phyllite	Dark gray; platy; fine grained; silky sheen. Similar to slate but more highly metamorphosed.	Western Metamorphic Belt
Schist	Gray; platy; large crystals; flakes of mica. Highly metamorphosed sandstone and shale.	Ladies Canyon
Greenstone	Green; fine- to coarse-grained. Metamorphosed pillow basalt and other volcanic rocks.	Western Metamorphic Belt
Marble	Light gray; mostly fine-grained. Metamorphosed limestone.	Crystal Cave
Hornfels	Dark; hard; non-foliated. Formed at intrusive contacts.	Ellery Lake

SIERRA NEVADA BATHOLITH

The granitic rocks that form the backbone of the Sierra Nevada are part of the large Sierra Nevada batholith. This batholith is not just one homogenous body of granite. Instead, it is made up of over one hundred individual *plutons.* Each pluton covers an area of from one to several hundred square miles and represents a separate intrusion of magma. Although most plutons are distinguished by their composition and age, plutons may have many other distinct characteristics. Some plutons are fine grained, some are coarse grained, and some have large phenocrysts. Some plutons have layering or segregation of the minerals. And some plutons have dark blobs, called *xenoliths,* formed when parts of the intruded roof or wall rock were assimilated in the magma. The plutons may also be cut by dikes of lighter or darker rocks. These dikes are usually formed during the final stages of crystallization when the last magma is injected into cracks in the previously crystallized parts of the pluton. Thus, there are many things to look for when you see granitic rocks, and many ways to distinguish one pluton from another.

Most of the granitic plutons of the Sierra Nevada were intruded from 80 to 150 million years ago, during the period of greatest subduction within the Franciscan subduction zone. At that time, the Franciscan subduction zone was located along the present-day Coast Ranges and the Farallon plate was being carried eastward into the subduction zone. Much of the Farallon plate consisted of oceanic crust and serpentine. As the rocks were carried deep into the subduction zone, high temperatures drove the water out of the serpentine. The water, which was a supercritical fluid at these high temperatures and pressures, rose into the overlying rocks and melted the rocks to form magma. The magma was lighter than the surrounding rocks, and rose within the crust. As the magma rose, it mixed with the silica-rich rocks of the crust and formed the silica-rich magma that resulted in the Sierra plutons. Most plutons were emplaced at depths of around six miles in the earth's crust, but there is evidence that some plutons were emplaced at depths of as much as twenty miles. The granite formed at these great depths is now exposed at the surface, indicating that the Sierra Nevada has been uplifted several miles, and that great thicknesses of overlying rock have been removed by erosion.

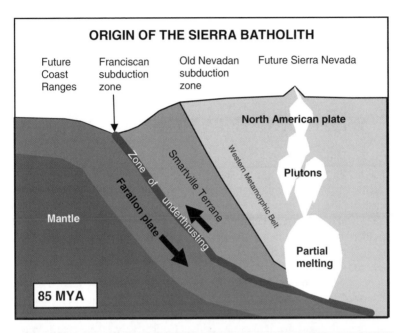

ORIGIN OF THE SIERRA BATHOLITH

Future Coast Ranges

Franciscan subduction zone

Old Nevadan subduction zone

Future Sierra Nevada

North American plate

Zone of underthrusting

Smartville Terrane

Western Metamorphic Belt

Farallon plate

Mantle

Plutons

Partial melting

85 MYA

The large rectangular grains in this photo are phenocrysts of potassium feldspar in the Cathedral Peak Granodiorite on Pothole Dome. The granodiorite was polished by glaciers during the last glacial episode. The hard phenoncrysts have retained the polish whereas most of the other minerals in the granodiorite have decomposed and lost their polish.

WESTERN METAMORPHIC BELT

The Western Metamorphic Belt is a broad band of metamorphic rocks that lie on the west side of the Sierra Nevada batholith and extend northwest for 200 miles through the foothills of the central and northern Sierra. The south end of the belt, near Mariposa, is about 30 miles wide and the belt thickens northward to about 60 miles in the northern Sierra. The belt is divided into three major rock units that also trend northwest. The Shoo Fly Complex lies on the eastern side of the belt, the Calaveras Complex forms the center, and the Foothills Terrane is on the western side. Each of these rock units is bounded and separated from the other units by large faults. Some of these faults extend the entire length of the metamorphic belt. The rocks within each unit are also cut by numerous faults. Collectively, these faults are known as the *Foothills fault system.*

The rocks of the Western Metamorphic Belt were deposited during Paleozoic to Jurassic time in a series of subduction zones that existed along what was then the western margin of North America. The subduction activity ended in late Jurassic time when all of the rocks of the metamorphic belt were subjected to a brief but intense period of deformation and metamorphism, referred to as the Nevadan orogeny. During this orogeny, the rocks in the metamorphic belt were squeezed, faulted, folded, metamorphosed, and added to the western margin of North America. After these rocks were added to the continent, the new margin of North America was along the western border of the Great Valley, and the new Franciscan subduction zone formed in what is now the Coast Ranges of California.

There are many different types of rocks in the metamorphic belt, including schist, slate, phyllite, greenstone, serpentine, chert, marble, and quartzite. These rocks have been faulted, folded, metamorphosed, and intruded by granite and other igneous rocks. Thus, the rocks of the Western Metamorphic Belt are extremely complex, and unraveling the geologic secrets of the metamorphic belt has been a long and difficult task for geologists. Nonetheless, based on the work of these geologists, a general picture has emerged of how the rocks in the metamorphic belt

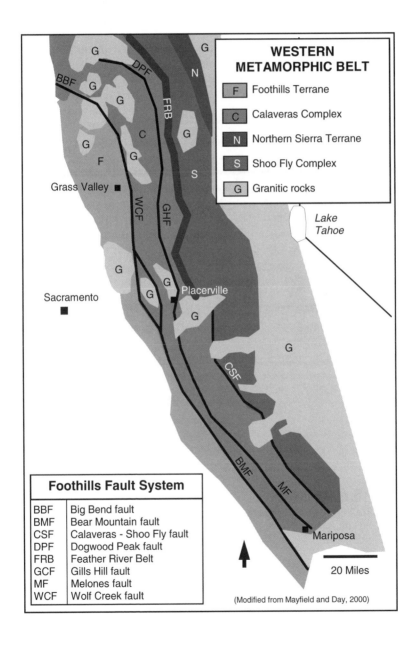

(Modified from Mayfield and Day, 2000)

were formed. Needless to say, this picture is subject to change as more information is squeezed from the rocks in the continuing work on the metamorphic belt.

The rocks and faults of the Western Metamorphic Belt all dip steeply to the east. This east dip can be seen almost everywhere that the rocks are exposed. In this stack of east-dipping metamorphic rocks, the oldest rocks, the Shoo Fly Complex, lie to the east, and are on the top of the stack. The youngest rocks, the Foothills Terrane, are on the west side of the belt and on the bottom of the stack. This is the opposite of what we normally see in sedimentary rocks. In layered sedimentary rocks, the oldest rocks are on the bottom of the stack and the youngest rocks on top. The reversal of the rocks in the Western Metamorphic Belt occurred as a result of subduction. When each new rock unit was carried into the subduction zone, it was inserted under the rocks that were already in the subduction zone. The east-dipping rocks thus piled up like pancakes on an east-tilted platter. However, on this platter, the newest pancakes were inserted under the pancakes that were already on the platter. To get a fresh pancake from this platter, you would need to take it from the bottom of the stack.

Within the Western Metamorphic Belt there are a number of plutons of granitic and mafic rocks that have been intruded into the metamorphic rocks. Some of these plutons are outliers of the Sierra Nevada batholith and others represent magma chambers for the volcanic arcs that formed at various times along the continental margin. There are also many fault slices of serpentine and other ultramafic rocks within the Western Metamorphic Belt. These ultramafic rocks represent pieces of oceanic crust that were torn off in the subduction zone. Serpentine also occurs along many of the faults of the Foothills fault system. This serpentine represents pieces of oceanic crust that were squeezed into and along the fault zones during the subduction process.

Shoo Fly Complex

The rocks of the Shoo Fly Complex are the oldest rocks in the metamorphic belt. They consist mainly of metamorphosed sedimentary rocks that were derived from the North American plate and deposited on the oceanic crust to the west. In mid-Devonian time, these rocks were subjected to a major period of subduction and mountain building known as the Antler orogeny. The Antler orogeny was brief and intense. During this period, the rocks of the Shoo Fly Complex were compressed, metamorphosed, cut by numerous thrust faults, intruded by igneous rocks, uplifted, and eroded.

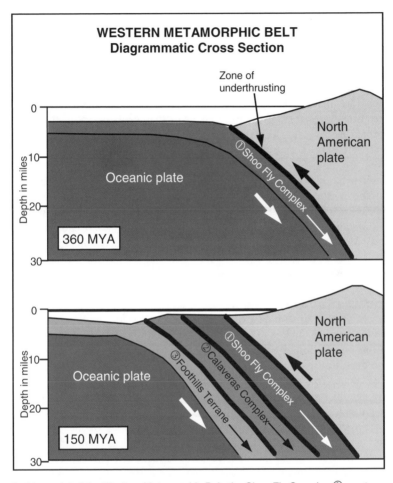

In this model of the Western Metamorphic Belt, the Shoo Fly Complex ① went into the subduction zone first, followed by the Calaveras Complex ② and the Foothills Terrane ③. During Cretaceous time, the rocks in the subduction zone were uplifted and eroded. Rocks that had been buried at depths of 30 miles or more were eventually exposed at the surface.

In the northern Sierra, the rocks of the Shoo Fly Complex are covered by several thousand feet of volcanic and volcaniclastic rocks known as the Northern Sierra Terrane. These rocks were derived from a series of island arcs that formed along the margin of the North American plate during late Devonian to Mesozoic time. The Sierra Buttes near Sierra City are formed from these rocks, and the rocks are also well exposed at Big Bear Lake, north of Sierra City.

Calaveras Complex

In mid-Devonian time, after the Antler orogeny, the margin of the North American plate was immediately west of the Shoo Fly Complex and a subduction zone was present west of the continental margin. The rocks of the Calaveras Complex accumulated in this subduction zone. These rocks are mainly black and green slate, schist, and greenstone. The greenstone was formed from basalt and other volcanic rocks that had erupted at spreading centers. The slate and schist represent sediments that were deposited in deep ocean trenches. Other rocks of many types were brought into the subduction zone from the west by plate movement. Many of these rocks were mixed together by faulting and folding in the subduction zone and now form a tectonic mixture of limestone, chert, basalt, and pieces of oceanic crust. The lubricant for this *melange* is mainly the clay that was deposited on the ocean floor. In early Mesozoic time, the rocks of the Calaveras Complex were added to the western margin of North America, and the stage was set for deposition of the Foothills Terrane.

Foothills Terrane

In late Triassic time, the Nevadan subduction zone formed to the west of the Calaveras Complex. The rocks of the Foothills Terrane accumulated in this subduction zone until the beginning of the Nevadan orogeny in late Jurassic time. The Foothills Terrane is mainly phyllite, slate, and greenstone. This rock unit also contains the well-known Mariposa Slate, which consists of platy black slate and serves as the host rock for many of the gold deposits of the Mother Lode. Another important rock unit, the Smartville Complex, occurs in the northern part of the Foothills Terrane. The Smartville Complex consists of a large slab of oceanic crust that was carried into the Nevadan subduction zone and thrust on top of the rocks that were already in the subduction zone. It is unusual to find exposures of oceanic crust such as this in continental areas.

Foothills Fault System

The Foothills fault system includes a number of major northwest-trending faults that cut through the rocks of the Western Metamorphic Belt. Several of these faults extend for tens of miles, and some extend for the entire length of the metamorphic belt. These faults separate the rocks of the Western Metamorphic Belt into many discrete fault-bounded units. Following is a brief description of some of the most important faults.

The Calaveras-Shoo Fly fault is the easternmost of the major faults and separates the Calaveras Complex from the Shoo Fly Complex. In the northern Sierra, the Calaveras-Shoo Fly fault bifurcates and becomes a thick zone of complexly faulted rocks referred to as the Feather River Belt. The Feather River Belt contains many ultramafic rocks. These rocks represent the remains of a large ocean basin that was carried into the subduction zone and squeezed between the Shoo Fly Complex and the Calaveras Complex.

The Melones fault cuts through the rocks of the Calaveras Complex. The fault dips steeply eastward and is marked by intensely sheared rocks, quartz veins, and lenses of serpentine. The shattered rocks along this fault are also impregnated with many different minerals, including gold, copper, zinc, and lead. The large gold deposits along the Mother Lode closely follow this fault from Placerville to Mariposa. Although the Melones fault is well-defined in the southern and central parts of the metamorphic belt, the fault splays to the north, and there is some uncertainty concerning its counterpart in the northern Sierra.

The Bear Mountain fault is the westernmost of the major faults. Along this fault, the rocks of the Foothills Terrane were thrust eastward under the rocks of the Calaveras Complex. In the northern Sierra, this fault is known as the Wolf Creek fault. The gold deposits in the Grass Valley area occur in fractured rocks near this fault.

The serpentine in this roadcut near Goodyears Bar is green, smooth, and has a waxy luster. The grooves on the surface of the serpentine were formed during movement of the serpentine in the subduction zone.

ROOF PENDANTS

The granitic rocks of the Sierra Nevada batholith are responsible for many of the best known scenic features in the range. However, not all of the glory goes to the granite. In many parts of the Sierra, there are large spectacular black and red mountains with steep ridges, spires, and cliffs. These mountains represent *roof pendants* of metamorphosed rock that are surrounded by the granitic rocks of the Sierra Nevada batholith. The roof pendants sit in the batholith like plums in a pudding, and add a little mystery and pizzazz to the geology of the Sierra.

The roof pendants are the remains of the Paleozoic and early Mesozoic rocks that once covered the magma chambers of the Sierra Nevada batholith. As the roof rocks were intruded by the granite, heat from the intrusions metamorphosed the overlying rocks. Most of these metamorphosed rocks were eroded and removed when the mountains were uplifted during Cretaceous and Tertiary time. The roof pendants occur in areas where the roof rocks were especially hard or thick, or where they formed deep roots between plutons.

The roof pendants include rocks of either Paleozoic or Mesozoic age. Good examples of the Paleozoic roof pendants can be seen in a string of mountains from Tioga Pass to Big Pine. These roof pendants have rocks from all of the Paleozoic periods. The oldest rocks are of Lower Cambrian age and occur in the Big Pine Roof Pendant. The Mt. Morrison Roof Pendant, a few miles north of the Big Pine Roof Pendant, has 32,000 feet of hornfels, chert, marble, slate and quartzite. These rocks provide a near-complete record of deposition in this area during Paleozoic time. Some of these Paleozoic rocks were deposited at the same time as the rocks of the Shoo Fly Complex in the Western Metamorphic Belt. Unmetamorphosed equivalents of many of these Paleozoic rocks occur in the Inyo and White Mountains to the east.

The Mesozoic roof pendants are well-exposed in a trend of mountains from Mt. Dana south to the Ritter Range. The Triassic and Jurassic volcanic rocks in these roof pendants reflect volcanic activity associated with the Nevadan subduction zone. The roof pendants of Cretaceous volcanic rocks were largely formed during intrusion of the Sierra Nevada batholith and reflect volcanic activity associated with the Franciscan subduction zone.

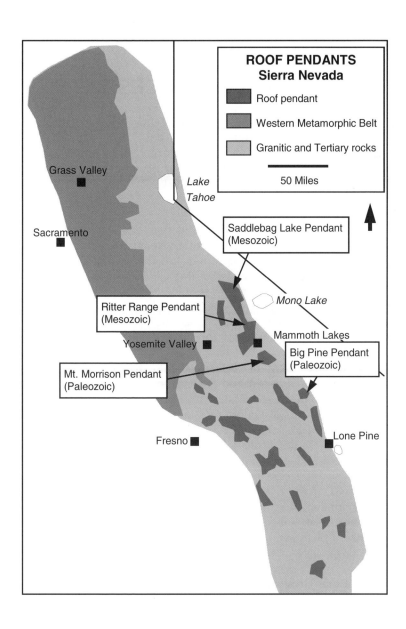

ROOF PENDANTS
Sierra Nevada

Roof pendant

Western Metamorphic Belt

Granitic and Tertiary rocks

50 Miles

Grass Valley

Lake Tahoe

Sacramento

Saddlebag Lake Pendant
(Mesozoic)

Mono Lake

Ritter Range Pendant
(Mesozoic)

Yosemite Valley

Mammoth Lakes

Big Pine Pendant
(Paleozoic)

Mt. Morrison Pendant
(Paleozoic)

Fresno

Lone Pine

TERTIARY ROCKS

As seen on the geologic map, most of the Tertiary rocks lie along the crest of the Sierra Nevada north of Lake Tahoe. These are mainly soft volcanic and sedimentary rocks, and are a small remnant of the Tertiary rocks that once covered most of the northern Sierra Nevada. Let's take a look at how these Tertiary rocks were formed.

Eocene Erosion Surface

During most of Cretaceous and Paleocene time, the Sierra Nevada was the site of a large mountain range that extended into Nevada and covered an area much larger than the present-day Sierra Nevada. The crest of these ancestral mountains was far east of the crest of the present-day Sierra. As the ancestral mountains were uplifted, they were also being eroded. Most of the erosion products from these ancestral mountains were carried into the Great Valley, where they formed thick layers of sedimentary rocks that now underlie much of the Great Valley.

By Eocene time, uplift of the ancestral Sierra had slowed down. However, erosion continued, and the ancestral mountains were deeply eroded to form a low range of hills with a gentle rolling landscape. This Eocene land surface was drained by a series of large rivers that flowed west into the Great Valley. Many of these rivers had their origin in Nevada, far to the east of the present-day Sierra rivers. Since this land surface was formed during Eocene time, it is generally referred to as the Eocene erosion surface. This erosion surface is marked in many areas by a thick zone of red soil that was formed by weathering in a humid climate during the long period of Eocene erosion. The Eocene erosion surface and its red soil are preserved in many places in the foothills of the northern Sierra and can be see along much of Highway 49 from Placerville through Auburn to Camptonville.

Eocene River Gravels

As described above, the low rolling hills of the Eocene erosion surface were drained by several large rivers that flowed west and northwest and emptied into the ocean that occupied the Great Valley at that time. Although these Eocene rivers had different courses from the present-day

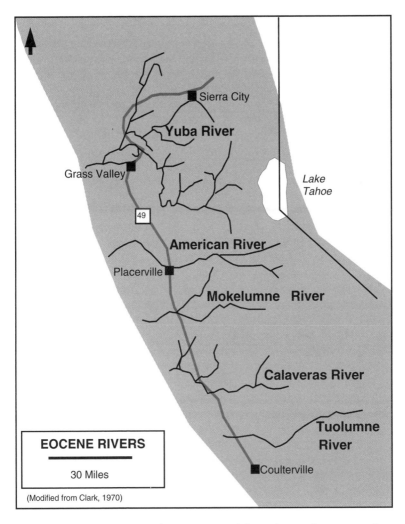

EOCENE RIVERS

30 Miles

(Modified from Clark, 1970)

rivers, most of the Eocene rivers are named from the nearby present-day rivers. From north to south, the major Eocene rivers are the Yuba, American, Mokelumne, Calaveras, and Tuolumne. Since these rivers had their headwaters east of the present-day Sierra and could not flow uphill to cross the Sierra, it is apparent that uplift of the present-day Sierra occurred after Eocene time.

We know much about these Eocene rivers, because the gravel in many of these rivers contained gold, and this gold has been extensively mined. You can see some of these gold mines at Gold Run on I-80 and at the Malakoff Diggins in the northern Sierra.

Valley Springs Formation

During Oligocene time there was intense volcanic activity in the Sierra Nevada and surrounding areas. Although the present-day Sierra had not yet been uplifted, a number of the volcanic centers lie along what is now the crest and east slope of the Sierra Nevada. Great quantities of tuffs and lava flows were ejected from these volcanic centers. Most of these rocks were rhyolitic in composition. This volcanic material rapidly covered the Eocene river gravels and filled the Eocene river valleys. These early Tertiary rhyolitic volcanic rocks are commonly referred to as the Valley Springs Formation. There are good exposures of the Valley Springs Formation near Sugar Bowl on the west side of Donner Pass.

Mehrten Formation

During Miocene time, volcanic material continued to be ejected from volcanic centers along the crest of the Sierra. Eventually, the central and northern Sierra Nevada was covered with a thick blanket of andesitic volcanic rocks known as the Mehrten Formation. These rocks include andesite conglomerates, welded tuffs, lava flows and lahars. While the Mehrten Formation was being deposited, new river channels were formed from time to time in the thick blanket of volcanic rocks that covered the Sierra. The positions of these channels changed often as the old channels were clogged by new volcanic rocks.

By late Miocene time, the Eocene erosion surface had been buried under a thick blanket of the sedimentary and volcanic rocks of the

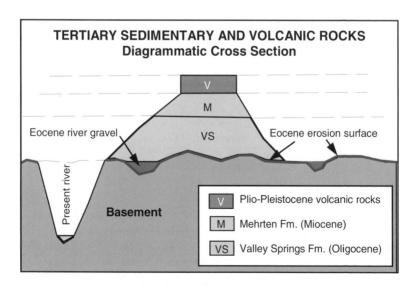

TERTIARY SEDIMENTARY AND VOLCANIC ROCKS
Diagrammatic Cross Section

Eocene river gravel

Eocene erosion surface

Present river

Basement

V	Plio-Pleistocene volcanic rocks
M	Mehrten Fm. (Miocene)
VS	Valley Springs Fm. (Oligocene)

Valley Springs and Mehrten Formations. When uplift of the present-day Sierra began in Pliocene time, the Tertiary rocks began to be rapidly eroded. The Tertiary rocks were soft and easily removed from the Eocene erosion surface. The Tertiary rocks that remain are mainly found along the ridges and crest of the northern Sierra, where erosion has not yet reached the soft rocks.

Plio-Pleistocene Volcanic Rocks

Volcanic rocks of Plio-Pleistocene age occur in many places along the eastern slope of the Sierra Nevada from Bishop to Mono Lake, and also in the area north of Lake Tahoe. Most of these volcanic rocks occur along faults and fractures that were formed during the Plio-Pleistocene uplift of the Sierra Nevada. The crustal rocks were weak in these intensely faulted areas and magma from deep in the earth worked its way to the surface along these weak rocks. The volcanism began in late Pliocene time and continues to the present day. The volcanic rocks erupted from volcanoes, domes, and fissures, and include basalt, rhyolite, obsidian, pumice, tuff, and ash. There are excellent exposures of these rocks in the Mammoth and Mono Lake areas.

This cliff at the Malakoff Diggins is formed from Eocene river gravel that was deposited in a channel of the Eocene Yuba River. The cliff has been exposed by hydraulic mining for the gold in gravel. Note the layers of coarse river gravel exposed in the cliff.

UPLIFT OF THE SIERRA NEVADA

If you had visited the Sierra Nevada five million years ago, you would have been disappointed. There was no high mountain range, just an area of low hills that extended eastward into Nevada, and a thick blanket of Tertiary sedimentary and volcanic rocks covered the northern part of these hills.

Uplift of the present-day Sierra Nevada began about five million years ago, in early Pliocene time. At that time, a large piece of the earth's crust began to be uplifted and tilted westward along a series of faults that cut through the earth's crust. The amount and timing of this uplift is recorded in the Tertiary sedimentary and volcanic rocks of the northern Sierra. These Tertiary rocks, which had been deposited at low elevations, were uplifted with the Sierra block. Based on their present elevation and tilt, it has been determined that the southern part of the Sierra has been uplifted about 10,000 feet and the northern part about 5,000 feet.

The uplift of the Sierra block is probably related to the formation of the Basin and Range province of Nevada and Utah. For the last 15 million years, the earth's crust under Nevada has been stretched and thinned, probably by convection currents. This crustal stretching began in central Nevada, and worked its way to the east and west from there. As the crust was stretched, it was broken into a jumble of large north-trending blocks. The blocks that remained high became mountain ranges and the low blocks became basins. These basins and ranges now form the Basin and Range province of Nevada and Utah.

About five million years ago, this crustal stretching reached eastern California. Large blocks of crust broke along faults and collapsed to form the Owens Valley, Mono Basin, Lake Tahoe basin, and a number of other basins. As these blocks collapsed, the Sierra Nevada block was uplifted and tilted to the west. The Sierra block was an unusually large block, and included the Great Valley. As the eastern part of this Sierra block was uplifted to form the Sierra Nevada, the western part was depressed to form the Great Valley.

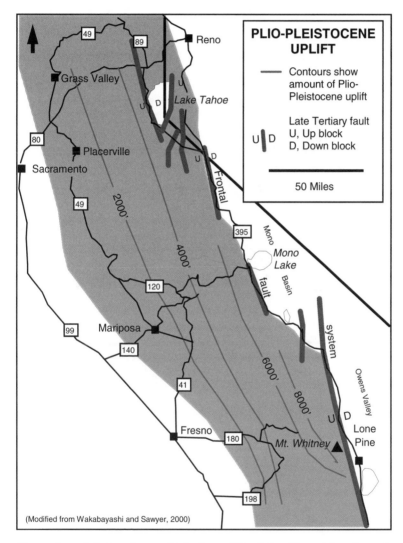

PLIO-PLEISTOCENE
UPLIFT

— Contours show
amount of Plio-
Pleistocene uplift

Late Tertiary fault
U, Up block
D, Down block

50 Miles

(Modified from Wakabayashi and Sawyer, 2000)

The series of faults along which the uplift of the Sierra Nevada took place is known as the Frontal fault system. Although several of these faults are long and well-defined, many are short and discontinuous. Uplift of the Sierra block was transferred from one fault to another along this complex zone of faulting.

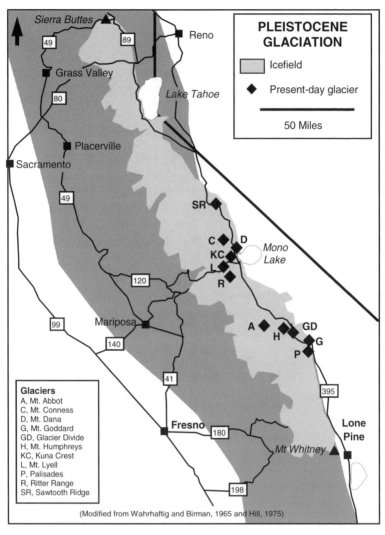

PLEISTOCENE GLACIATION	
▢	Icefield
◆	Present-day glacier
———— 50 Miles	

Glaciers
A, Mt. Abbot
C, Mt. Conness
D, Mt. Dana
G, Mt. Goddard
GD, Glacier Divide
H, Mt. Humphreys
KC, Kuna Crest
L, Mt. Lyell
P, Palisades
R, Ritter Range
SR, Sawtooth Ridge

(Modified from Wahrhaftig and Birman, 1965 and Hill, 1975)

GLACIAL EPISODES
Sierra Nevada

Glacial episode	Years before present
Tioga	19,000-26,000
Tahoe	70,000-150,000
Sherwin	about 1,000,000
McGee	about 1,500,000

GLACIATION

During the last two million years, glaciers have covered the high country of the Sierra Nevada a number of times. The glaciers carved mountains into new shapes, deepened and steepened valleys, formed hundreds of lakes and waterfalls, and left mounds of clay, sand, gravel, and boulders scattered throughout the Sierra. Glaciers have had a profound affect on the landscape of the Sierra Nevada, and the results of their work can be seen almost everywhere in the mountains.

Four major episodes of glaciation are generally recognized in the Sierra Nevada. From oldest to youngest, these are the McGee, Sherwin, Tahoe, and Tioga. During each episode, a thick sheet of glacial ice covered the high country from Mt. Whitney north to the Sierra Buttes. The areas that were covered by these icefields have been stripped of their soil cover, leaving fresh rocks exposed. The landscape in these areas is dotted by lakes that were scoured by the ice and punctuated by craggy peaks that once poked through the icefield.

Many rivers of ice spread out from the icefield. To the west, glaciers flowed down the valleys of the Kings, San Joaquin, Merced, Tuolumne, Stanislaus, Mokelumne, American and Yuba Rivers. To the east, the icefield sent tongues of ice over the crest of the Sierra and down many of the steep canyons of the eastern slope, such as Lee Vining Creek, Rush Creek, McGee Creek, and the Truckee River valley.

During each glacial episode, the icefield and the glaciers pulsated with numerous advances and retreats. At the end of each glacial episode, the glaciers retreated up their respective valleys into the icefield, and then the icefield melted. As the glaciers and icefield melted, they deposited mounds of rock that had been carried in and on the ice. These *moraines* of glacial debris have been used to sort out the glacial history of the Sierras. This has been a complex job. The moraines have no fossils, so it is difficult to accurately date the moraines and to correlate the moraines on the east side of the Sierra with those on the west side. In addition, each glacial episode removed and redistributed the earlier moraines. Just bits and pieces of the early moraines remain. Most of the moraines we see today are from the last glacial episode, the Tioga.

Glacial Erosion and Deposition

A glacier is like a thick river of ice moving slowly down a valley at several inches to several feet per day. The glacier is fed by snow that accumulates in an *icefield* at the head of the valley. The snow turns into ice as it is buried by new snow. Over time, the ice in the icefield can accumulate to thickness of up to several thousand feet. After reaching a critical thickness, the ice flows from the icefield under its own weight, like cold molasses. As the glacier moves down the valley, it scrapes the rocks along the floor and walls of the valley. If the rocks are soft, it gouges out the rocks and leaves indentations in the floor and walls of the valley. If the rocks are hard, the glacier polishes and smoothes the rough edges of the rocks. If the rocks are hard and jointed, the glacier quarries the jointed blocks. As the rocks are removed along the path of the glacier, the walls of the valley become steeper and the floor of the valley becomes wider, giving the valley a "U" shape. As the sides of the valley are steepened, the lower courses of tributary rivers are cut off, leaving the truncated valleys hanging from the sides of the main valley. If some of the rocks in the glaciated valley are soft and some are hard, the glacier will remove the soft rocks, leaving a depression in the valley floor that may later be filled by a lake. Some glacial valleys have a staircase of benches formed when the glacier quarried rocks along vertical and horizontal joints. Other valleys have a chain of lakes, where the lake basins have been cut from the softer rocks. Glaciers on the flanks of the higher mountains carve amphitheaters, called *cirques*. Small lakes, called *tarns*, are commonly scooped out of the rocks at the base of the cirque.

As the glacier scrapes and cuts into the rocks in its path, it carries the rock that has been removed and deposits the rock where the ice melts. The rocks left behind by the glacier are of many different sizes, including clay, silt, sand, gravel, and boulders. Rocks deposited by a glacier are referred to as *till*. Some till ends up in piles of rocks deposited at the end of the glacier or along the sides of the glacier. These piles of till are called *moraines*. *Lateral moraines* are formed along the sides of the glacier. The rocks deposited at the end of the glacier are called *terminal moraines*. Successive piles of till deposited at the end of the glacier while it is retreating are called *recessional moraines*. During retreat, a glacier is simply melting faster than it is advancing. *Medial moraines* form where two valley glaciers join and their lateral moraines coalesce. Terminal and recessional moraines can dam the water in the valley, forming a moraine-dammed lake. Large boulders carried by the glacier and left behind after the glacier melted are called *erratics*.

By the end of the last glacial episode, the Tioga, all of the glaciers in the Sierra Nevada had completely melted. Since then, there have been several periods during which small glaciers have formed on the higher peaks. These glaciers have advanced and retreated during historic time, in response to variations in historic climate.

Presently, there are about 80 glaciers in the Sierra Nevada. These are all on the east or northeast sides of mountain peaks and at elevations greater than 10,500 feet. The largest of these is the Palisade glacier, which covers about one-fourth of a square mile. Another well-known glacier is the Mt. Dana glacier on the northeast side of Mt. Dana south of Tioga Pass.

The polish on this granite at Olmstead Point was formed during Pleistocene glaciation when a thick icefield moved across this area. Most of the polish has been destroyed by weathering in the 10,000 years since glaciers melted, but some patches like this remain. Striations on the polished surface indicate the direction of ice movement. This patch is about a foot long.

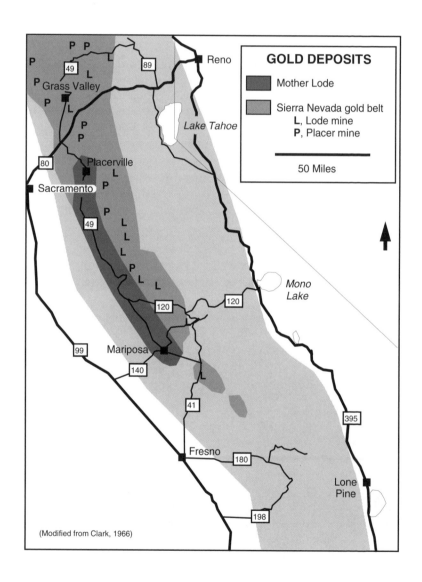

GOLD DEPOSITS

Mother Lode

Sierra Nevada gold belt
L, Lode mine
P, Placer mine

50 Miles

Reno

Lake Tahoe

Grass Valley

Placerville

Sacramento

Mono Lake

Mariposa

Fresno

Lone Pine

(Modified from Clark, 1966)

THE SIERRA NEVADA GOLD BELT

When gold was discovered at Sutter's mill in Coloma on January 24, 1848, there were less than 15,000 people in California, not counting Native Americans. The gold rush began shortly after this discovery. Gold mining at that time was not particularly high-tech. Because gold is heavy and commonly occurs in the native form, it is easily separated from sand, gravel, and other host rock using various agitating and collecting devices, usually with water. At the beginning of the gold rush, all that was needed was a gold pan and a good eye to pick up the gold— or so it was thought. Four months after the gold discovery, there were 800 miners working in the vicinity of Coloma. A month later, there were 2,000 miners in the Sierra foothills, including almost the entire population of San Francisco. During the next year, 1849, thousands of prospectors headed for California by ship and wagon train from all parts of the United States and many other countries as well. By the end of the gold rush, in 1852, the population of California had swelled to 225,000.

Thousands of gold discoveries were made in the foothills of the Sierra Nevada during and after the gold rush. Hundreds of these discoveries were developed into commercial gold mines, and a few dozen of these mines produced large quantities of gold. Most of this gold was found in a belt of gold deposits about 30 to 50 miles wide that extended from Mariposa to Sierra City. This trend of gold deposits is generally referred to as the Sierra Nevada gold belt. The richest part of the gold belt was within a mile or so of the Melones fault between Mariposa and Placerville. This string of rich gold mines is known as the Mother Lode.

No one knows how much gold was produced from these mines. Production figures in the early years of the gold rush were in dollars rather than ounces, and many of the early production figures are missing or incomplete. Nonetheless, if you value gold at $300/oz., the total production from California mines from 1848 to present is estimated at approximately thirty billion dollars. The periods of greatest production were from 1850-65, from 1879-84, and from 1936-1941. Most of the mines closed during World War II. A few mines were able to open after the war, but operations were expensive and difficult. Only a few mines are operating at present.

Origin of the Gold

Gold is ubiquitous in nature, and small quantities occur in many different rocks. The average igneous rock contains 0.0000005 percent gold. The main problem for the prospector is to find gold in concentrations that are profitable to mine, in the range of 1/3 ounce/ton. Mother Nature, using several different chemical and physical processes, did a remarkable job in concentrating gold in the Sierra Nevada gold belt.

Most of the Sierra gold occurs in the rocks of the Western Metamorphic Belt. These rocks accumulated in a series of subduction zones that were present in this area from early Paleozoic to Jurassic time. During this period, thousands of miles of oceanic crust were swept into these subduction zones. Although most of this oceanic crust was carried under the North American plate and returned to the mantle, some of the oceanic crust remained in the subduction zone, and some of these rocks contained small amounts of gold. However, this gold still needed to be concentrated. The Nevadan orogeny would help in this process.

This mine tunnel in the Gold Bug Mine near Placerville is open to the public. White veins of quartz cut through the dark metamorphic rock on the walls of the tunnel. When the mine was operating, the fuses at the end of the tunnel would have set off dynamite that was packed into holes drilled into the hard rock.

During the late Jurassic Nevadan orogeny, the rocks in the subduction zone were subjected to intense heat and pressure. As the rocks were heated, the gold was removed from the rocks and concentrated in CO_2-rich solutions. During early Cretaceous time, at the beginning of the Franciscan subduction, these gold-bearing solutions were forced upward by the heat in the subduction zone and injected into the overlying rocks. The gold-bearing solutions mainly followed the weak and shattered rocks along the major fault zones of the Western Metamorphic Belt, since this was the easiest route to the surface. During this upward trip, gold and other minerals were precipitated along the fracture zones wherever the solutions reached sympathetic conditions of temperature, pressure, and local chemistry.

Most of the gold was precipitated in fractured rocks near the fault zones. The rocks consisted of schist, greenstones, slate, granite, or any other rock that was fractured. The gold was often deposited with quartz in veins that filled fractures in the rock. Some gold was also deposited in open fractures, where gold crystals had space to grow into their delicate shapes. Other minerals often accompanied the gold and were deposited along with the gold. These minerals include copper, zinc, lead, iron, silver, and mercury. In some places, gold was chemically combined to form gold compounds. After the gold and other minerals were deposited, the solutions continued to the surface and were expelled in hot springs. By early Cretaceous time, most of the gold had been deposited in the veins and shear zones in the metamorphic rocks of the gold belt. The gold was ready to begin the next stage of concentration.

PROPERTIES OF GOLD	
Chemical symbol	Au
Atomic number	79
Atomic weight	169.9665
Density	18.88 at 68°F
Boiling point	5,576°F
Melting point	1,948°F
Crystal habit	Cubic, octahedral, dodecahedral Commonly dendritic, reticulated or spongy Also occurs as nuggets, flattened grains, or scales
Hardness	2.5-3
Color	Yellow, silver white; opaque

As the gold was being deposited in the veins along the gold belt, the ancestral Sierra began to be uplifted, and the gold veins in the Western Metamorphic Belt were exposed to weathering and erosion. Uplift and erosion continued through Cretaceous and Paleocene time, and by Eocene time the ancestral Sierra had been eroded to a low range of hills that was drained by large rivers. During this long period of uplift and erosion, large quantities of gold were removed from the gold veins and concentrated on the Eocene erosion surface. Since the gold was heavy, most of it remained in the vicinity of the weathered veins.

Some of the gold on the Eocene erosion surface was swept into the Eocene rivers and deposited with the gravel in the deep river channels. Large quantities of gold eventually accumulated in these Eocene river gravels, and these gravels have been extensively mined in the northern Sierra. Some of the gold also remained in the gold veins of the Western Metamorphic Belt. Most of the large gold mines along the Mother Lode extracted ore from these veins. Some of the gold also accumulated in the channels of the present-day Sierra rivers. This placer gold was washed into the rivers where the rivers had cut through gold veins and through gold-bearing Eocene river gravels.

The placer gold was easily and quickly extracted during the early days of the gold rush. However, more creative and effective methods would be needed to mine the low-grade gold deposits, the gold deposits in hard rock, and the gold that lay deep underground.

PRINCIPAL GOLD DISTRICTS OF THE SIERRA NEVADA (Based on Clark, 1970)		
District	**Type**	**Production ($MM)**
Grass Valley	Lode	300
Jackson-Plymouth	Lode	180
Hammonton	Dredge field	130
Folsom	Dredge field	125
Columbia	Placer	87
Oroville	Dredge field	55
Nevada City	Lode and placer	50
Alleghany	Lode and placer	50
Sierra City	Lode	30
Angels Camp	Lode, some placer	30
Jamestown	Lode	30
Placerville	Placer and lode	27
Carson Hill	Lode	27

Gold Mining

Although gold had been found and used by local Native Americans in the Sierra foothills for many years prior to the gold rush, it was not considered valuable and was of no particular significance. All of that changed rapidly with the 1848 gold discovery at Coloma. With that discovery, the gold rush began. Although the first discoveries were in the channels of the present-day Sierra rivers, gold was soon found in the Eocene and Oligocene river gravels and in the quartz veins and sheared metamorphic rocks of the Western Metamorphic Belt. Some of these gold deposits were rich and others were low grade. Some of the deposits were at or near the surface of the ground. Others extended hundreds or thousands of feet underground. Some of the gold ore was hard and difficult to process. Other gold ore was soft and easy to mine. Since the gold occurred in a wide variety of conditions, many different methods were used to mine the gold. The most common mining methods were placer, hydraulic, dredge, lode, drift, and open pit.

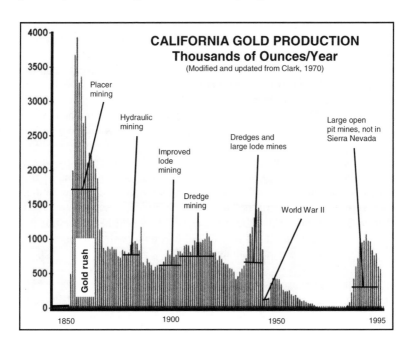

Placer Mining: Most of the gold found at the beginning of the gold rush was extracted from rich placer deposits in the present-day rivers. In the first few months, all that a prospector had to do was pick up the gold nuggets from the stream channels. Sometimes a knife or pick was helpful in prying out the nuggets. Needless to say, this didn't last long, and other devices were soon used to separate the gold from the river gravel. Most of these devices separated the heavy gold from the lighter rock fragments by washing the gold-bearing alluvium with water. The lighter rock fragments would be washed away and the heavy gold would remain.

Gold pans were used by many early miners to extract the gold from the alluvial deposits. The pans were inexpensive and easily portable. However, panning was slow and labor intensive. It worked for very rich gold deposits, but was not practical for recovering large quantities of gold from medium- and low-grade deposits. Rapidly, other methods were found to separate the gold.

One of the favorite methods of the Chinese miners was the rocker. This consisted of a small box with a screen on top. River gravel was shoveled into the box and the box was rocked using a handle. The screen kept the larger rock fragments out of the box and let the smaller fragments pass into the lower part of the box. Water flowed through the lower part of the box across a series of slanted riffles, which separated the gold from the alluvium.

Long toms were even more efficient. A typical long tom was a wooden trough about 12 feet long and eight inches deep. The upper end of the trough was a foot or so wide, and the trough widened to about twice that distance at the lower end. The bottom of the box was a perforated sheet of iron. Below that, there was a riffle box. The gold-bearing alluvium was shoveled into the upper part of the box and washed through with water. The gold accumulated along the riffles.

Sluice boxes were used to handle even larger volumes of alluvium. The sluice box was a wooden trough, usually about 12 feet long. Alluvium was shoveled into the box and washed through with large amounts of water. The gold was caught in riffles at the end of the sluice. Often, many sluice boxes were strung together to make a sluice up to several hundred feet long. Sometimes a ditch in the ground would be used as a sluice rather than a wooded box. The gold would be trapped in a riffle box placed at the end of the ditch. This was called ground sluicing. Long toms and sluices required lots of water, a problem in many areas.

Lode Mining: In most areas where placer mining was in progress, miners quickly traced the gold upslope to its source. The source was often a gold-bearing quartz vein, referred to as a *lode* by the early prospectors. Soon they would be mining the vein with pick and shovel. At first, the gold vein was rich and easy to work. The gold had been concentrated in the weathered rocks near the surface. In a short time, however, the rich gold in the weathered rocks was gone and further mining required hard work. The unweathered rock was usually hard, and the ore in the fresh vein was not as rich as the surface ore. The vein would be followed into the ground with a tunnel or shaft, and this would come to be known as lode mining.

In general, lode mining required more work, more capital, more expertise, and larger operations than placer mining. Large lode mines also required experienced labor willing to work for minimal wages under extremely difficult and dangerous conditions. Many foreigners were imported to handle this work. When successful, the lode mines were major sustained operations. More gold was recovered from lode mines than from placers. During the late 1800's, there were hundreds of lode mines all along Sierra foothills. The largest operations were along the Mother Lode between Jackson and Plymouth and in the northern Sierra near Grass Valley. Some of these mines would eventually follow the gold ore to depths of over a mile and have up to 200 miles of tunnels and other workings. At present, there is very little lode mining in the Sierra

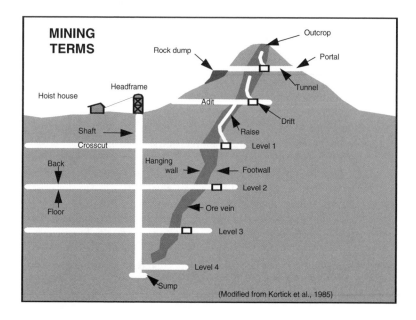

(Modified from Kortick et al., 1985)

foothills. Most of the lode mines were closed during World War II. Although gold is still present in many of these mines, the mine workings have deteriorated and it would be very costly to reopen the mines.

Drift Mining: Drift mining is similar to lode mining, except the mining is done horizontally. Most of the drift mines in the Sierra Nevada gold belt were in rich gold-bearing Eocene river channels. The miners dug into hillsides and followed the river channels into the hill, twisting and turning with every whim of the channel. They followed the deepest part of the channel, which contained the richest gold, and thus neatly defined the direction and extent of the old river channels. Some drift mines extended as much as a mile or so into the hillside. However, the rich gold-bearing gravels were usually only a few feet thick and were often discontinuous. Drift mining was thus difficult and risky in most areas. There were many drift mines near Placerville and Nevada City, but none are now operational or accessible.

Hydraulic Mining: Many Eocene river channel deposits were mined hydraulically. The gold-bearing gravel in these channels was from a few feet to 600 feet thick. Most of the gold was in the lowest part of the gravel, and there was little, if any, gold in the upper part. To get at the rich gold in the lower part of the channel it was necessary to remove the overlying gravel. However, removing this overburden was difficult and expensive if the gravel was thick—until someone found that you could simply wash down the entire bank of gravel with a hose and recover the gold as the gravel was washed through a sluice. With the discovery of this hydraulic mining method, large deposits of Eocene river gravel could be mined that could not be economically mined any other way. Hydraulic mining grew rapidly and was used in many major mining operations in the northern Sierra. The largest of these hydraulic mines was the Malakoff Diggins near North Bloomfield.

Dredge Mining: Most of the gold nuggets and flakes in the Sierra rivers were not carried far beyond their source in the Gold Belt, and most of this gold was recovered during the early placer mining operations. However, large quantities of very fine flakes of gold were carried many miles downstream from the gold belt and were deposited in the gravel along lower courses of most of the major Sierra rivers. The concentration of the very fine gold in these gravels was usually quite low, a few cents worth of gold per cubic yard of gravel. However, there was a lot of gravel, and the gravel could be profitably mined by large dredges. The dredges scooped up the gravel in huge buckets, recovered the gold, and redeposited the tailings back into the river channel. The dredges floated in a pond that moved along with the dredge as it consumed the river gravel. The Feather, Yuba, American, and Merced rivers all had large dredge mining operations at the base of the foothills. One of the largest of these operations, at Hammonton on the lower Yuba River, operated from 1903 to 1968. Large amounts of gold were recovered from these operations. There is no dredge mining at present.

Open Pit Mining: A few gold mines in the Sierra foothills have been mined by open pit mining, where large quantities of low-grade ore are excavated from the surface using large trucks and other surface equipment. Two of the largest of these mines were the Harvard Mine and Carson Hill Mine, both near Sonora. Some leaching operations were also carried out where gold was leached from mine tailing by cyanide solutions and then recovered from the cyanide solution.

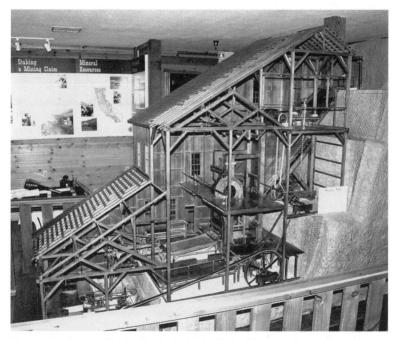

This model stamp mill at the California State Mining Museum shows how gold was recovered from gold ore. The ore entered the mill at the upper right where it was crushed into bite-sized pieces. The crushed ore was then powdered in the stamp mill in the center of the model. The powder was next washed across the sloping copper plate and the gold was recovered as an amalgam ready for refining.

Milling and Refining

During the first days of the gold rush, the recovery of the gold was easy, as long as an abundant supply of water was available. The gold nuggets and gold dust were heavy and easily separated from the sand and gravel placer deposits. However, most of this easy-to-recover gold was mined out within a year or two. Much of the remaining gold occurred as very fine particles that were dispersed in a variety of hard rocks, including quartz veins, schist, slate, phyllite, and granodiorite. Most of this gold ore was low grade. Recovering gold from this ore required a large milling and refining operation.

Most of the gold mills were built on a slope below the mine portal. Ore that was removed from the mine was dumped into large jaw crushers at the top of the mill. The crushers, like a giant human jaw, broke the rock into two-inch or smaller pieces. The rock was then fed into a stamp mill, where the rock was crushed into powder by large iron stamps. A small mill commonly had five stamps, and larger mills could have 100 or more stamps. Each stamp consisted of a vertical iron rod, about 14 feet high, with a large iron cylinder on the lower end. The rod and cylinder were lifted on a cam, and then dropped so that the cylinder struck an iron mortar that was in place below the cylinder. Water was fed into the mortar during the stamping. The slurry from the stamp was washed over a sloping apron plate made of copper that was coated with mercury. The finely divided gold combined with the mercury to form an amalgam, and the tailings were passed on to a tailings pile. Once a day or so the stamping would be halted and the gold-bearing amalgam would be recovered from the copper plate.

The amalgam was sent to a refinery for processing. There, the amalgam was placed in a retorting furnace, where the mercury was vaporized, leaving a porous mass of gold sponge. The mercury was condensed, recovered, and used again. The spongy mass of gold was then heated in a crucible, the impurities were skimmed from the molten gold, and the gold was poured into a cast-iron mold.

A stamp mill was not a pleasant place to work. The mill operated continuously. The roar of the stamp mill could be heard for miles. The noise of the stamps often caused hearing loss for the mill workers within weeks. Pieces of breaking rock from the stamp were like bullets, another hazard to mill workers. The mercury, if not handled properly, was still another health hazard. Nonetheless, jobs in the mill were preferable to the underground jobs in the mines.

The large open pit mine at Carson Hill has removed much of the original Carson Hill. The Carson Hill Gold Mine is no longer in operation, but the pit is being mined for gravel.

This ten-stamp mill at the Empire Mine near Grass Valley was used to crush gold ore into powder during the milling process. At its peak, the mill at the Empire Mine had 80 stamps that operated 24 hours a day and could be heard for miles.

GEOLOGIC HISTORY

The Sierra Nevada has had a relatively short life - but a life full of violence, drama, and mystery. The oldest rocks in the mountains were formed in early Paleozoic time. At that time, the area of the present-day Sierra was part of a large ocean basin and the margin of the North American continent was in Nevada. The rocks of the Shoo Fly Complex were deposited in this ocean basin. During the Antler orogeny, in mid-Devonian time, the rocks of the Shoo Fly Complex were folded, faulted, uplifted, and eroded. After this short but violent event, a series of island arcs formed in this area and the volcanic rocks of the Northern Sierra Terrane were deposited on top of the Shoo Fly Complex. By late Paleozoic time, the rocks of the Shoo Fly Complex and Northern Sierra Terrane had been added to the western margin of North America and a new subduction zone developed further west.

The Calaveras Complex accumulated in this new subduction zone. In contrast to the Shoo Fly Complex, most of the rocks of the Calaveras Complex were not derived from the North American continent. Instead, these rocks represent terranes that were carried into the subduction zone by plate movement. These exotic and mysterious terranes include large slabs of limestone, quartzite, and schist. The Calaveras Complex also includes island arcs, volcanic rocks, and deep ocean sediments that were formed within the subduction zone.

By early Jurassic time, the rocks of the Calaveras Complex had been added to the western edge of North America and a new subduction zone, the Nevadan, formed to the west of the Calaveras Complex. The rocks of the Foothills Terrane were deposited in the Nevadan subduction zone during most of Jurassic time. These rocks are mainly phyllite, slate, and greenstone, and were largely generated within or near the subduction zone. In late Jurassic time, the rocks of the Foothills Terrane were metamorphosed and added to the western edge of North American during the Nevadan orogeny. The Nevadan orogeny was especially intense, and affected the rocks of the Calaveras Complex and Shoo Fly Complex as well as those of the Foothills Terrane. These three units of metamorphosed rock are collectively known as the Western Metamorphic Belt. The Nevadan orogeny ended in late Jurassic time when the large Smartville Terrane was carried into the Nevadan subduction zone and plugged the subduction zone. When this happened,

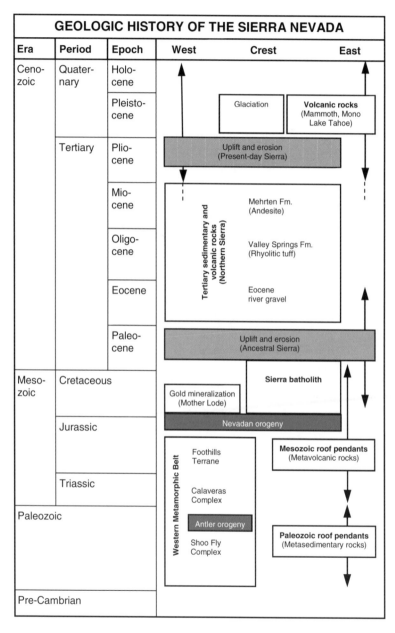

the Smartville block was added to the western margin of North America, and the Franciscan subduction zone was formed along the new continental margin west of the Smartville block.

With the beginning of Franciscan subduction zone, several important things began to happen along the new continental margin:

1) Gold-bearing solutions that had been generated in the Nevadan subduction were injected into the faulted and fractured rocks of the Western Metamorphic Belt. These are now the gold deposits of the Mother Lode.

2) Plutons of granitic rocks that were formed in the Franciscan subduction zone began to be intruded along the new continental margin. These intrusions now form the Sierra Nevada batholith.

3) The new continental margin began to be uplifted, and this uplift continued into Paleocene time. The uplifted area formed a high mountain range that extended from the present-day Sierra foothills into western Nevada. As the ancestral Sierra Nevada was uplifted, the mountains were also eroded, and the erosion products were carried into the Great Valley. These eroded sediments now underlie much of the Great Valley.

By Eocene time, the northern part of the ancestral Sierra Nevada had been eroded to a low rolling landscape. This Eocene erosion surface was drained by a vast system of rivers, and thick river gravels were deposited along the channels of these rivers. Some of these river gravels are gold-bearing and have been mined extensively in the northern Sierra. During Oligocene and Miocene time, the soft sedimentary and volcanic rocks of the Valley Springs and Mehrten Formations were deposited on top of the Eocene erosion surface. By the end of Miocene time, these rocks covered much of the northern part of the ancestral Sierra Nevada, but never extended into the southern part of the ancestral mountains.

While Tertiary sedimentary and volcanic rocks were being deposited, there was very little uplift of the ancestral Sierra. Then, about five million years ago, the present-day Sierra Nevada began to form as the Sierra block was rapidly uplifted and rotated to the west along the newly-formed Frontal fault system. As the range was uplifted, the blanket of soft Tertiary sedimentary and volcanic rocks was rapidly eroded from much of the central and northern Sierra. The uplift was also accompanied by extensive volcanism along the eastern slope and in the area north of Lake Tahoe.

During Pleistocene time, the mountains were subjected to four major episodes of glaciation. These glaciers played a major role in developing the dramatic landscape of the High Sierra and in forming many of the best-known scenic features of the mountain range.

PART III

THE GEOLOGIC TRIPS

OVERVIEW OF THE TRIPS

The Sierra Nevada is large and it is not possible in this book to visit all of the features of geologic interest. Instead, I've tried to select several areas that emphasize different aspects of the geology of the mountains. The trip to Lone Pine explores the faults and uplift of the mountains. At Mammoth Lakes, you'll see the volcanoes, domes, craters and many volcanic rocks that accompanied the uplift. The trip to the Mono Lake area takes a look at the moraines and lakes that were formed along the east slope of the Sierra during Pleistocene glaciation. At Lake Tahoe, you will see how the lake was made by a combination of faulting and volcanism, and examine the role that glaciers played in forming the lakes and bays of the Tahoe area. The northern Sierra is a good place to see the Tertiary sedimentary and volcanic rocks that once blanketed the Sierra. On this trip you'll also see the largest hydraulic mine and the largest lode gold mine in the Sierra. The trip along the Mother Lode visits many famous mines and mining towns of the gold rush. In Yosemite Valley, you'll learn how its majestic scenic features were formed. At Tuolumne Meadows you'll see how the large Tuolumne icefield shaped many of the landforms of the High Sierra. During the trip to the southern Sierra, you'll visit one of the deepest canyons in North America and examine several roof pendants of metamorphic rocks. These nine trips provide a good sampling of the many aspects of the geology of the Sierra Nevada. Armed with this geologic background, you should be able to appreciate the geology of most any other part of the Sierra.

Each trip is divided into several different localities, and each locality has one or more specific geologic sites. The geologic localities and sites are identified in the book in this manner:

❷ Geologic Locality

Each geologic locality emphasizes a specific aspect of the geology of the Sierra Nevada and is identified with a number that is keyed to the location map for the trip. Each locality also has a map that shows the important geologic features for the locality and the locations of the geologic sites that will be visited.

Geologic Site - *Directions to the site.*
Description of the site.

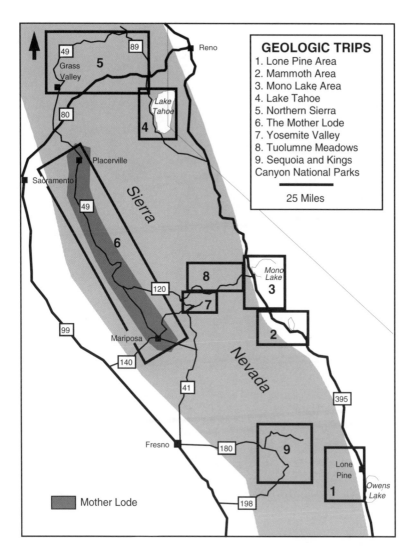

GEOLOGIC TRIPS
1. Lone Pine Area
2. Mammoth Area
3. Mono Lake Area
4. Lake Tahoe
5. Northern Sierra
6. The Mother Lode
7. Yosemite Valley
8. Tuolumne Meadows
9. Sequoia and Kings Canyon National Parks

25 Miles

Mother Lode

Use caution and common sense while on the trips. Get local trail guides and follow the local hiking rules and regulations when leaving the highway. Drive, park and hike safely. Collecting rocks is prohibited in most of these areas, so it is best not to collect unless you have received permission. To see the details of the rocks, bring a hand lens or magnifying glass if you have one. You may be surprised at what you see. Have a good trip!

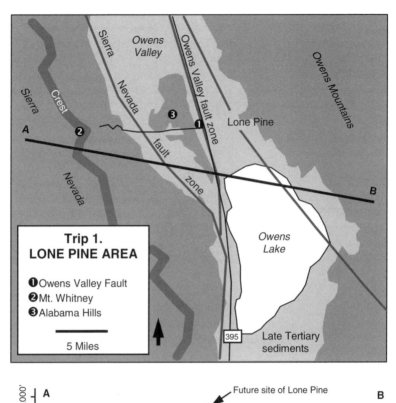

Trip 1.
LONE PINE AREA

❶ Owens Valley Fault
❷ Mt. Whitney
❸ Alabama Hills

5 Miles

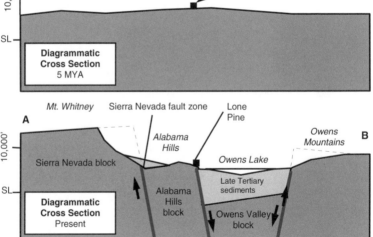

The upper cross section shows the Lone Pine area prior to uplift of the Sierra Nevada. The lower section shows the present landscape, formed by uplift and tilting of the Sierra Nevada block and subsidence of the Owens Valley block.

LONE PINE AREA
Uplift of the Sierra Nevada

The view of Mount Whitney (14,496') from Lone Pine is impressive. The mountain is the highest of several peaks along the steep escarpment of the southern Sierra Nevada. When looking at Mt. Whitney from Lone Pine, it is hard to believe that only five million years ago there was no Sierra Nevada, no Owens Mountains, no Owens Valley, no Owens Lake, and no Mt. Whitney. Instead, there was a low range of hills that extended from the present-day Sierra foothills into western Nevada.

About five million years ago, these low hills began to be broken by a series of northwest trending faults. During the next five million years, the Sierra Nevada was uplifted and tilted westward along these faults. Uplift was greatest in the south, near Lone Pine, and decreased northward. As the Sierra block was uplifted, the crust to the east of the faults subsided, forming a number of basins to the east of the Sierra, including the Owens Valley, Mono Valley, and Lake Tahoe basins.

The series of faults along which the Sierra Nevada was uplifted and the adjacent basins subsided is referred to as the Frontal fault system. Nowhere can the effect of the uplift be better seen than at Lone Pine. Here, the Frontal fault system is split into two major fault zones, the Sierra Nevada fault zone and the Owens Valley fault zone. The Sierra Nevada block has been uplifted about 10,000 feet along the Sierra Nevada fault zone and the Owens Valley block has been dropped over 5,000 feet along the Owens Valley fault zone. The Alabama Hills lie between these two fault zones. The Alabama Hills block represents a sliver of the earth's crust that was neither uplifted with the Sierra Nevada block nor down-dropped with the Owens Valley block. As the Sierra block was uplifted, it began to be eroded. The higher the uplift, the greater the erosion. Many of these erosion products were deposited as sedimentary rocks in the sinking Owens Valley block.

During this trip, you'll take a look at recent faulting along the Owens Valley fault zone, drive across the Sierra Nevada fault zone on the way to Whitney Portal, and investigate how and why the unusual scenic features of the Alabama Hills were formed.

❶ Owens Valley Fault

The Owens Valley fault zone goes through the town of Lone Pine. The Alabama Hills are on the west side of the fault and Owens Valley is on the east side. Owens Valley has subsided about 5,000 feet along this fault zone during the last five million years. The fault is active, and the movement is still going on, as evidenced by a number of recent small fault scarps along the fault zone. Some of these scarps were formed as recently as 1872, when the town of Lone Pine was destroyed by the Owens Valley earthquake. This M8.0 earthquake was one of the largest earthquakes ever recorded in California, and was about the same magnitude as the 1906 San Francisco earthquake. Of the 300 residents in Lone Pine at the time of the earthquake, 23 were killed by collapsing homes and buildings. During the earthquake, the ground was ruptured for a distance of over 100 miles and left a series of discontinuous scarps between Olancha and Big Pine.

In and near Lone Pine, you can see several of the fault scarps that were formed during the 1872 earthquake. We'll visit several of these scarps. However, don't expect to see a fresh scarp and fresh rocks. In the 130 years since the earthquake, most of the scarps have been covered by grass, rocks and shrubs, and some have been modified by man. Nonetheless, the linear trend and general shape of the scarps is evident. Although many of these scarps are only a few feet high and may not be impressive, keep in mind that many small offsets like this can add up to a large amount of uplift given a long period of time. Assuming an average rate of uplift of only 2.4 inches per century, the Sierra block would be uplifted 10,000 feet in five million years.

It takes a huge break, probably through the entire earth's crust, to cause an earthquake as large as the 1872 Owens Valley earthquake. A break of this magnitude would normally extend laterally for tens of miles, and the rocks along the break would be offset from several feet to as much as twenty or thirty feet. Earthquakes of this size are very effective in releasing stress along a fault. It usually takes a long time for stress to build up and cause another major earthquake, perhaps several decades to several hundred years. It is virtually certain that another large earthquake will eventually occur in the Lone Pine area, but no one really knows when that will happen.

→Mt. Whitney, in the center of the photo, is the highest point along the crest of the Sierra Nevada. The Sierra crest represents the eroded eastern edge of the large west-tilted Sierra Nevada fault block.

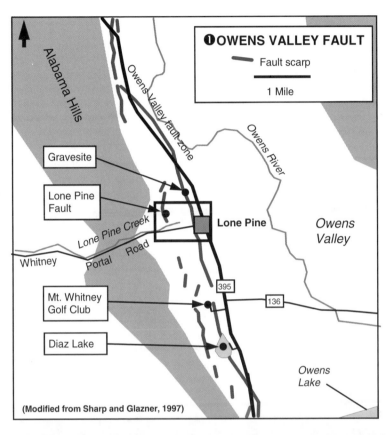

Diaz Lake: *From the junction of Hwy. 130 and Hwy. 395 go 1 mi. S on Hwy. 395; turn W into the Diaz Lake Recreational Area.*

Diaz Lake is a popular recreational area, with boating, fishing, water sports, picnic grounds, camping, and trails. The lake and the surrounding area is owned by the Los Angeles Department of Water and Power and is leased as a recreational facility by Inyo County. The Los Angeles Aqueduct lies immediately west of the lake along the base of the Alabama Hills.

The lake is named for the Diaz family, who had established and operated a successful cattle ranch here in the late 1860's. Prior to the 1872 Owens Valley earthquake, this part of the ranch was a spring-fed wetland with cattails and reeds. During the earthquake, the ground on the east side of the fault dropped 20 feet. New springs developed and fed into this depression to form Diaz Lake. Down-dropped blocks like this are common along major fault zones and reflect minor surface adjustments to very deep movement along the fault zone.

Diaz Lake lies within the Owens Valley fault zone, and was formed when this area subsided 20 feet during the 1872 Owens Valley earthquake. The Alabama Hills can be seen on the far side of the lake and the Sierra crest in the distance.

For information, maps, and books on the Owens Valley, Death Valley, eastern Sierra, and Yosemite, drop by the Interagency Visitor Center 1.5 miles south of Lone Pine at the intersection of Highways 395 and 136 (760-876-6222).

Mt. Whitney Golf Club - *The Mt. Whitney Golf Club is on the W side of Hwy. 395 near the junction with Hwy. 130; follow the entrance road to the clubhouse.*

The Mt. Whitney Golf Club is in the Owens Valley fault zone just north of Diaz Lake. One of the fault scarps formed during the 1872 earthquake goes through the golf course. Although the scarp has been modified by development at the golf course, it can still be seen as a low north-trending embankment that runs along the western side of the golf course. The clubhouse and the tee for hole six are on the top of the east-facing scarp and most of the remainder of the golf course is on the downdropped block. During the earthquake, the ground to the east of the scarp dropped about 15 feet. The road to the clubhouse climbs the fault scarp, and a remnant of the unmodified scarp can be seen on the south side of the road as it crosses the scarp.

This view looks north along the Owens Valley fault scarp at the Mt. Whitney Golf Club. The clubhouse, at the left side of the photo, is on the top of the scarp and the low area at the right is at the base of the scarp. The large tree is on the gentle slope of the fault scarp. The fault scarp was formed during the 1872 Owens Valley earthquake.

For information about Lone Pine, Owens Lake, the Alabama Hills, and nearby areas, visit the Lone Pine Chamber of Commerce, 126 S. Main St., Lone Pine (760-876-4444)

Lone Pine Fault - *From the junction of Hwy. 395 and Whitney Portal Rd. go 0.6 mi. W on Whitney Portal Rd.; park at the information pullout on the right side of the road; hike back 0.1 mi. to the gravel road just W of the L. A. Aqueduct; go N 0.1 mi. on this road, turn right on the narrow dirt road just beyond Lone Pine Creek; continue on this road for 0.1 mi. to the base of the fault scarp; the scarp lies immediately W and continues N for 0.5 mi.; the dirt road runs between the fault scarp and the L. A. Aqueduct.*

The Lone Pine fault is one of several faults that lie within the Owens Valley fault zone. This fault has a well-developed scarp just north of Lone Pine Creek and immediately west of the Los Angeles Aqueduct. The east-facing scarp is 15 feet high and trends north. The scarp offsets an alluvial fan with large boulders, and the boulders are exposed on the face of the scarp. This scarp was probably formed during several different earthquakes along the Lone Pine fault. The latest movement was during the 1872 Owens Valley earthquake, when the east side of the fault moved down an estimated eight feet and the west side of the block moved north several feet.

Gravesite - *Drive N on Hwy. 395 to the sign marking the north entrance to Lone Pine; the gravesite is on the W side of Hwy. 395 immediately S of the sign.*

The plaque at this locality marks the common gravesite for the victims of the 1872 earthquake. The gravesite is on the top of a scarp along the Owens Valley fault and Highway 395 is at the base of the scarp. The scarp continues north from the gravesite, and can be seen as an east-facing scarp on the west side of the highway for several miles to the north of Lone Pine.

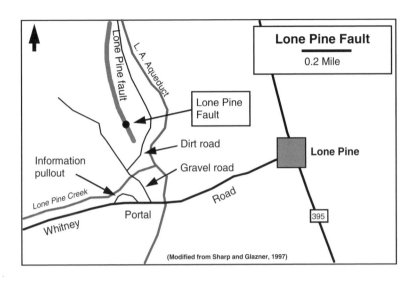

↑The boulder-covered Lone Pine fault scarp on the left side of the photo extends north for about half a mile.

←The steep boulder-covered slope in this photo is the east face of the Lone Pine fault scarp near Lone Pine Creek. The fault cuts through an alluvial fan, exposing the boulders in the fan. The Alabama Hills are in the middle ground on the right and the crest of the Sierra Nevada is in the distance.

❷ Mt. Whitney

Mt. Whitney lies 13 miles west of Lone Pine, and is the highest point along the steep eastern escarpment of the Sierra Nevada. This escarpment is a deeply eroded fault scarp that was formed by faulting along the Sierra Nevada fault zone. During the last five million years, the Sierra block was uplifted over 10,000 feet along this fault zone. The Sierra Nevada fault zone is not exposed along Whitney Portal Road, but lies along the mountain front where it is buried by alluvium that has washed down from the eroding fault scarp.

Although you cannot see the other side of Mt. Whitney from here, the west slope of the mountain is quite different. It slopes gently to the west and is part of the old Miocene pre-uplift land surface that has been preserved. The westward tilt of the surface records the westward tilting of the Sierra Nevada block during uplift. This low-relief west-tilted surface occurs along the west side of many peaks along the Sierra crest.

Lone Pine Campground - *From Lone Pine go 8 mi. W on Whitney Portal Rd.* The Lone Pine Campground is near the top of the large alluvial fan that extends from the Sierra Nevada mountain front to the Alabama Hills. The alluvial fan rises 3,000 feet as you climb up Whitney Portal Road from the Alabama Hills. The fan is composed of rocks and debris that have eroded from the uplifted Sierra block to the west. Note the many large granite boulders on the upper part of the fan that have eroded from the fault scarp.

Whitney Portal - *From the Lone Pine Campground drive 5 mi. W to the end of Whitney Portal Rd. If you wish to go to the summit of Mt. Whitney, a permit is required. From Whitney Portal, the summit is a strenuous 21.4-mi. round-trip hike along the rugged Mt. Whitney Trail.*
Just west of the Lone Pine Campground, Whitney Portal Road leaves the alluvial fan along the mountain front and begins its steep climb up the eroded fault scarp of the Sierra Nevada fault zone. Along the road there are many exposures of medium gray granodiorite with dark xenoliths. This granodiorite is part of the Whitney Intrusive Suite, a large granitic intrusion that extends from here through Mt. Whitney to Roads End in Kings Canyon National Park. The steep east face of Mt. Whitney has a large number of vertical indentations that give this side of the mountain a fluted appearance. These indentations are formed by intersecting vertical joints in the granodiorite. The granodiorite breaks into blocks along these joints, aided by the freeze and thaw action of water. This type of erosion is common in the High Sierra where rocks are jointed, and where there is water and freezing temperatures.

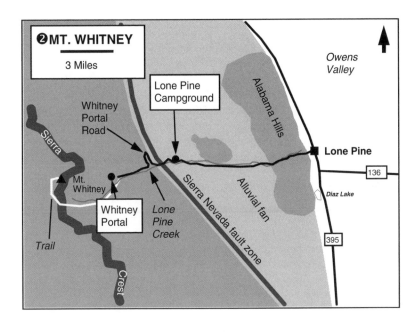

The steep buttresses on the east face of Mt. Whitney are formed by intersecting vertical joints in the granite. This photo was taken from near Whitney Portal.

❸ Alabama Hills

The Alabama Hills are famous for the scenic rounded rocks that have formed the backdrop for some 200 movies and many television programs. The rocks of the Alabama Hills are the same granitic and metamorphic rocks that occur in the Sierra Nevada. However, the granite in the Alabama Hills is not clean and fresh like the granite in the High Sierra, but is deeply weathered and crumbles easily. The granite is cut by a number of joints, and the deep weathering of the granite along these joints has given the Alabama Hills their striking scenery.

The granite of the Alabama Hills is typically cut by three sets of joints, two vertical and one near horizontal. If all three sets of joints are well-developed and equally-spaced, they cut the granite into cubes. However, in most areas, the joints are irregular and discontinuous. Some joints are wide-spaced and others close-spaced. In some places, vertical joints are dominant. In other places, horizontal joints are dominant. These irregular and discontinuous joints cleave the granite into a variety of slabs, spires, ledges, and blocks.

The joints provide pathways along which the granite has been subjected to weathering and decomposition. Much of the weathering probably took place prior to uplift of the Sierra Nevada. At that time, this area had heavy rainfall and the granite was covered by thick soil and vegetation. Under these humid conditions, the joints were wet much of the time and the granite along the joint surfaces rapidly disintegrated into quartz grains and clay. The sharp edges and corners of the jointed blocks were rounded more rapidly than the flat surfaces because the edges and corners had more surfaces that were subjected to decomposition. In this manner, cubes of granite were rounded into boulders, spires were rounded into columns, and slabs and ledges developed curved edges.

When the Sierra Nevada block was uplifted during Plio-Pleistocene time, the Alabama Hills came into the rain shadow of the new mountains and the climate of the Alabama Hills became arid. Under these arid conditions, the soil cover was removed from the granite, the joints were cleaned out, and the rounded rocks were exposed in their full glory. The rocks were no longer buried under a deep cover of soil and vegetation. Since the Alabama Hills were not uplifted with the Sierra Nevada, they were never subjected to glaciation. If the Alabama Hills had been glaciated, the glaciers would have cleaned off the loose decomposed rocks and left fresh clean granite like you see in the High Sierra.

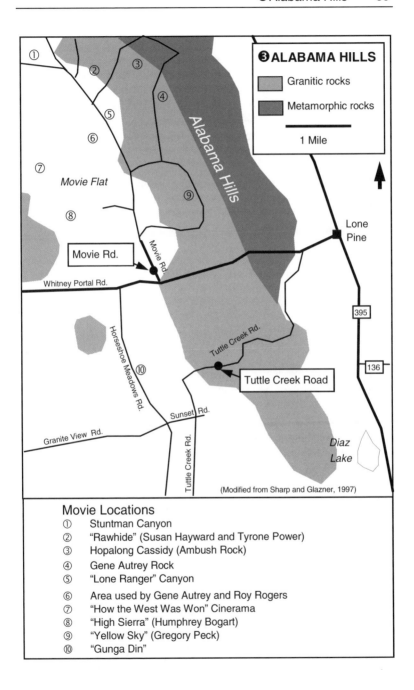

❸ALABAMA HILLS

Granitic rocks

Metamorphic rocks

1 Mile

Alabama Hills

① Movie Flat
Movie Rd.
Whitney Portal Rd.
Lone Pine
Movie Rd.

Horseshoe Meadows Rd.

Tuttle Creek Rd.

Tuttle Creek Road

395

136

Sunset Rd.

Granite View Rd.

Tuttle Creek Rd.

Diaz Lake

(Modified from Sharp and Glazner, 1997)

Movie Locations

① Stuntman Canyon
② "Rawhide" (Susan Hayward and Tyrone Power)
③ Hopalong Cassidy (Ambush Rock)
④ Gene Autrey Rock
⑤ "Lone Ranger" Canyon
⑥ Area used by Gene Autrey and Roy Rogers
⑦ "How the West Was Won" Cinerama
⑧ "High Sierra" (Humphrey Bogart)
⑨ "Yellow Sky" (Gregory Peck)
⑩ "Gunga Din"

Movie Road - *From Lone Pine, go W on Whitney Portal Rd. 3 mi. to Movie Rd.; turn right and drive 0.5 mi. to Movie Flat.*
Only the first part of Movie Road is paved. After that, it becomes a good gravel road. Dozens of dirt roads branch from this road, leading to many scenic locations. If you are interested in movie locations, get one of the guidebooks available locally. With these guides, you can find the locations of specific scenes from your favorite movies.

When looking at a specific rock outcrop in the Alabama Hills, try to identify which joints formed the feature. If one set of vertical joints dominate, you will see vertical slabs. Spires and columns are formed from intersecting vertical joints. Rounded boulders and blocks form where vertical and horizontal joints are all well-developed. Ledges form where there are good horizontal joints. Also, note that the surface of the granite is rough and that the grains of quartz and feldspar easily rub off the decomposing granite. These coarse grains form the sandy floor of Movie Flat.

Tuttle Creek Road - *From Movie Rd. go W on Whitney Portal Rd. 1 mi.; turn S on Horseshoe Meadows Rd.; go 2 mi. and turn E on Sunset Rd.; go 0.2 mi. and turn left on Tuttle Creek Rd.; follow Tuttle Creek Rd. back to Whitney Portal Rd.*
Narrow, winding Tuttle Creek Road follows Tuttle Creek as it cuts across the southern part of the Alabama Hills. From this road, there are many excellent views of odd-shaped jointed and rounded granite. Some of these picturesque rocks have been given names such as The Owl, Polar Bear, Walrus, Eagle, The Bishop, Peter's Pumpkin, and Cougar. Local guidebooks will identify this cast of characters.

The rounded granitic rocks of the Alabama Hills are in the foreground and Mt. Whitney in the center background.

The vertical joints are well-developed in this granite in the Alabama Hills. Note the rough texture on the surface of the weathered granite in the left foreground.

These large granite monoliths in the Alabama Hills are formed from wide-spaced intersecting vertical and horizontal joints. Note the individual for scale.

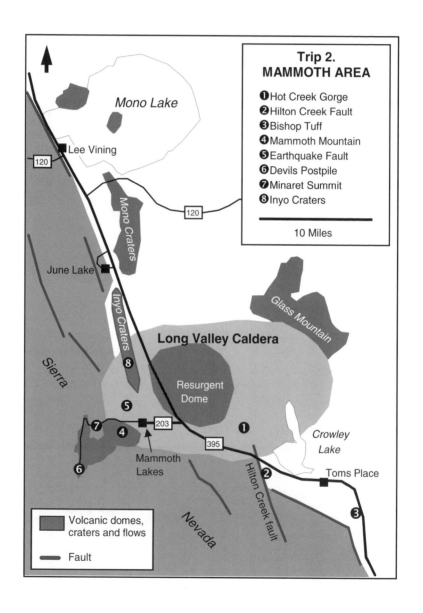

Trip 2.
MAMMOTH AREA

1. Hot Creek Gorge
2. Hilton Creek Fault
3. Bishop Tuff
4. Mammoth Mountain
5. Earthquake Fault
6. Devils Postpile
7. Minaret Summit
8. Inyo Craters

10 Miles

Mono Lake

Lee Vining

120

120

Mono Craters

June Lake

Inyo Craters

Glass Mountain

Long Valley Caldera

8

Resurgent
Dome

5

7

203

4

Mammoth
Lakes

6

395

1

Crowley
Lake

2

Toms Place

3

Sierra

Hilton Creek fault

Nevada

Volcanic domes,
craters and flows

Fault

MAMMOTH AREA
Volcanoes, Domes and Craters

The Mammoth area is one of the most volcanically active areas in the lower 48 States. From Bishop to Mono Lake, you are never out of sight of volcanoes, domes, craters, fumaroles, hot springs, and many different types of volcanic rocks, including rhyolite, andesite, basalt, obsidian, pumice, tuff, and welded tuff. During this trip, you'll see examples of all of these volcanic features and volcanic rocks.

Much of this volcanic activity is associated with the Long Valley Caldera, the remains of a huge volcano that erupted 760,000 years ago. Most of the remaining volcanic activity is associated with the Inyo and Mono Craters, a trend of domes and craters that extend from the Long Valley Caldera north to Mono Lake.

All of the volcanic features in this area lie along the fault zones that define the eastern escarpment of the Sierra Nevada and appear to be related to the uplift of the Sierra. The volcanism began four million years ago, about the same time that the uplift began, and has continued up to the present time. During uplift, the earth's crust was stretched, faulted and broken along the mountain front and magma from deep within the crust made its way upward along the broken rocks in the fault zones.

The early volcanic activity was mainly basaltic. However, the composition changed over time and most of the later volcanic rocks are rhyolitic. Rhyolite magma, which has a high content of silica, is stiff and does not flow easily. Depending on the water content and other conditions, rhyolite magma can form volcanic rocks that look quite different. If the magma is rich in water, the magma may erupt as tuff and frothy white pumice. If there is less water and the magma cools slowly, the magma may form a stiff, pasty rhyolite flow. If there is no water, and the magma chills rapidly, the magma may form a black obsidian flow. Many of the volcanic features in the Mammoth area are made up of combinations of rhyolite, obsidian, tuff, and pumice that were formed during different phases of the same eruption.

Long Valley Caldera

The Long Valley Caldera is a large oval depression, about 20 miles across, that lies north and northwest of Lake Crowley. The caldera was formed during the eruption of the Long Valley volcano 760,000 years ago. During this eruption, 150 cubic miles of superheated ash was expelled from the volcano. Half of this ash was thrown into the air and formed a column of ash eight miles high. The larger fragments of ash fell back to the ground near the volcano and the smaller fragments were carried by the jet stream as far east as Kansas and Nebraska. The other half of the eruption consisted of clouds of ash that flowed down the flanks of the volcano. The fragments of this ash were suspended by the gas emitted from the ash. Some of these ash flows extended north from the caldera, but most of the flows went south down the Owens Valley and reached as far as Big Pine. The air-fall ash and ash flows that were deposited during the eruption of the Long Valley Caldera are known as the Bishop Tuff. The Volcanic Tableland that covers much of the Owens Valley from Lake Crowley to Bishop is formed from numerous ash flows in the Bishop Tuff.

Following the eruption of the Long Valley volcano, the magma chamber under the volcano was nearly empty, so the volcano collapsed into itself, forming the large depression of the Long Valley Caldera. Immediately after the eruption, the caldera was about two miles deep. However, much of the erupted ash fell back into the depression, filling about two-thirds of the caldera. After the eruption, more magma arrived in the magma chamber and pushed up a dome in the center of the caldera. This *resurgent dome* now rises 1,500 feet above the valley floor. Some of the magma under the caldera later erupted to form rhyolite domes and volcanoes in and along the edges of the caldera. Mammoth Mountain is one of these volcanoes. The Long Valley Caldera is still volcanically active. A large magma chamber under the caldera provides the heat for numerous hot springs, hot creeks, and fumaroles in the caldera. From time to time, the magma moves, causing earthquakes, faults, and renewed uplift of the resurgent dome.

During the last of the glacial episodes, a large lake occupied the depression of the Long Valley Caldera. Shorelines of this lake can be seen around the edges of the caldera. The resurgent dome was an island in this lake. The lake was dammed by the Bishop Tuff at the south end of Lake Crowley. Owens Gorge was formed when this Pleistocene lake cut through the dam and then carved a steep gorge through the ash flows of the Bishop Tuff.

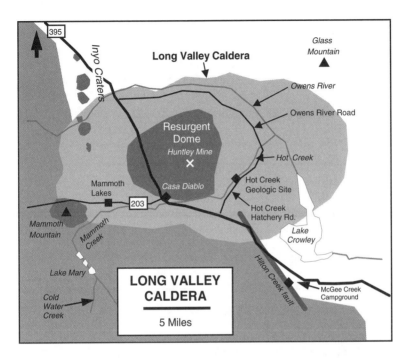

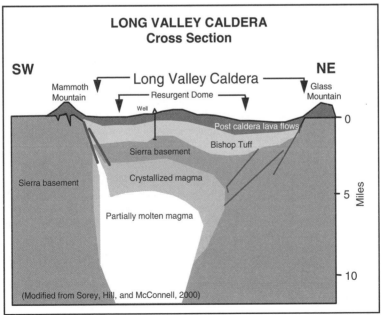

LONG VALLEY CALDERA
Cross Section

(Modified from Sorey, Hill, and McConnell, 2000)

❶ Hot Creek Gorge

There are many hot springs and geothermal areas in the Mammoth and Mono Lake areas. Most of these were formed when surface water or groundwater from the eastern slope of the Sierra Nevada was heated by magma at shallow depths. One of the best known of these geothermal areas is Hot Creek Gorge, which lies within the Long Valley Caldera.

Hot Creek Geological Site - *From the junction Hwy. 395 and Hot Creek Hatchery Rd. drive 3.5 mi. E on Hot Creek Hatchery Rd. to the Hot Creek Geological Site; the site has a good viewing area and several paths to the bottom of the gorge.*
Hot Creek lies at the bottom of a 100-foot gorge that cuts across the southeast flank of the resurgent dome. The creek flowed through this area prior to uplift of the resurgent dome, and the gorge was cut as the creek maintained its established course during uplift of the dome.

The water in Hot Creek has its source in the Mammoth area where a number of snow-fed creeks combine to form Mammoth Creek. Mammoth Creek then flows eastward into the Long Valley Caldera. In the caldera, much of the cold water soaks into the ground and is heated by the magma under the caldera. Near Casa Diablo, this hot groundwater mingles with the surface water from Mammoth Creek. The creek then changes its name to Hot Creek, and continues to flow eastward through Hot Creek Gorge. Further east, Hot Creek leaves the gorge, spreads out on the floor of the eastern part of the caldera, and eventually makes its way into the Owens River and Lake Crowley.

The temperature of the water in Hot Creek can rise dramatically after earthquake activity. Many of the earthquakes in this area are caused by movement of magma under the caldera, and the moving magma provides new sources of heat for the groundwater that flows into Hot Creek. Hot Creek is a popular swimming area, but test the water before you plunge in, particularly after an earthquake!

The rocks in the walls of Hot Creek Gorge are a rhyolite lava flow that erupted from a vent on the southern rim of the Long Valley Caldera about 300,000 years ago. The lava flow is about three miles long and 500 feet thick. Along the creek, the rhyolite has been bleached, oxidized, and altered to white clay by the hot water in many places. Hydrothermal alteration of rhyolite is common in volcanic areas, and can result in large deposits of clay. The kaolinite deposits at the Huntley Mine in the center of the resurgent dome were formed in this manner.

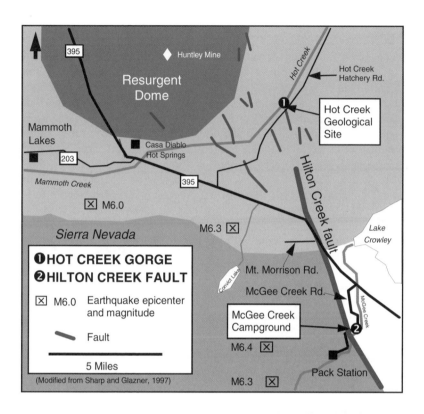

Hot Creek Gorge at the Geological Site. The Sierra Nevada is on the horizon.

❷ Hilton Creek Fault

The Hilton Creek fault is one of the many faults that make up the Frontal fault system of the Sierra Nevada. The fault begins south of Hilton Creek, cuts through the McGee Creek Campground, and then continues north into the Long Valley Caldera, where it splays into a number of small faults and dies out. This fault is of special interest because it has been recently active and this activity seems to be related to the current volcanism in the Long Valley Caldera. In May of 1980, a series of four earthquakes (M6.0 to M6.4) occurred within a few miles of the Hilton Creek fault. The earthquakes were accompanied by a number of surface ruptures along the fault. Most of these ruptures were less than a mile long and had vertical movements less than six inches. There were also a large number of ruptures in the southern part of the resurgent dome and these ruptures are on trend with the Hilton Creek fault. It appears that magma under the caldera is intermittently making its way upward along fractured rocks in the fault zone. The 1980 faulting in this area is the most significant earthquake activity on the east side of the Sierra Nevada since the 1872 Owens Valley earthquake. One of the best places to see the Hilton Creek fault is at the McGee Creek Campground.

McGee Creek Campground - *From Hwy. 203 and Hwy. 395, drive S 8 mi. on Hwy. 395; turn right on McGee Creek Rd. and go 2 mi. to the McGee Creek Campground.*

During the Pleistocene glacial episodes, a glacier flowed down McGee Creek and extended about a mile beyond the mountain front. When the glacier melted, it left behind the huge pile of terminal, recessional, and lateral moraines that can easily be seen from Highway 395. McGee Creek Road climbs up this pile of glacial material. The McGee Creek Campground lies in a flat valley along McGee Creek, and is flanked by two large lateral moraines. The flat floor of the valley was formed from glacial outwash sediments. At the campground, the flat valley floor and the flanking lateral moraines are cut by a 50-foot high scarp formed by the Hilton Creek fault. The scarp appears as a steep embankment at the west end of the campground, and provides a neat windbreak for the campground. On the hillside above the campground, you can see where the fault scarp cuts through the lateral moraines. McGee Creek Road continues beyond the campground and makes a jog where it crosses the fault scarp on the northern lateral moraine. The outwash plain and lateral moraines at the McGee Creek Campground were deposited during the last glacial episode. The faulting must have occurred after this glacial episode. It is rare for a fault scarp of this magnitude to be preserved, and it is rare for a fault scarp to cut glacial material that is this young.

This view of the eastern front of the Sierra at McGee Creek shows the large pile of glacial till left by the McGee Creek glacier. The till appears as the low flat-topped ridge in the center of the photo. The Hilton Creek fault lies along the mountain front and cuts through some of this glacial material.

The Hilton Creek fault scarp lies at the west end of the McGee Creek Campground. The thin horizontal line of snow follows the top of the fault scarp. To the right, the scarp crosses McGee Creek Road and then climbs up the north wall of the valley.

❸ Bishop Tuff

The volcanic ash that was deposited during eruption of the Long Valley volcano is referred to as the Bishop Tuff. There are many exposures of the Bishop Tuff in the vicinity of the Long Valley Caldera. However, the most extensive exposures are southeast of the Long Valley Caldera, where the tuff extends for 20 miles across Owens Valley and as far south as Bishop and Big Pine.

The Bishop Tuff includes several different units. At the base is a layer of unconsolidated white ash and pumice, about ten to fifteen feet thick, that was thrown into the air at the beginning of the eruption and fell to the ground near the volcano. This air-fall ash is overlain by a series of ash flows that streamed down the flanks of the Long Valley volcano during its eruption. The ash flows are as much as 500 feet thick. Where the ash flows were thick, mainly in the center of the flow, the hot ash fused together to form welded tuff. The welded tuff is extremely hard and forms the rough, desolate Volcanic Tableland that lies between Bishop and the Long Valley Caldera. Where the ash flows were thin, mainly along the margins of the flow, the ash was not welded, and consists of white unconsolidated tuff. You will see the air-fall tuff and the unconsolidated ash-flow tuff at the Big Pumice Cut south of Toms Place, and the welded tuff and Volcanic Tableland during the trip to Owens Gorge.

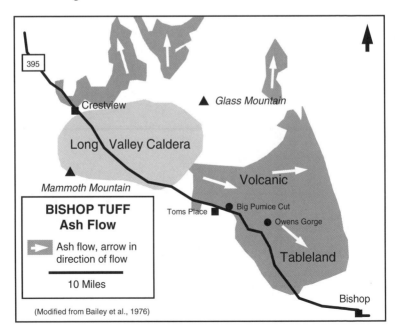

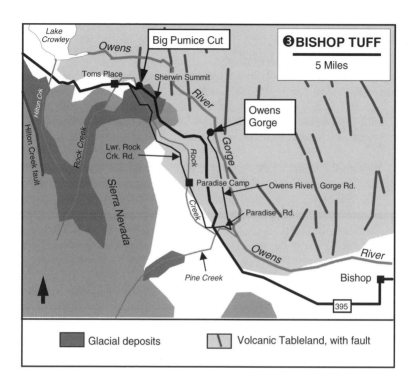

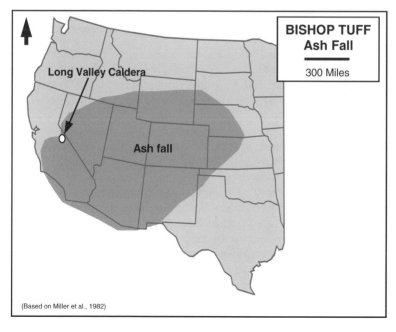

(Based on Miller et al., 1982)

Big Pumice Cut – *From Toms Place go S on Hwy. 395 1 mi.; park in the large pullout on the W side of the highway immediately S of Lower Rock Creek Rd. The Big Pumice cut is on the E side of Hwy. 395.*

The Big Pumice cut is a large roadcut along Highway 395 that exposes the unconsolidated rocks that were deposited along the western edge of the ash flows that form the Bishop Tuff. The white tuff and pumice in the roadcut erodes rapidly, so there are few good, clean exposures. However, there is still much to see.

Before the Bishop Tuff was deposited, much of the Sierra mountain front south and west of this area was covered by the Sherwin Till. The Sherwin Till was deposited about 800,000 years ago, during the second oldest glacial episode in the Sierra Nevada. When the Bishop Tuff was deposited, it covered the Sherwin Till in this area. You can see the Sherwin Till at the north end of the Big Pumice cut, where the brush is growing. The till is composed of partially decomposed boulders and other poorly sorted glacial debris. In the roadcut, note that the Bishop Tuff lies on top of the Sherwin Till and that the contact between the till and the tuff slopes gently to the right. Since the tuff was deposited on top of the till, the Sherwin till is obviously older than the tuff. This roadcut is one of the few places that the age relationship between the Sherwin Till and the Bishop Tuff can be seen, and was the subject of a technical publication by Sharp in 1968.

The lowermost 15 feet of the Bishop Tuff that overlies the Sherwin Till consists of a layer of pumice and ash. This is the material that had been thrown into the air at the beginning of the eruption of the Long Valley volcano. This air-fall pumice is mainly fine-grained and forms well-bedded layers. In this roadcut, these layers follow the surface of the underlying Sherwin Till and slope gently to the right. The remainder of the tuff in the roadcut is mainly coarse, poorly-sorted pumice. In clean exposures, very faint near-horizontal layering can be seen. This pumice was deposited as a series of ash flows. The faint layering probably represents different pulses during the flow. These rocks were at the edge of the ash flow and never became welded. You will see that these rocks are quite different from the welded tuffs at the Gorge Overlook. In the center of the roadcut, several near-vertical clastic dikes cut through the Bishop Tuff. These dikes consist of sand and gravel that has fallen into cracks in the tuff from the overlying surface rocks. The sand and gravel in these dikes is harder than the pumice, so the dikes are quite prominent in the outcrop.

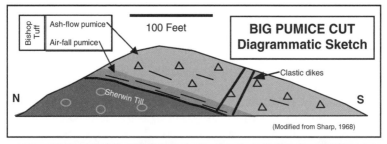

The Sherwin Till is exposed on the lower brush-covered slope to the left. Note the large boulders in the till. The till is overlain by the white rocks of the Bishop Tuff in the upper part of the roadcut.

Two clastic dikes cut through the Bishop Tuff in the center of the Big Pumice cut. The banded layer between the dikes is air-fall pumice and the overlying white rocks are ash-flow pumice.

Owens Gorge - *From Toms Place drive 11 mi. S on Hwy. 395; turn E on Paradise Rd. and drive 1 mi.; turn N on Gorge Rd. and drive 6 mi. to the Upper Power Plant; park near the closed gate.*

As you drive along Gorge Road to the Upper Power Plant, you are driving on the Volcanic Tableland. The tableland is an extremely hard surface that resists erosion and is formed from welded tuff. The welded tuff is part of the Bishop Tuff, and the tableland represents the upper surface of the thick ash flows that were deposited during eruption of the Long Valley volcano. The ash flows were several hundred feet thick in this area, and the hot ash cooled slowly. The tuff fragments were welded together as the ash cooled. During the cooling period, gas that had been trapped in the ash flows was expelled to the surface through vents. These vents now appear as scattered small conical hills on the tableland, and are locally known as pimples. You can see many of these pimples along Gorge Road.

When the ash flows were first deposited in this area, the surface of the tableland sloped gently south from the Long Valley volcano to Big Pine. Since then, Bishop and Big Pine have dropped over 2,000 feet relative to Long Valley. Some of this downward movement was by down-warping of the ground and some by faulting that took place along a number of small faults. These faults cut across the tableland, and each fault offsets and drops the surface of the tableland 20 feet or so. Most of the faults are on the east side of the Owens Gorge, so they are not apparent along Gorge Road.

From the pullout near the Upper Power Plant you can get a good view of the Owens Gorge and the welded tuff that is exposed in the walls of the gorge. The tuff has well-developed columnar joints that form large vertical columns along the steep walls of the gorge. In some places, the joints are not vertical, but form spectacular radiating columns. These columns formed around the gas vents in the flow. The vents represented a cooling surface to the flow, and the columns formed perpendicular to that cooling surface. These vents formed the pimples on the surface of the flow.

The welded tuff is very hard and erodes into steep cliffs. In fresh exposures, the rock is mostly pink, but the rock is brown on weathered surfaces. If you look at the rock with a magnifying glass, you will see small fragments of pumice, clear fragments of feldspar and quartz, and many small pieces of other nondescript volcanic rocks. In the walls of the gorge, you can see evidence of multiple ash flows. Some white pumice is also found within the flows near the Upper Power Plant.

Owens Gorge at the Upper Power Plant is cut into the hard welded ash flows of the Bishop Tuff. The top of the Bishop Tuff forms the Volcanic Tableland. Columnar joints in the welded tuff form pillars that line the walls of the gorge.

Radiating columnar joints in the Bishop Tuff are exposed in the wall of Owens Gorge near the Upper Power Plant. The joints formed around a vent where gas escaped from the ash flow. The "pimple" on the surface of the ash flow was also formed by the escaping gas.

❹ *Mammoth Mountain*

Mammoth Mountain is a volcano that lies along the southwestern rim of the Long Valley Caldera. The volcano began to take shape 200,000 years ago and was built up over the next 160,000 years by a series of a dozen or so eruptions of rhyolite and andesite interspersed with layers of tuff, scoria, and pumice. The last of these eruptions was about 40,000 years ago.

Summit - *From the main ski lodge at Mammoth Mountain take the gondola to the top, then hike 0.25 mi. to the S summit; go in the summer when there is no snow.*
You can see some of the volcanic rocks that make up Mammoth Mountain along the short hike from the summit gondola station to the south summit of the mountain. Most of the rocks along the trail are purple and gray andesite with crystals of quartz, feldspar, biotite, and hornblende. Some of these rocks have been altered by hot steam and fluids that have destroyed the biotite and hornblende and turned the feldspar into clay. From the summit, you can see across the Long Valley Caldera to Glass Mountain, just beyond the east side of the caldera.

Now that you have enjoyed the view from the summit, there is something else that I should tell you. You are standing on top of an active volcano. In May of 1980, a number of earthquakes were recorded at Mammoth Mountain. These earthquakes were caused by surges of magma in a magma chamber that lies below the mountain. In 1989, another swarm of earthquakes was caused by upward intrusion of a dike of magma that lies one to two miles below the mountain. Large volumes of gas are still being expelled from the magma below Mammoth Mountain. In most volcanoes, this gas would make its way upward and come out of a vent at the summit. However, at Mammoth Mountain impermeable rocks above the magma chamber stop this upward flow. The gas is, instead, forced to rise along the flanks of the volcano, and some escapes from fumaroles on the flanks of the mountain. Gondola 2 passes near one of these fumaroles on its way to the summit. Other gas rises around the base of the volcano, where it locally permeates the ground. Following the 1980 earthquakes, there was an increase in water temperature and flow at most of the fumaroles on Mammoth Mountain. After the 1989 earthquakes, there was an increase in CO_2 gas derived from the magma. The earthquakes and CO_2 gas emissions at Mammoth Mountain have been under intense study by the U.S. Geological Survey for many years. For an update on the volcanic activity for the Long Valley Caldera, go to their website: http://quake.wr.usgs.gov/VOLCANOES/LongValley.

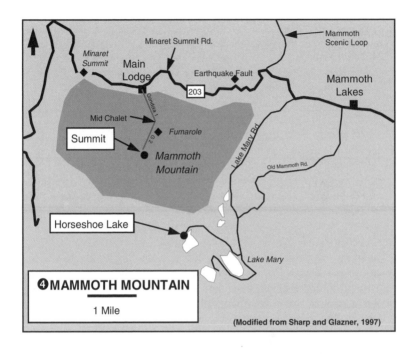

Minaret Summit Rd.

Mammoth
Scenic Loop

Minaret
Summit

Main
Lodge

Earthquake Fault

Mammoth
Lakes

203

Gondola

Mid Chalet

Fumarole

Lake Mary Rd.

Summit

Mammoth
Mountain

Old Mammoth Rd.

Horseshoe Lake

Lake Mary

❹**MAMMOTH MOUNTAIN**

1 Mile

(Modified from Sharp and Glazner, 1997)

A steep cliff of the andesitic volcanic rocks that form Mammoth Mountain can be seen from the gondola to the summit. The reflections in the upper right are from the window of the gondola.

Horseshoe Lake - *Drive to the end of Lake Mary Road; park in the parking lot for the abandoned Horseshoe Lake campground.*

From the parking lot at Horseshoe Lake, you can see a large area of dead trees. In 1990, the Forest Service first noticed that the trees were dying in this area. Soon, it was recognized that this tree kill was due to abnormally large concentrations of CO_2 in the soil. Chemical analysis of the gas indicated that the gas was coming from a magmatic source rather than from groundwater. The swarm of earthquakes that occurred at Mammoth Mountain in 1989 was attributed to movement of magma below Mammoth Mountain. The gas was probably released from the magma at that time. Earthquakes related to movement of magma have occurred periodically since 1989, so the problem has not yet passed.

When the CO_2 gas was released from the magma during the 1989 earthquake, some of the gas escaped from fumaroles. However, most of the gas simply percolated upward through the ground around the base of the mountain. Since CO_2 is heavier than air, the gas can build up to abnormally high concentrations in low spots on the ground. High concentrations also occur when the CO_2 is trapped under heavy snow cover and not allowed to dissipate.

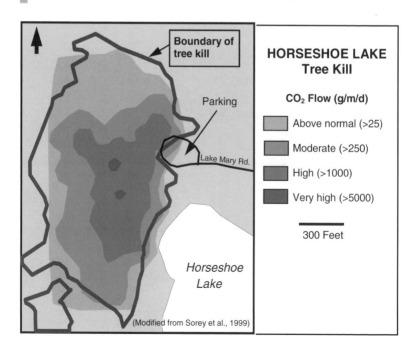

Boundary of tree kill

Parking

Lake Mary Rd.

Horseshoe Lake

HORSESHOE LAKE Tree Kill

CO_2 Flow (g/m/d)

Above normal (>25)

Moderate (>250)

High (>1000)

Very high (>5000)

300 Feet

(Modified from Sorey et al., 1999)

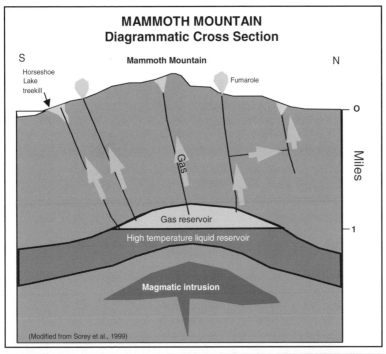

These trees near the parking lot at Horseshoe Lake have been killed by excess CO_2 that has permeated the soil. The CO_2 is coming from a magma reservoir that lies below Mammoth Mountain.

❺ *Earthquake Fault*

The earthquake fault is on the north slope of Mammoth Mountain and at the south end of the Inyo Craters. Despite its billing, the earthquake fault is not a fault and it is unlikely that it was caused by an earthquake. In fact, no one really knows how the crack was formed. Take a look and see if you have any ideas.

Earthquake Fault - *From the junction of Mammoth Scenic Loop and Hwy. 203 drive W on Hwy. 203 1 mi. to the earthquake fault turnoff; take the short drive to the parking area.*

From the parking area you can take a short walk to the earthquake fault and then go along the fault for some distance. The fault is a large open crack, up to 10 feet wide and 50 feet deep, that extends north-south for somewhat less than a mile. The crack occurs in a rhyolite lava flow, one of the many flows that make up Mammoth Mountain. If you look at the irregularities in the rocks on either side of the crack, it appears that that there is no offset along the crack, but that the sides were simply pulled apart. No one really knows how the crack was formed. It doesn't appear to be a fault because

The earthquake fault is a deep crack in a rhyolite flow on the north flank of Mammoth Mountain. The origin of the crack is not known, but it is doubtful that the crack was formed by an earthquake.

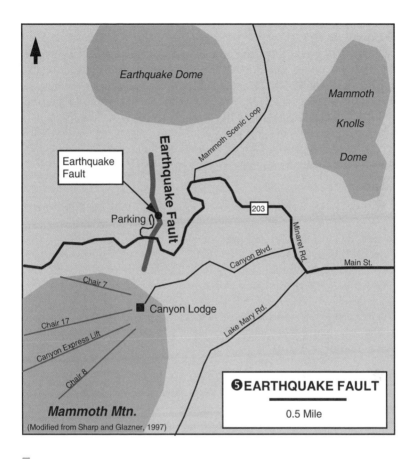

the sides are not offset. The crack was not caused by cooling of the lava flow because the flow occurred over 50,000 years ago. Any crack formed at that time would have been filled long ago. One possibility is that the crack formed when the lava flow was bent by a deep-seated intrusion of magma at the south end of the Inyo Craters. There has been a great deal of volcanic activity along the Inyo Craters during the last 2,000 years. If the crack had occurred in most other types of rock, it probably would not have survived long. However, the rhyolite flow is hard, brittle rock, and does not erode rapidly.

From the viewing area, the earthquake fault extends south to Highway 203, which goes across the crack. Immediately south of the highway the crack continues as a shallow trench, and then dies out as it heads for the ski area near Canyon Lodge.

❻ Devils Postpile

The Devils Postpile is the most spectacular and best-known example of columnar jointing in California. The basalt that forms the postpile came from vents on the valley floor near the Upper Soda Springs Campground about 100,000 years ago, during the Tahoe glacial episode. After leaving the vent, the lava flowed down the valley of the Middle Fork of the San Joaquin River about 2.5 miles. At that point it encountered an obstruction in the valley, perhaps a glacial moraine, and ponded in back of the obstruction until it reached a thickness of 400 feet - much thicker than most basalt flows.

It took an unusual set of geologic circumstances to form the long curved columns at Devils Postpile. The lava was thick and homogeneous, with no flow banding. There was little gas in the flow, so few vesicles were formed. This thick mass of lava cooled very slowly. As it cooled, it contracted evenly, and formed very regular contraction joints. Typically, contraction joints break lava flows into six-sided columns that are perpendicular to the cooling surface. In a tabular flow, these columns are usually vertical. However, the thick Devils Postpile flow was not tabular, but pinched out along the sides of the valley. The columns at Devils Postpile thus curve toward the edges of the valley.

Shortly after the lava flow, glaciers moved down the river valley and overrode the basalt. The glaciers also quarried the basalt along the columnar joints, and eventually removed much of the flow from the central part of the valley. Devils Postpile represents a small remnant of the original flow that clings to the east side of the valley. After glaciation, many of the basalt columns subsequently broke from the side of the flow and accumulated in the large pile seen at the base of the cliff.

Viewpoint - *From Minaret Summit drive 7 mi. W on Hwy. 203 to the Devils Postpile Ranger Station; from there take the short hike to the Devils Postpile viewpoint. Accessible mid-June to mid-Oct. In summer, take the shuttle from Mammoth Mtn. Inn 7AM to 7PM daily. For details, phone 760-934-2289 or check website www.nps.gov/depo.*
From the base of the Devils Postpile you can see the tall basalt columns exposed in the cliff on the east side of the river valley. In the center of the postpile, the columns are near vertical, but along the edges, the columns are curved so that they lie at a steep angle. Individual columns are as much as 60 feet long, and many are two to three feet in diameter. Note that most of the basalt columns have six sides, but you can also find columns with three, four, five, and seven sides. This is typical for most basalt flows. The basalt is dark gray, fine grained, and has phenocrysts of plagioclase and olivine.

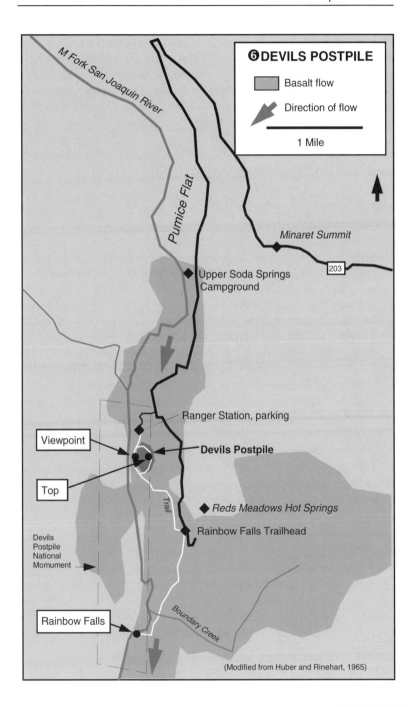

❻DEVILS POSTPILE

Basalt flow

Direction of flow

1 Mile

M Fork San Joaquin River

Pumice Flat

Minaret Summit

203

Upper Soda Springs Campground

Ranger Station, parking

Viewpoint

Devils Postpile

Top

Trail

Reds Meadows Hot Springs

Rainbow Falls Trailhead

Devils Postpile National Momument

Rainbow Falls

Boundary Creek

(Modified from Huber and Rinehart, 1965)

Top - *From the viewpoint, take the short loop trail to the top of the postpile.*
After this short hike, you will be standing on top of the Devils Postpile lava flow. The tops of the basalt columns have been polished and striated by the Pleistocene glaciers and look like polished tiles on a rounded dance floor. The striations indicate the direction of movement of the glacier.

Rainbow Falls - *Take the trail from Devils Postpile (4 mi. RT) or from Rainbow Falls trailhead (2 mi. RT); a stairway and short trail lead to the bottom of the falls.*
At Rainbow Falls, the Middle Fork of the San Joaquin River drops 101 feet over a cliff of the same lava flow that formed Devils Postpile. It appears that two separate geologic steps were needed to make these falls:

1) When the last glacier melted at the end of the last ice age, the Middle Fork of the San Joaquin River flowed downstream from the Devils Postpile on the west side of the lava flow. The basalt cliff along the western edge of the lava flow was formed by river erosion when the river occupied this course.

2) Later, upstream from Rainbow Falls, the river was diverted eastward and began to flow on the top of the lava flow. The river then plunged over the edge of the flow, forming Rainbow Falls. At the base of the falls, the river returned to its original channel and continued to flow south.

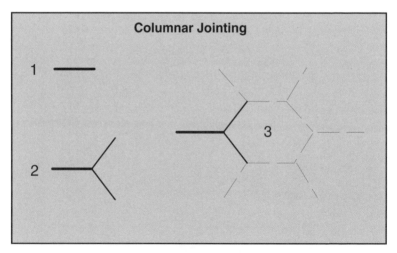

Columnar Jointing

1. As the lava cooled, it shrank, and small contraction cracks began to form.
2. After the cracks extended about ten inches, they branched to form an angle of about 120°. This provided the maximum stress relief.
3. After each new crack extended another ten inches, it branched again, forming six-sided columns.

Devils Postpile is one of the most spectacular examples of columnar jointing of a basalt lava flow in California.

At the top of Devils Postpile, the basalt columns have been polished by glaciers to resemble a curved tiled dance floor. Striations on the polished surface indicate the direction of movement of the glacier.

❼ Minaret Summit

The Minaret Summit is a low point along the Sierra Nevada drainage divide. Moisture-laden winter storms from the west are funneled through this divide and directed toward Mammoth Mountain. Mammoth Mountain soaks up the moisture from these storms in thick blankets of snow and then sends the dehumidified air on to Owens Valley and Nevada. Mammoth Mountain thus accumulates large amounts of snow during the winter, whereas most of the other peaks east of the Sierra crest get little moisture and little snow. Mammoth Mountain is ideally situated to capture the winter snow from the west, and still provide easy access from the protected eastern slope of the Sierra.

Minaret Summit - *From Old Mammoth Rd. and Hwy. 203 drive 5 mi. W on Hwy. 203 to the Minaret Summit; take the short turnoff to the view area.*

From Minaret Summit, you can get an excellent view of the Minarets, which appear as a series of sharp rugged spires that dominate the horizon six miles to the west. The Minarets are formed from metamorphosed Cretaceous volcanic rocks, and the weathering and erosion of these dark volcanic rocks has given the Minarets its distinctive topography. In a 1994 publication, Fiske and Tobisch showed that these volcanic rocks are composed largely of pyroclastic flows and were formed along the western margin of a large Cretaceous caldera. The Minarets Caldera is similar in size to the nearby and more recent Long Valley Caldera.

The Minarets Caldera is part of the large Ritter Range roof pendant, which consists of 30,000 feet of dark metamorphosed Cretaceous volcanic rocks that have been only slightly deformed. This roof pendant is a remnant of the Cretaceous volcanic rocks that once covered the Sierra Nevada batholith. The volcanic rocks were formed at the surface while the plutons of the Sierra Nevada batholith were being intruded at depth. During Cretaceous time, this part of the Sierra must have been somewhat similar to the present-day Andes, where numerous volcanoes erupt at the surface as plutons are formed at depth.

After the volcanic rocks of the Ritter Range were deposited, some were reheated to high temperatures by the underlying granite magma of the Sierra Nevada batholith. Where this has occurred, the volcanic rocks have been altered and new minerals have been formed. One of the most common of these minerals is garnet, which occurs as small red crystals in the metamorphosed volcanic rocks. Rocks altered by heating in this manner are called hornfels and are common in the Ritter Range.

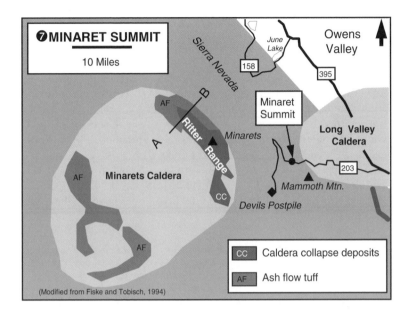

Diagrammatic Cross Section

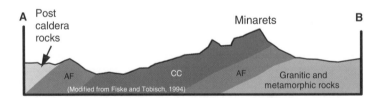

The Minarets consist of dark metamorphosed Cretaceous volcanic rocks that were formed along the east side of the Minarets Caldera.

❽ *Inyo Craters*

The Inyo Craters are a six-mile-long chain of craters, domes, flows, explosion pits, faults, and cracks that extend from Mammoth Mountain north to Obsidian Dome. This volcanic trend crosses the rim of the Long Valley Caldera without any apparent change. It also crosses the Hartley Springs fault, one of the major frontal faults of the Sierra Nevada, without effect. All of the volcanic activity along this trend is quite recent. The oldest volcanic activity was the formation of the North Deadman Dome several thousand years ago. The most recent activity occurred approximately 500 to 600 years ago and resulted in the formation of Obsidian Dome, South Glass Creek Dome, South Deadman Dome, Dear Mountain, and the Inyo Crater Lakes at the south end of the trend.

> **Inyo Crater Lakes** - *From the junction of Hwy. 203 and Mammoth Scenic Loop drive N on the Mammoth Scenic Loop 2.5 mi.; turn W at the "Inyo Craters" turnoff and follow the unpaved road 1 mi. to the parking area; hike 0.3 mi. to the craters.*
> There are three craters in this group. The hike from the parking area takes you to the two smaller craters. Each of these is about 600 feet across. The southern crater is about 200 feet deep and the northern crater about 100 feet deep. Both are filled by small lakes. The third crater of the group is at the top of Deer Mountain, immediately to the north. These craters were formed about 500 years ago when magma, rising along a dike, encountered groundwater. The

This pit at the southern Inyo Crater Lake was formed by an explosion of steam when rising magma encountered groundwater near the surface.

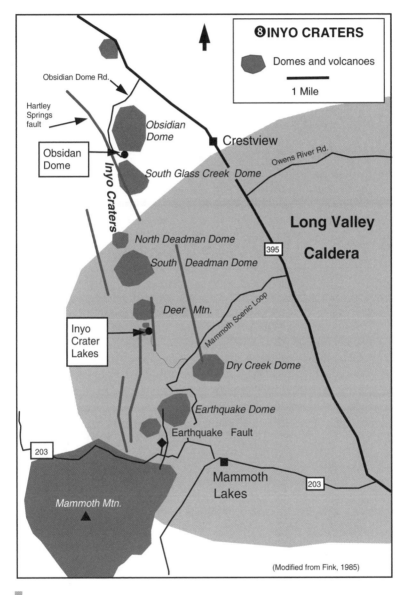

❽INYO CRATERS

Domes and volcanoes

1 Mile

Obsidian Dome Rd.

Hartley Springs fault

Obsidan Dome

Inyo Craters

Obsidian Dome

Crestview

Owens River Rd.

South Glass Creek Dome

Long Valley

North Deadman Dome

South Deadman Dome

395

Caldera

Deer Mtn.

Mammoth Scenic Loop

Inyo Crater Lakes

Dry Creek Dome

Earthquake Dome

Earthquake Fault

203

Mammoth Mtn.

Mammoth Lakes

203

(Modified from Fink, 1985)

groundwater turned to steam, forming *phreatic* explosions that blasted the craters from the country rock. No volcanic rocks erupted from the craters at the time of the explosions. The walls of the craters consist of near-horizontal layers of tuff and lava flows that came from other earlier eruptive centers. If the steam had vented slowly rather than explosively, there would have been fumaroles at this locality rather than craters.

Obsidian Dome - *From the junction of Hwy. 158 and Hwy. 395 go S 3.7 mi. on Hwy. 395; turn W on Obsidian Dome Rd.; go 1.5 mi. to the parking area for Obsidian Dome.*

Obsidian Dome is a small dome near the north end of the Inyo Craters. The dome was formed when viscous rhyolite magma oozed from a vent about 600 years ago. At the beginning of the eruption, volcanic tuff was ejected from the vent and carried northeast, where it formed a blanket several feet thick near the vent.

To see the rocks that form the dome, hike up the short gated road to the abandoned rock quarry at the top of the dome. The rocks along the road and at the top consist of layers of obsidian, stony rhyolite and pumice. The obsidian looks like black glass and breaks into hard sharp fragments with curved surfaces. The stony rhyolite is dull and colored gray, orange and pink. The pumice is light gray, foamy, and very light weight. Blocks of pumice quarried at Obsidian Dome were used as decorative rock.

The obsidian, stony rhyolite, and pumice at Obsidian Dome are essentially the same composition and were formed from viscous rhyolitic magma. The differences in composition are due mainly to the amount of gas in the magma and the cooling history of the magma. The obsidian formed from gas-poor rhyolitic magma that chilled so fast that crystals did not have time to form. Crystallization was slow because the magma was viscous and the elements had trouble combining into crystals. The stony rhyolite formed from magma that cooled more slowly, and small crystals had time to form. The pumice formed from frothy layers of gas-rich magma that chilled rapidly.

Obsidian is common in young rhyolite eruptions. However, obsidian is a supercooled liquid, and over time obsidian crystallizes into stony rhyolite. Thus, old obsidian flows are rare. The process by which obsidian changes to stony rhyolite is referred to as *devitrification*. Devitrification begins at the surface of the obsidian, which is exposed to weathering, and works toward the interior. Old obsidian flows have a rind of devitrified glass. The older the flow, the thicker the rind, assuming the same climatic conditions. If the rate of devitrification is known, then the age of the obsidian can be determined. Many of the obsidian flows along the Inyo and Mono Craters have been dated using this method.

This obsidian flow at Obsidian Dome has near-vertical flow banding and is broken into large blocks that formed as the obsidian cooled. Note the striated surfaces that were formed like grooves in toothpaste squeezed from a tube.

In this close up view of the flow you can see bands of black obsidian, gray rhyolite, and white frothy pumice. The pen at lower left provides scale.

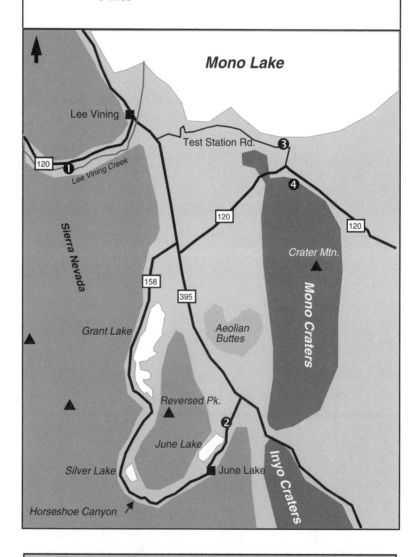

Trip 3.
MONO LAKE AREA

3 Miles

❶ Lee Vining Canyon
❷ June Lake Loop
❸ Tufa Towers
❹ Mono Craters

Mono Lake

Lee Vining

Test Station Rd. ❸

120

❶ Lee Vining Creek

❹

Sierra Nevada

120

120

Crater Mtn.

158

395

Mono Craters

Grant Lake

Aeolian
Buttes

Reversed Pk.

❷

June Lake

Inyo Craters

Silver Lake

June Lake

Horseshoe Canyon

The Mono Basin Scenic Area Visitor Center, located on Highway 395 just north of Lee Vining, has interactive exhibits on Mono Lake and guided walking tours along the shoreline (760-647-3044).

MONO LAKE AREA
Glaciers on the Eastern Slope

Mono Lake occupies a low spot in the Mono Basin, one of the many basins in the Basin and Range Province. The Mono Basin was formed when a large block of the earth's crust subsided along a major fault that goes through Lee Vining. The Sierra block was uplifted along this fault as the Mono Basin subsided. Most of this faulting occurred over the last five million years. As the Sierra Nevada was uplifted, the mountains were eroded and the erosion products were conveniently deposited in the subsiding Mono Basin. From time to time, volcanic rocks were added to the sediments as the basin subsided. To date, an estimated 10,000 feet of sediments and volcanic rocks have been dumped into Mono Basin from the Sierra Nevada.

Mono Lake is an enclosed saline lake. The lake gets most of its water from the Sierra, but has no outlet. Since the Mono Basin is arid, evaporation of the lake water has increased the salinity of the lake and the lake is now more saline than seawater. This saline water supports a large population of brine shrimp, which attract birds and other wildlife. The lake is also noted for its unusual tufa pinnacles that are found locally along the shoreline.

Until 1941, Mono Lake had been supplied with fresh water that flowed into the lake along Rush, Parker, Walker and Lee Vining Creeks. In 1941, the Los Angeles Department of Water and Power began to divert this water to Los Angeles through a newly completed tunnel and aqueduct system. Since these creeks had been the main water supply for Mono Lake, the water level of the lake began to drop at a rate of over one foot per year. By 1982, the water level had dropped 45 feet and the existence of the lake and the associated wildlife began to be seriously threatened. Concerned groups sounded the alarm and started a major movement for restoration of the lake. As a result of this movement, in 1985 the lake was declared a natural preserve and in 1994 the Department of Water and Power agreed to maintain the elevation of the lake at 6,392 feet. This elevation is 20 feet above the 1982 low-point and 25 feet below the pre-diversion level. The lake is not expected to reach its mandated level until 2014.

Lake Russell

Although the Mono Lake area is now arid, Mono Lake looked quite different during the Pleistocene glacial episodes. The glacial-age lake, referred to as Lake Russell, was much larger than the present lake and over 600 feet higher. Glaciers, fed mainly by the large Tuolumne icefield in the High Sierra, came down Lundy Canyon, Lee Vining Canyon, Bloody Canyon, Rush Creek and Reversed Creek and pushed their glacial ice and debris into the western shore of Lake Russell. In route, the glaciers carved and widened their valleys, scooped out bedrock that would later be filled by lakes, and carried a large load of rock debris. When the glaciers melted at the end of the glacial episodes, they left a number of large lateral, terminal, and recessional moraines along the eastern slope of the Sierra Nevada, from Robinson Creek in the north to Reversed Creek in the south. Some of this glacial debris was pushed over a mile beyond the mountain front.

Prior to eruption of the Long Valley Caldera, Lake Russell drained south into the Owens River, and from there into Owens Lake. However, this outlet was plugged by the eruption of the Long Valley volcano. From that time to present, the lake has had no outlet and the lake level has risen and fallen, depending on the supply of water, the rate of evaporation, and the thirst of Los Angeles. The lake level was high

The horizontal lines along the lower part of the Sierra mountain front, as seen from the Mono Basin Visitor Center, define several old shorelines of Pleistocene Lake Russell.

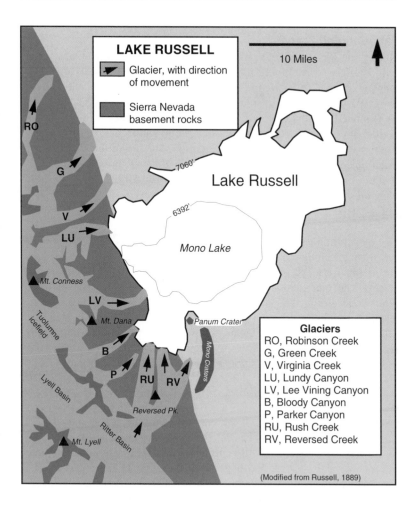

LAKE RUSSELL

Glacier, with direction of movement

Sierra Nevada basement rocks

10 Miles

RO

7060'

Lake Russell

6392'

G

V

LU

Mt. Conness

Mono Lake

Tuolumne Icefield

LV

Mt. Dana

Panum Crater

Lyell Basin

B

P

RU   RV

Mono Craters

Glaciers
RO, Robinson Creek
G, Green Creek
V, Virginia Creek
LU, Lundy Canyon
LV, Lee Vining Canyon
B, Bloody Canyon
P, Parker Canyon
RU, Rush Creek
RV, Reversed Creek

Reversed Pk.

Ritter Basin

Mt. Lyell

(Modified from Russell, 1889)

during the glacial episodes and low during interglacial times. Many of the shorelines of these earlier lakes can be seen as faint lines encircling the lake.

During the trip to the Mono Lake area, you will see the lateral, terminal and recessional moraines and some of the other glacial features formed by the Pleistocene glaciers in Lee Vining Canyon and in the June Lake area. You will also walk along the shoreline of Mono Lake, see the famed tufa towers, and learn how these unusual features were formed. Finally, you will visit the Mono Craters, see how the craters were formed, and get a close look at the volcanic rocks that make up the Mono Craters.

❶ *Lee Vining Canyon*

During the Pleistocene glacial episodes, Lee Vining Canyon was filled with the large Lee Vining glacier, which abruptly terminated in Lake Russell. The glacier started in the Tuolumne icefield, which spilled over Tioga Pass, and was then joined by glaciers from several side canyons as it moved down Lee Vining Canyon. When the Lee Vining glacier melted, it deposited its load of rocks as lateral and recessional moraines. There were at least four major glacial episodes during the Pleistocene. Each episode brought new glaciers that bulldozed through the earlier moraines and left their own moraines. Thus, many of the early moraines were destroyed, and most of the moraines that we see today are from the latest glacial episodes, the Tahoe and Tioga.

The most prominent moraines are the lateral moraines that form the high linear ridges along the sides of lower Lee Vining Canyon. These ridges are as much as 700 feet high and have two crests on each side of the valley. The outer crest was formed during Tahoe glaciation and the inner crest during the younger Tioga glaciation. There is also a large terminal moraine at the end of Lee Vining Canyon, just east of the information pullout on Highway 120. In addition a number of smaller recessional moraines appear as a series of low ridges that cross the lower part of Lee Vining Canyon west of the information pullout.

Utility Road - *From Lee Vining, go W on Hwy. 120 1 mi.; turn N on Utility Rd. and park in the first pullout.*
Utility Road cuts through the terminal moraine at the end of Lee Vining Canyon and you can see the rocks that make up this moraine in the roadcuts along Utility Road. These rocks are unsorted, and include clay, gravel, and huge boulders. Most of the boulders and smaller stones are rounded or subangular. A few have grooves and striations that were formed when the rock was ground against resistant bedrock. The moraine is 500 feet high at Utility Road.

Lower Lee Vining Campground – *From Lee Vining go W 2.5 mi. on Hwy. 120; park at the entrance to Lower Lee Vining Campground.*
Lower Lee Vining Campground lies immediately east of one of the recessional moraines in the lower part of Lee Vining Canyon. The moraine forms a 20-foot high ridge that extends across the valley between the two large lateral moraines on the sides of the valley. This recessional moraine briefly served as a dam for Lee Vining Creek, but the creek now cuts through the moraine. Further up the valley over the next two miles there are many other recessional moraines. Cattleguard and Moraine campgrounds are both built on recessional moraines.

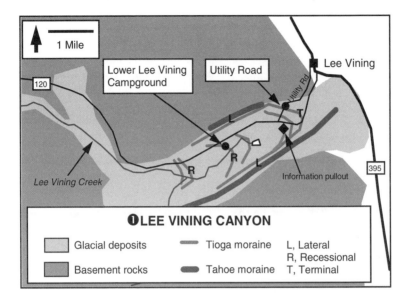

Lower Lee Vining Campground

Utility Road

Lee Vining

Utility Rd

120

Lee Vining Creek

Information pullout

395

L

R

R

L

T

❶LEE VINING CANYON

Glacial deposits

Tioga moraine

L, Lateral
R, Recessional

Basement rocks

Tahoe moraine

T, Terminal

This photo is at the entrance to the Lower Lee Vining Campground. The ridge at the right with the patch of snow is a recessional moraine (RM) that was deposited during retreat of the Lee Vining glacier at the end of the last glacial episode. The valley wall in the background is the large lateral moraine (LM) that was deposited on the south side of the Lee Vining glacier.

❷ *June Lake Loop*

When going from Lee Vining to Mammoth Lakes, make a detour along the June Lake Loop. It only takes a few extra minutes, but you'll see some great scenery and geology. The loop begins four miles south of Lee Vining and follows Highway 158 for twelve miles through a large horseshoe-shaped valley that cuts into the eastern front of the Sierra Nevada. Reversed Peak lies in the center of the horseshoe. Highway 158 bends around the west side of the peak as it loops to the south.

This horseshoe-shaped valley was formed by the Rush Creek and Reversed Creek glaciers. These are actually two lobes of the same glacier that were split by Reversed Peak. These glaciers gave the horseshoe valley its unique shape. The Rush Creek glacier had its origin in the icefields of the High Sierra, where large quantities of ice crossed the crest of the Sierra and followed Rush Creek down the eastern slope. On this part of its journey, the Rush Creek glacier gouged out the basins for the Marie Lakes, Waugh Lake, Gem Lake and Agnew Lake. Immediately east of Agnew Lake, the Rush Creek glacier tumbled down a steep fault scarp along the Frontal fault system, and then encountered the weak fractured rocks in the fault zone at the base of the scarp. On the east side of the fault zone, the glacier bumped into the hard rocks of Reversed Peak. Since the glacier could not go over Reversed Peak, it split and sent one lobe north and the other lobe south. The main part of the Rush Creek glacier took the northern route. For the first mile, this lobe followed the fractured rocks in the fault zone and carved out the basin for Silver Lake from the weak rocks in the fault zone. The Rush Creek lobe then turned northeast, flowed along the northwest side of Reversed Peak and entered Pleistocene Lake Russell about six miles north of the peak. The southern fork of the Rush Creek glacier followed the fault zone south from Silver Lake for about a mile, then turned northeast, carved out the basins for Gull Lake and June Lake, and entered Lake Russell on the southeast side of Reversed Peak. The Rush Creek and Reversed Creek glaciers reached a maximum thickness of 1,600 feet, but never covered Reversed Peak, which stands 2,000 feet above the lakes.

The Rush Creek glacier picked up a large amount of rock and debris from the Sierra Nevada as it worked its way across the Sierra crest, down the eastern slope, and along the Frontal fault zone. When the Rush Creek and Reversed Creek glaciers melted, this debris was deposited as moraines and till in and along both valleys. This till covers much of the area on the east side of Reversed Peak between June Lake and Grant Lake and as far east as Highway 395.

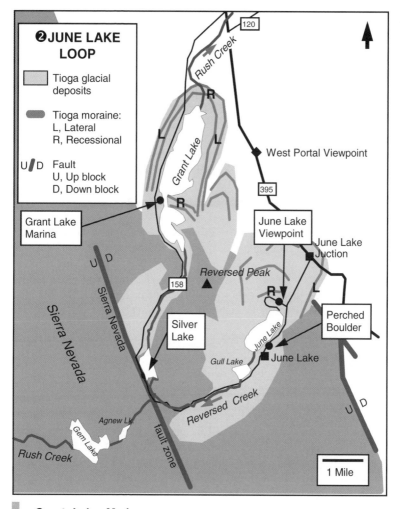

❷JUNE LAKE LOOP

Tioga glacial deposits

Tioga moraine:
L, Lateral
R, Recessional

U/D Fault
U, Up block
D, Down block

Grant Lake Marina

West Portal Viewpoint

June Lake Viewpoint

June Lake Juction

Perched Boulder

Reversed Peak

Silver Lake

Gull Lake

June Lake

Grant Lake

Rush Creek

Sierra Nevada

fault zone

Reversed Creek

Agnew Lk

Gem Lake

Rush Creek

1 Mile

Grant Lake Marina - *From Lee Vining drive S 4 mi. on Hwy. 395; turn W on Hwy. 158 and park at the Grant Lake Marina.*

Grant Lake is used as the collecting reservoir for most of the Mono Basin water that is being diverted to Los Angeles. From here the water goes under Highway 395, around Aeolian Buttes, through a tunnel under the Mono Craters, into the Owens River, and then travels south 400 miles to Los Angeles. Grant Lake rests almost entirely in sediments deposited from the Rush Creek glacier. The sides of the lake are formed from the large lateral moraines of the glacier, and the dam at the north end is a large recessional moraine, enhanced by a man-made dam. The marina is on another recessional moraine that nearly bisects the lake.

Silver Lake - *From the Grant Lake Marina drive 3 mi. S on Hwy. 158; park in the parking lot on the SW side of Silver Lake.*

Silver Lake was carved out of the fractured rocks along a major fault zone in the Sierra Nevada fault zone. The Sierra block was uplifted several thousand feet along this fault. The steep slope from Agnew Lake to Silver Lake is a fault scarp formed by the fault and cleaned off by the Rush Creek glacier. At Silver Lake, the road follows the fault. Just south of the lake, the fault can be seen cutting across the granitic rocks at the base of the escarpment. This fault zone is responsible for putting the bottom of the "U" in the horseshoe. Without the fault zone, there would be no Silver Lake.

Perched Boulder - *From Silver Lake, continue 4 mi. S on Hwy. 158 to the fire station at the N end of the community of June Lake.*

Adjacent to the June Lake Fire Station there is a large boulder perched on an outcrop on the north side of the road. The boulder is a glacial erratic that is 18 feet high and weighs 150 tons. This boulder was picked by the Rush Creek glacier from somewhere in the Sierra and carried to this locality. When the glacier melted, the boulder was stranded on top of a small roche moutonnée.

June Lake Viewpoint - *From June Lake go N 1 mi. on Hwy. 158 to the Oh! Ridge viewpoint.*

This viewpoint is on a large recessional moraine that lies at the eastern end of June Lake. From the viewpoint, you can look southwest across June Lake down the Reversed Creek valley toward the Sierra escarpment. Reversed Creek begins at June Lake, flows through Gull Lake, and joins Rush Creek just south of Silver Lake. From there, Rush Creek flows through Silver Lake to Grant Lake. Prior to diversion of the Mono Basin water to Los Angeles, Rush Creek flowed from Grant Lake into Mono Lake, and was the main water supply for Mono Lake.

Reversed Creek is unique. It is the only creek along the entire eastern Sierra that flows west toward the mountain front rather than away from the mountains. The reversed drainage was formed when the Reversed Creek glacier encountered hard rock in the valley floor after it left the fault zone at the base of the Sierra escarpment. The glacier rode up and over these hard rocks as it continued northeast toward Mono Lake. The direction of movement of a glacier depends on the slope of ice surface, not on the slope of the valley floor. As a glacier flows down a canyon, the bottom of the glacier can scoop out low spots and benches. Thus, the ice at the bottom of the glacier can travel upslope for some distance.

The long sloping ridge on the northwest side of Grant Lake, as seen in the center of this photo, is a large lateral moraine (LM) that was deposited by the Rush Creek glacier.

This large perched boulder near the June Lake Fire Station is a glacial erratic that was left here when the Reversed Creek glacier melted. The boulder sits on a small roche moutonnée that is being broken apart by jointing.

❸ Tufa Towers

At several places along the shoreline of Mono Lake there are clusters of spectacular white towers that form spires and rounded knobs up to ten feet high. These towers are formed from tufa. Tufa is one of many forms of calcium carbonate, and is of the same composition as the stalactites and stalagmites that occur in limestone caves. In Mono Lake, these towers form where fresh water springs feed into the bottom waters of the lake. The fresh spring water contains calcium in solution, and the lake water contains sodium and potassium carbonate in solution. When the fresh water wells up into the lake water, it is lighter and begins to rise through the lake water. As the fresh water rises, the calcium in the fresh water and the carbonate in the lake water combine to form tufa. The tufa in the towers is porous, so the fresh water flows through this porous structure until it finds a surface where it comes into contact with the lake water. The intricate spires and knobs of the towers are formed by this process. Although tufa is found in other alkaline bodies of water, the quantity, size, and variety of the tufa towers at Mono Lake is unique.

In many places, tufa towers can be found along higher shorelines of Mono Lake. Since tufa towers can only be formed in lake water, we know that these towers were formed when the lake was at a higher level and covered these areas. Some of the towers along the older shorelines of the lake formed as much as 13,000 years ago.

South Tufa Reserve - *From Lee Vining go S 4 mi. on Hwy. 395; turn E on Hwy. 120 and drive 5 mi. to the turnoff to the South Tufa Reserve; drive 1 mi. and park at the reserve. Seasonal tours at 1 PM Saturday and Sunday.*
The South Tufa Reserve has many groups of tufa towers and is the largest and best developed of the tufa areas. These towers were formed mostly between 200 to 900 years ago. The towers were exposed when the level of the lake dropped following diversion of the water to Los Angeles. The lake level is rising again. When it reaches the planned level in 2014, the shoreline of the lake will be near the parking lot and many of these towers will again be covered.

County Park - *From Lee Vining drive 4 mi. N on Hwy. 395; turn R on Cemetery Rd.; drive 0.5 mi. to the Mono Lake County Park.*
There is an elevated wood walkway at Mono Lake County Park that makes it easy to investigate the shoreline of the lake and the tufa towers along the shoreline. This site is well worth a visit, even if time is short.

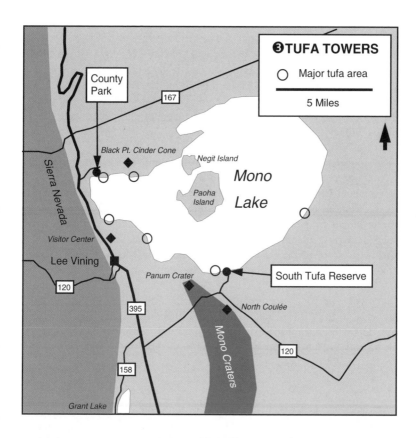

❸TUFA TOWERS

○ Major tufa area

5 Miles

County Park

167

Black Pt. Cinder Cone

Negit Island

Mono

Paoha Island

Lake

Sierra Nevada

Visitor Center

Lee Vining

120

Panum Crater

South Tufa Reserve

395

North Coulée

Mono Craters

120

158

Grant Lake

Tufa towers in Mono Lake at the South Tufa Reserve.

❹ Mono Craters

As you drive south from Lee Vining on Highway 395, you will see a low range of light-gray mountains to the east. These are the Mono Craters. They extend from Panum Crater on the south shore of Mono Lake southward for about ten miles to Devils Punch Bowl. The highest peaks rise 2,000 feet above Mono Lake and many of the peaks have steep slopes with craters at the top.

The Mono Craters were formed by volcanic activity that started about 40,000 years ago and has continued up to the present time. Paoha and Negit islands in Mono Lake are on a northern extension of this volcanic chain. Negit Island formed during volcanic eruptions 1,700 years ago. Paoha Island formed 325 years ago when lake-bottom sediments were pushed up by volcanic activity. The Black Point cinder cone at the northwest shore of the lake erupted during the last high stand of Mono Lake. Panum Crater also erupted about the same time.

Older volcanic rocks are also present in this area. The Aeolian Buttes, just west of the Mono Craters, are formed from the Bishop Tuff, which was deposited during the eruption of the Long Valley volcano. A layer of Bishop Tuff was also encountered at a depth of 1,400 feet under Paoha Island when an oil exploration well was drilled in 1908.

There are about 30 volcanic centers along the Mono Craters. Most eruptions followed a general sequence of events. The eruption would begin when stiff rhyolite magma forced its way to the surface along a crack in the earth's crust. Ash and coarse pumice were then thrown from the vent. After this, the vent would clear its throat with a large explosion that created a crater with a rim of pumice, rock debris, and fragments of bedrock. Stiff rhyolite magma would then ooze from the vent like toothpaste, leaving a small rhyolite plug in the center of the crater.

An eruption could stop at any of the above phases. If the eruption continued, the rhyolite magma would slowly ooze out of the vent until the crater was filled and formed a circular steep-sided dome. Following this, the rhyolite magma might either push through the older overlying volcanic material or squeeze out beneath the older material. On some domes, the rhyolite magma flowed over the crater wall and enveloped the original crater. In some places, after spilling over the wall of the crater, the flow continued as a stream of stiff molten glass that extended for up to two miles from the crater. These glass flows are known as coulées. Some domes have small secondary craters formed when gas built up behind a plug and was released in an explosion. The trips to

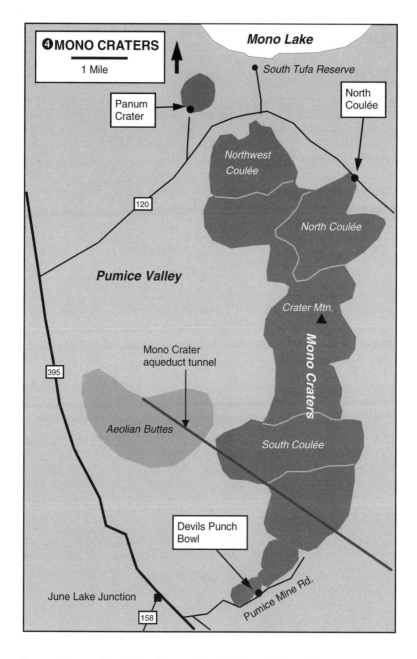

❹MONO CRATERS

1 Mile

Mono Lake

South Tufa Reserve

Panum Crater

North Coulée

Northwest Coulée

North Coulée

120

Pumice Valley

Crater Mtn.

Mono Crater aqueduct tunnel

Mono Craters

Aeolian Buttes

395

South Coulée

Devils Punch Bowl

June Lake Junction

Pumice Mine Rd.

158

Panum Crater, North Coulée, and Devils Punch Bowl illustrate several different types of eruptions that have occurred along this trend.

This photo shows two of the larger eruptive centers along the Mono Craters. There are about 30 eruptive centers along this ten-mile trend of rhyolitic domes and craters.

The North Coulée obsidian flow is formed from rhyolitic magma that flowed from a vent at the north end of the Mono Craters about 630 years ago.

Panum Crater - *From the junction of Hwy. 395 and 120, drive 3 mi. E on Hwy. 120; turn N at the sign for Panum Crater; drive 1 mi. on the gravel road to the parking area.*

Panum Crater erupted in about 1320, and has changed little since then. From the parking area, take the short trail to the rim of the crater. From the rim, you will see that the crater is about 2,000 feet across and has a prominent rhyolite dome in the center. Follow the trail around the rim. Note that the rocks that make up the rim are mainly tuff and pumice. If you look hard, you will also find a few smooth rounded pebbles mixed in with the tuff and pumice. The material that makes up the rim was ejected from the vent at the beginning of the eruption. The rounded pebbles came from the layer of gravel upon which Panum Crater was built. This gravel was part of a delta formed by Rush Creek during the last glacial episode.

Next, take the short trail across the moat to the rhyolite dome in the center of the crater. Note that the rhyolite is splintered. This happened when the dome was shattered by an explosion during formation of the dome. The explosion blew a gap in the tuff ring and threw glass blocks through the gap into Mono Lake. The gap in the tuff ring was partly filled by pumice from later eruptions.

The jagged rocks in the middle of the photo are part of the rhyolite dome that lies in the center of Panum Crater. The low brush-covered slope that extends across the center of the photo is the tuff ring that forms the rim of the crater.

North Coulée *– From Hwy. 120 and the Panum Dome turnoff drive 3.5 mi. E on Hwy. 120 to milepost 20.00; park in the pullout where the coulée is near the road.*

Along the trend of the Mono Craters, there are three large coulées, South Coulée, North Coulée and Northwest Coulée. These coulées are made up of thick obsidian flows that extend for one to two miles from their vents. Obsidian flows of this length are unusual. Most rhyolite magma forms domes and plugs because it is too viscous to flow for any significant distance. All three of these coulées are young. The flows that formed the North Coulée occurred about 630 years ago, and the flows that formed the South Coulée occurred about 700 years ago.

North Coulée has two lobes. This geologic site is at the northern lobe. You can see the southern lobe about half a mile to the south. Each lobe represents a different flow. The flows began from vents about one mile to the west. The flow is 200 to 300 feet thick, the sides are steep, and there is talus at the base of the flow. The rocks at the surface of the flow chilled rapidly, forming glassy blocks that were broken during movement of the flow. As the flow progressed, the front of the flow carried debris that was eventually overridden and incorporated into the flow. This jumble of broken sharp glass makes quite a mess – not good for climbing without lots of bandages.

The steep front of the North Coulée obsidian flow consists of a jumble of obsidian blocks and other volcanic debris.

Devils Punch Bowl - *From June Lake Junction drive S on Hwy. 395 for 0.4 mi.; turn E on Pumice Mine Rd. (gravel) and drive 1.5 mi. to the "Punch Bowl" sign; follow the dirt road 0.1 mi. to the rim of Devils Punch Bowl.*

The Devils Punch Bowl is a small crater, about 1,200 feet in diameter and 140 feet deep, at the south end of the Mono Craters. This crater was formed by an explosion at the beginning of the eruption, and differs from Panum Crater in that there is no significant tuff ring around the crater. The small rhyolite dome in the center of Devils Punch Bowl was formed about 700 years ago and is younger than the nearby domes.

Devils Punch Bowl illustrates an early stage in the development of the craters and domes along the Mono Craters trend. This eruption simply quit early, and it is unlikely that Devils Punch Bowl will later develop into a large dome or coulée.

The crater that forms Devils Punch Bowl was blasted out of the preexisting volcanic rocks about 700 years ago. Note the small rhyolite plug (RP) in the center of the crater.

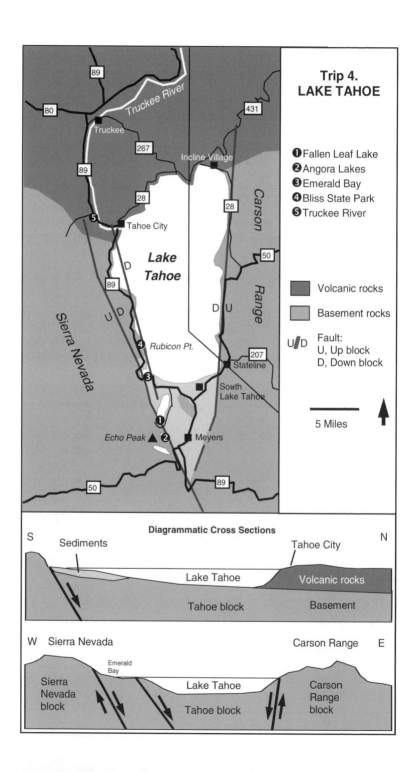

**Trip 4.
LAKE TAHOE**

❶ Fallen Leaf Lake
❷ Angora Lakes
❸ Emerald Bay
❹ Bliss State Park
❺ Truckee River

Volcanic rocks

Basement rocks

U/D Fault:
U, Up block
D, Down block

5 Miles

Truckee River

80

89

89

Truckee

267

Incline Village

431

28

28

Tahoe City

*Lake
Tahoe*

D

89

U D

50

D U

4 *Rubicon Pt.*

207

Stateline

3

South
Lake Tahoe

Sierra Nevada

Carson Range

1

Echo Peak ▲ 2

Meyers

50

89

Diagrammatic Cross Sections

S

Sediments

N

Tahoe City

Lake Tahoe

Volcanic rocks

Tahoe block

Basement

W Sierra Nevada

Carson Range E

Emerald
Bay

Sierra
Nevada
block

Lake Tahoe

Carson
Range
block

Tahoe block

Trip 4
LAKE TAHOE
Faults, Glaciers, and Lakes

Lake Tahoe is the largest and deepest lake in the Sierra Nevada, and certainly one of the most scenic. On this trip we'll take a look at how the lake was made, and how glaciers played an important role in the formation of many of the other lakes and scenic features in the Tahoe area.

The first step in the formation of Lake Tahoe began during the Plio-Pleistocene uplift of the Sierra Nevada. When the crust in the Tahoe area was uplifted and stretched, it broke into several large blocks. One of these blocks, the Tahoe block, dropped about 5,000 feet along a series of large faults that splayed and opened to the north. As the Tahoe block dropped, the adjacent Sierra Nevada and Carson Range blocks were uplifted, forming a deep valley between the Sierra Nevada and the Carson Range. This valley sloped to the north and was drained by a north-flowing river. The second step in the formation of the lake occurred when the north part of this valley was filled with a thick pile of volcanic rocks that formed a dam in the river valley. The waters of Lake Tahoe are held in place by this dam. The volcanic rocks at the north end of Lake Tahoe extend from Tahoe City and Incline Village north to Sierraville, and from Truckee east to Floristan.

The water for Lake Tahoe is supplied mainly by rivers and creeks along the south and west sides of the lake that are fed from the abundant snow in the Sierra Nevada. Since more water is supplied to the lake than the lake can hold, the level of the lake depends on the height of the dam at the outlet. Presently, the lake is 1,645 feet deep. However, during Pleistocene glaciation, the level of the lake moved up and down as much as 600 feet as glaciers and moraines dammed the outlet and then receded and/or were breached.

Glaciers have had a profound influence on the landscape along the western margin of Lake Tahoe. Most of the moisture from Pacific storms was trapped by the mountains west of the lake, so there are few glaciers on the east side of the lake. Lake Tahoe itself was never covered by glaciers. Like Mono Lake and Owens Lake, Lake Tahoe was the terminus of the glaciers and a depository for glacial debris and water.

Glaciers left their mark on the landscape in many ways. They carved cirques and glacial valleys in the high country. They entered the lake and dumped their glacial debris into the lake. They also left behind polished granitic rocks and exotic blocks that can be found in many places around the lake.

All four of the major Sierra glacial episodes were present in the Tahoe area. During each episode, a thick icefield covered the high Desolation Wilderness area west of the lake. This icefield stripped the Desolation Wilderness of its weathered rock and soil cover and exposed large areas of fresh granitic and metamorphic rocks. The moving ice in the icefield also scooped out numerous small lake basins and carved dozens of jagged peaks in the Desolation Wilderness. From the icefield, a number of glaciers extended east down the steep fault scarps that formed the western side of the Tahoe basin. As the glaciers moved down the canyons and into Lake Tahoe, they gouged out lake basins, formed cliffs, and steepened the walls of the valleys. The glaciers also carried a large amount of rock material and dumped it into the western and southern part of the lake. Some of this glacial material was deposited as lateral, terminal, and recessional moraines. You can see these moraines today at Fallen Leaf Lake, Angora Lake, Cascade Lake, and Emerald Bay.

Much of the work done in the early glacial episodes was covered and reworked during the later glacial episodes. Thus, most of the moraines that we see today were formed by the large Tahoe glacial episode, 70,000 to 150,000 years ago, and the younger but smaller Tioga episode, 19,000 to 26,000 years ago.

The Truckee River serves as the outlet for Lake Tahoe. The overflow water leaves the lake at the outlet just south of Tahoe City. From there, the water flows north to Truckee, and then east to Reno. During glacial episodes, glaciers filled the Truckee River valley from time to time and blocked the outlet of the lake. When this happened, the lake rose as much as 600 feet and covered much of the low area south of the present lake. The communities of South Lake Tahoe and Meyers are built on sediments that were deposited when the lake was at these higher levels. Shorelines that were formed at the high lake levels can be seen in a number of places around the lake basin. When the dams of glacial ice suddenly broke, it must have been quite a sight. But more about that later, during the trip to the Truckee River.

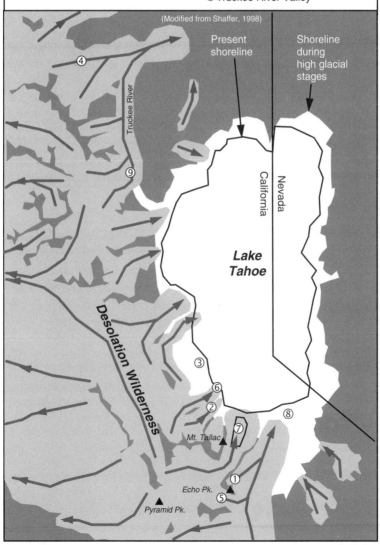

LAKE TAHOE
Tahoe Glacial Episode
(70,000-150,000 Years Ago)

 Icefield/glacier, arrow shows direction of movement

5 Miles

Locations
① Angora Lakes
② Cascade Lake
③ D.L. Bliss State Park
④ Donner Lake
⑤ Echo Lake
⑥ Emerald Bay
⑦ Fallen Leaf Lake
⑧ South Lake Tahoe
⑨ Truckee River Valley

(Modified from Shaffer, 1998)

Present shoreline

Shoreline during high glacial stages

Truckee River

California   Nevada

Lake Tahoe

Desolation Wilderness

Mt. Tallac

Echo Pk.

Pyramid Pk.

The Bottom of the Lake

Unfortunately, from a geologic standpoint, the beautiful blue waters of Lake Tahoe hide the bottom of the lake and some of the interesting geology that could otherwise be seen on the lake bottom. In order to get an understanding of this geology, the U.S. Geological Survey recently published a detailed bathymetric map and report that describes the bottom of the lake (Gardner et al., 1999). Based on this study, the central part of the lake has a relatively flat bottom that slopes gently to the north and is at depths of 1,500 to 1,645 feet below the present shoreline. The margins of the lake are made up of sediments brought into the lake by rivers and glaciers. These sediments typically form a shallow shelf from the shoreline to water depths of about a hundred feet. Below this shelf, there is a steep slope that has gullies, trenches, ridges, cliffs, mounds, blocks, and fans. Here are some of the geologic features described in the USGS study:

① The entire east side of the lake has a narrow shallow shelf and then a steep slope to the flat bottom of the lake. Very little sediment has entered the lake from this side, so only a narrow bench of sediment has built up along the shoreline.

② Immediately east of Stateline Point, at the north end of the lake, there is an underwater cliff that is 1,400 feet high. The cliff probably represents a fault scarp. Crystal Bay is on the down-thrown side of the fault and the water in Crystal Bay is up to 1,500 feet deep.

③ On the west side of the lake, near Tahoe Pines, a five mile section of the shelf of the lake has collapsed. The glacial sediments that made up the shelf broke off and formed an underwater avalanche. This avalanche carried the sediments into deep water and deposited them in an irregular fan that is five miles wide, six miles long, and as much as 660 feet deep. The fan includes large blocks and mounds of avalanche material that traveled almost across the lake before settling on the flat bottom. One of these blocks is nearly a mile long, half a mile wide and 400 feet high.

④ East of Rubicon Point there is a 1,400-foot underwater cliff. The cliff is likely the scarp of one of the boundary faults of the Tahoe block.

⑤ The south margin of the lake from Fallen Leaf Lake to Stateline is formed from glacial-outwash sediments deposited in front of glaciers. This steep gullied slope is interrupted in at least two places by large blocks of sediment pushed to the margin of Lake Tahoe by large glaciers.

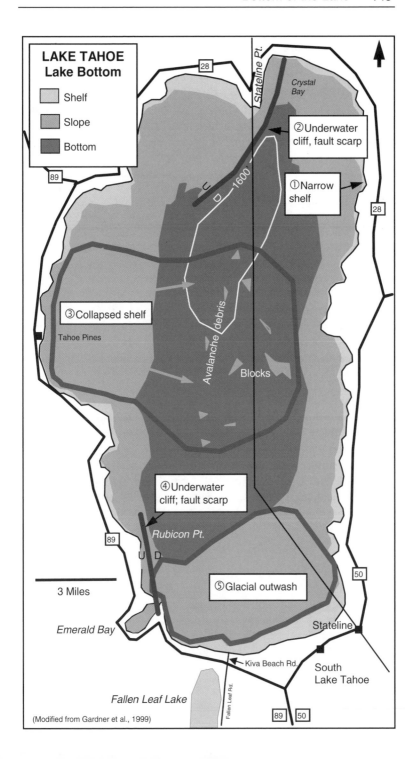

LAKE TAHOE
Lake Bottom

- Shelf
- Slope
- Bottom

28

89

Stateline Pt.

Crystal Bay

②Underwater cliff, fault scarp

①Narrow shelf

28

1600'

③Collapsed shelf

Tahoe Pines

Avalanche debris

Blocks

④Underwater cliff; fault scarp

89

Rubicon Pt.

U D

3 Miles

⑤Glacial outwash

50

Emerald Bay

Stateline

Kiva Beach Rd.

South Lake Tahoe

Fallen Leaf Lake

Fallen Leaf Rd.

89 50

(Modified from Gardner et al., 1999)

❶ *Fallen Leaf Lake*

Fallen Leaf Lake was formed by glacial moraines. The east and west sides of the three-mile-long lake are bounded by lateral moraines and the lake is separated from Lake Tahoe by a series of recessional moraines. Fallen Leaf Lake is 150 feet above Lake Tahoe and drains into Lake Tahoe through Taylor Creek, which cuts through these recessional moraines. If there were no lateral and recessional moraines, there would be no Fallen Leaf Lake.

The south end of Fallen Leaf Lake lies at the base of one of the large faults along which the Tahoe block was downfaulted several thousand feet. The lake sits in a pile of glacial debris that was carried down the scarp of this fault by Pleistocene glaciers. This glacial debris fills in much of the southern part of the Tahoe basin. As the lake was filled in, the glaciers rode over the older glacial material and continued to dump their debris into the lake.

The glacier that formed Fallen Leaf Lake began in a thick icefield that covered the Desolation Wilderness west of Fallen Leaf Lake. From this icefield, the glacier flowed down the valley of Glen Alpine Creek and formed numerous small lakes and falls as it tumbled down the steep slope into the Lake Tahoe basin. From the marina at Fallen Leaf Lake, you can see how this glacier formed the lake.

Marina - *From the junction of Hwys. 50 and 89 in South Lake Tahoe drive 3 mi. N on Hwy. 89; turn left on Fallen Leaf Rd. and drive 5.5 mi. to the marina.*
The marina at Fallen Leaf Lake lies near the base of one of the large faults that form the southwest border of the Lake Tahoe basin. You can't see the actual fault, but you know that it is there because the marina and the south end of Fallen Leaf Lake are underlain by young lake and glacial sediments, and the granitic basement rocks can be found along Glen Alpine Creek immediately west of the marina.

Fallen Leaf Campground lies on the recessional moraines that can be seen at the far end of the lake. This recessional moraine is composed of a series of linear ridges that cut across the valley. The high ridge on the southeast side of the lake is a large lateral moraine that formed between the Glen Alpine glacier and the Angora glacier. This moraine is up to 900 feet high. The ridge along the northwest side of the lake is the lateral moraine that formed between the Glen Alpine and Tallac Creek glaciers.

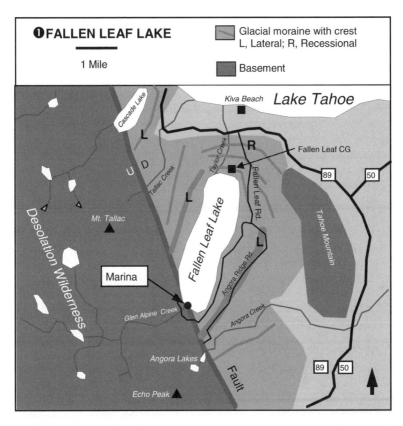

❶FALLEN LEAF LAKE

1 Mile

Glacial moraine with crest
L, Lateral; R, Recessional

Basement

Cascade Lake

Kiva Beach *Lake Tahoe*

L

U   D

Taylor Creek

Tallac Creek

R

Fallen Leaf CG

Fallen Leaf Rd.

89   50

L

Mt. Tallac

Fallen Leaf Lake

Desolation Wilderness

Tahoe Mountain

L

Marina

Angora Ridge Rd.

Glen Alpine Creek

Angora Creek

Angora Lakes

89   50

Echo Peak

Fault

Fallen Leaf Lake from Angora Ridge Road.

❷ Angora Lakes

Although the Angora Lakes lie only a mile south of Fallen Leaf Lake, they are quite different. Fallen Leaf Lake lies on the downthrown side of the boundary fault for the Tahoe basin, whereas the Angora Lakes are on the upthrown side of the same fault, about 1,000 feet above Fallen Leaf Lake. Another major difference is that the Angora Lakes have been carved out of the granitic basement rocks of the Sierra Nevada by glacial erosion. In contrast, Fallen Leaf Lake sits in a pile of glacial debris—very scenic glacial debris. During the drive from Fallen Leaf Lake to Angora Lakes, you climb the lateral moraine on the south side of Fallen Leaf Lake and then ride along the crest of this moraine for about a mile. The road ends in a meadow on the high side of the boundary fault for the Tahoe basin. From there, it is a short hike to the Angora Lakes.

Angora Ridge - *From the junction of Hwy. 50 and Fallen Leaf Rd. drive S on Fallen Leaf Rd. 2.0 mi.; turn left on Tahoe Mountain Rd. and drive 0.4 mi.; turn right on Angora Ridge Rd. and drive 2 mi.; park at one of the pullouts on the ridge just beyond the fire lookout.*

The high ridge that you have been driving along is a lateral moraine that was formed between the Glen Alpine and Angora glaciers. You can see the glacial till that makes up the moraine all along the ridge. Some of the boulders are quite large, and these are mixed with rounded rocks of all sizes, as well as sand, silt, and clay. From the ridge, you can look down 900 feet onto Fallen Leaf Lake. When the glaciers were active, they were at least as high as this lateral moraine. The lateral moraine makes a convenient ramp to get to the Angora Lakes. If it were not for this lateral moraine, these lakes would not be easily accessible by car.

Upper Angora Lake - *From the fire lookout continue 1 mi. to the parking lot at end of Angora Ridge Rd.; hike along the closed road 0.5 mi. to Upper Angora Lake.*

Upper Angora Lake lies in a glacial cirque on the east side of Angora Peak and the north side of Echo Peak. The steep semicircular wall of the cirque and the basin for Upper Angora Lake were excavated from Angora and Echo Peaks as meltwater from the Angora glacier alternately froze and thawed the jointed granite. Note the steep granite cliffs at the base of the cirque at the far side of the lake. Upper Angora Lake is one of hundreds of cirque lakes formed in the Sierra high country during the ice ages. Lower Angora Lake was formed when the Angora glacier excavated some of the weaker jointed granite along Angora Creek. This lake is partly dammed by a moraine left during retreat of the last Angora glacier.

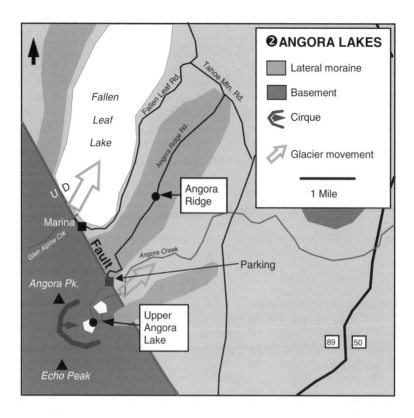

❷ANGORA LAKES

- Lateral moraine
- Basement
- Cirque
- Glacier movement

1 Mile

Fallen Leaf Lake

Fallen Leaf Rd.

Tahoe Mtn. Rd.

Angora Ridge Rd.

Angora Ridge

Marina

Glen Alpine Crk.

Angora Creek

Parking

Angora Pk.

Upper Angora Lake

Echo Peak

89 50

U D

Fault

Upper Angora Lake is a cirque formed by a glacier that covered the east side of Angora Peak. While enjoying the view of the lake and Angora Peak, top center, have a lemonade at the Angora Lakes Resort. Lemonade has been a tradition of the resort for over half a century.

❸ Emerald Bay

Scenic Emerald Bay is geologically similar to Fallen Leaf Lake. However, the recessional moraines at Fallen Leaf Lake formed a dam for the lake, whereas Emerald Bay enters Lake Tahoe through a narrow gap in its recessional moraine. The glacier responsible for Emerald Bay began in the Desolation Wilderness icefield and scooped out the basins for Velma Lakes and Eagle Lake on its way to Lake Tahoe. When the glacier reached Lake Tahoe, it crossed a large fault on the west side of the Tahoe basin and abruptly entered the lake. Upon entering the lake, the glacier began to melt and dump its load of glacial debris along the shoreline. At the end of the last glacial episode, the glacier retreated and left the large lateral moraine that now forms the southeast side of Emerald Bay and the recessional moraine that nearly closes the mouth of the bay. Eagle Point and Emerald Point are on this recessional moraine.

Inspiration Point - *From Fallen Leaf Rd. drive N on Hwy. 89 5 mi. to the Inspiration Point parking area on the S side of Emerald Bay.*

One mile south of Inspiration Point, Highway 89 begins to climb the large lateral moraine on the south side of Emerald Bay. The road then follows the crest of this moraine to Inspiration Point. From the crest of the moraine there are good views of Emerald Bay to the north and Cascade Lake to the south. Cascade Lake is formed by lateral and recessional moraines deposited by a glacier that moved down Cascade Creek. At Inspiration Point, the highway crosses a fault. The Sierra Nevada was uplifted on the west of this fault and the Tahoe basin subsided on the east side. This same fault forms the head of Cascade Lake and Fallen Leaf Lake. The fault dies out rapidly to the north, and the downfaulting of the Tahoe block is transferred to another fault that lies in Lake Tahoe just east of Rubicon Point.

Vikingsholm Parking - *From Inspiration Point drive 1 mi. N to the Vikingsholm parking area. Vikingsholm, a Scandinavian-style mansion built in 1929, is a one-mile hike from the Vikingsholm parking area; guided tours in the summer. Emerald Bay is in Emerald Bay State Park (530-525-7277).*

From here there is an excellent view of Emerald Bay and the recessional moraine at the mouth of the bay. The head of the bay lies in the granitic rocks of the Sierra Nevada batholith, and there are good exposures of these granitic rocks at the Vikingsholm parking area. Fannette Island is a small roche moutonnée of basement rock that was overridden by the Emerald Bay glacier. As shown on the Tahoe location map (p. 140), the bay lies on a sliver of basement rock between two of the large boundary faults on the west side of downdropped Tahoe block.

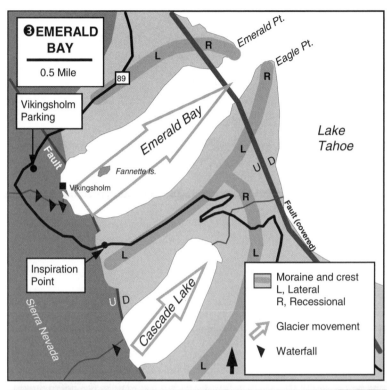

The low ridge at the mouth of Emerald Bay is a recessional moraine. The bay is connected to Lake Tahoe through a narrow gap in this moraine. Fannette Island in the center of the bay is an outcrop of granite that rises 150' from the water.

❹ Bliss State Park

Most of the granitic rocks in the High Sierra are fresh and hard, since they were scoured and cleaned by glaciers during the Pleistocene glacial episodes. However, the granitic rocks at D. L. Bliss State Park are deeply weathered. The weathered rocks were preserved here because this area lies between the Emerald Bay glacier to the south and the Meeks Bay glacier to the north, and this area was never covered by glaciers.

The deep weathering of these granitic rocks has produced a number of large rounded boulders that can be seen throughout the park. This weathering has been taking place for several million years. As in the Alabama Hills, the weathering follows the joints in the granite, and the granite along the joints slowly decomposes and is washed away. Granite that is cut by intersecting joints develops rounded ledges and boulders, depending on the joint pattern. Many of these rounded boulders can be seen in the roadcuts along Highway 89 just south of the park entrance. However, the most impressive example of a large rounded boulder is in the park, at Balancing Rock.

Balancing Rock - *The entrance to D.L. Bliss State Park (entrance fee) is on Hwy. 89 2 mi. N of the Vikingsholm Parking area; from the park entrance drive 2 mi. to the Balancing Rock Nature Trail; hike the 0.5 mi. loop trail; easy. For information, phone 530-525-7277 or visit the website www.parks.ca.gov.*

There are many good examples of rounded granite boulders and ledges along the Balancing Rock nature trail. However, the highlight along the trail is Balancing Rock, a 130-ton granite boulder perched on a granite base. The boulder is separated from the base by a large near-horizontal joint, and the granite along that joint is in the process of weathering. In fact, you can see a hole through this joint if you look at the right angle. The height of Balancing Rock gives an indication to the amount of weathering that has occurred in this area. The original granite surface was once at least as high as the top of the rock.

Rubicon Point - *From Balancing Rock, drive 1 mi. east to Rubicon Point parking area.*

Rubicon Point is a 600-foot high granite promontory that lies at the south end of Rubicon Bay. Immediately east of Rubicon Point, the shoreline drops 1,411 feet vertically to the bottom of Lake Tahoe. This steep underwater cliff is a fault scarp, one of the many faults that were responsible for the downdropping of the Tahoe block. The fault scarp is preserved because it was not covered by younger glacial debris.

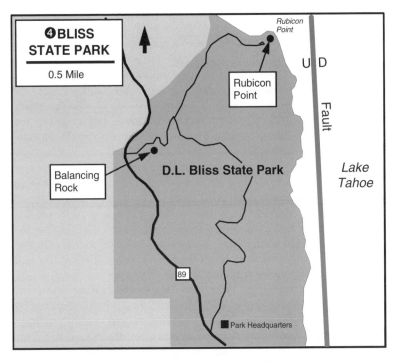

❹BLISS STATE PARK

0.5 Mile

Rubicon Point

Rubicon Point

Balancing Rock

D.L. Bliss State Park

U | D

Fault

Lake Tahoe

89

Park Headquarters

Balancing Rock in D. L. Bliss State Park is a large rounded boulder of granitic rock formed by deep weathering along jointed granite.

❺ *Truckee River*

The water level of Lake Tahoe remains constant at 6,229 feet. This level is maintained because more water enters the lake than is lost by evaporation. The excess water flows into the Truckee River through the Outlet Gates, just south of Tahoe City. From the Outlet Gates, the Truckee River flows north through a narrow, deep, 12 mile-long river valley as it drops 400 feet on its way to Truckee. This section of the river cuts through the volcanic rocks that form the northern dam for the lake.

The water level of Lake Tahoe has not always been constant. Ever since the volcanic rocks began to dam the lake, the level of the lake has risen as the outlet was blocked by eruptions of new volcanic material and has fallen as the volcanic rocks were eroded by the river. The level of the lake also fluctuated during the Pleistocene glacial episodes, rising as much as 600 feet when glaciers blocked the Truckee River valley and falling during interglacial episodes. Ice does not make a very good dam. When the water level behind an ice dam reaches about 9/10's the thickness of the ice, the ice begins to float and the dam is undermined by the water. When this happens, the dam fails catastrophically and huge amounts of lake water are suddenly released down the river valley. This happened repeatedly along the Truckee River during Pleistocene glaciation. Large boulders, as much as ten feet in diameter, were carried by these floods along the Truckee River as far as Reno.

> **Alpine Meadows Road** - *From the junction of Hwys. 89 and 28 in Tahoe City drive 3.5 miles N on Hwy. 89 to Alpine Meadows Road; park.*
> From its intersection with Highway 89, Alpine Meadows Road goes west up the Bear Creek valley to the community of Alpine Meadows. During the Pleistocene glacial episodes, the Bear Creek glacier flowed down this valley and then north along the Truckee River valley where it was joined by other glaciers and continued to Truckee. When these glaciers melted, they left behind lateral moraines and other piles of glacial debris. On the east side of this road intersection, you can see some of this glacial material along the side of the valley. The moraines are composed of a great variety of poorly sorted volcanic and igneous rocks in a jumbled mass.

At Layton State Park you can see the Outlet Gates for Lake Tahoe. The park is on the south side of the HW 89 bridge across the Truckee River. The outlet was first dammed in 1870 with rock and timber. The present dam was built in 1910. The park is also the site of the North Lake Tahoe Historical Society Museum (530-583-1762).

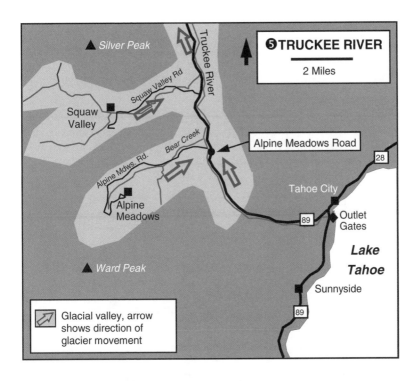

The Truckee River valley one mile south of Alpine Meadows Road. During the Pleistocene glacial episodes, glaciers periodically blocked this valley and formed a dam that raised the water level of Lake Tahoe as much as 600 feet.

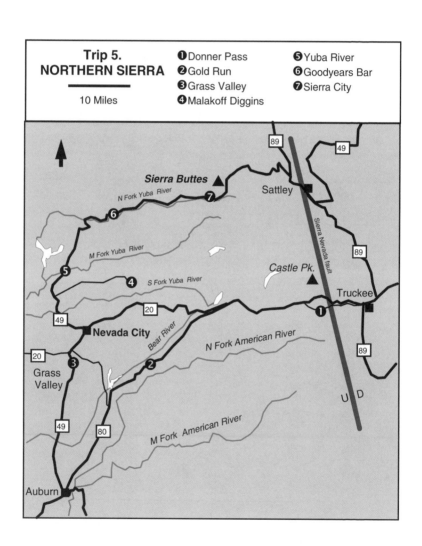

Trip 5.
NORTHERN SIERRA

10 Miles

❶ Donner Pass
❷ Gold Run
❸ Grass Valley
❹ Malakoff Diggins

❺ Yuba River
❻ Goodyears Bar
❼ Sierra City

Sierra Buttes

N Fork Yuba River

❼

❻

Sattley

89

49

M Fork Yuba River

S Fork Yuba River

❺

❹

Castle Pk.

Sierra Nevada fault

89

Truckee

❶

20

49

Nevada City

Bear River

N Fork American River

89

20

❸

❷

U   D

Grass
Valley

49

80

M Fork American River

Auburn

Trip 5
NORTHERN SIERRA
Tertiary Sedimentary and Volcanic Rocks

Geologically, the northern Sierra differs from the central and southern Sierra in several ways. Most importantly, the northern Sierra is not as high. It was uplifted only about 5,000 feet during the Plio-Pleistocene compared to more than 10,000 feet of uplift in the southern Sierra. Due to the smaller uplift, the river valleys in the northern Sierra are not as deep and the Tertiary rocks have been preserved over large areas.

The Western Metamorphic Belt is also wider and more complex in the northern Sierra and contains several metamorphic rock units that do not occur in the central Sierra. These units, which include the Smartville Complex, Feather River Belt, and Northern Sierra Terrane, provide critical information about the geologic history of the Sierra Nevada and about the development of the western margin of North America during Paleozoic and Mesozoic time.

The gold belt in the northern Sierra is also different. The Mother Lode does not extend into the northern Sierra. Instead, the gold belt in the northern Sierra is wider and the gold occurs under more varied geologic conditions. The northern Sierra also had the largest hydraulic gold mining operations of the entire gold belt. Most of the hydraulic gold was mined from gravel that was deposited by the Eocene Yuba River. These Eocene river gravels are thick and widespread in the northern Sierra, and are not present at all in the southern Sierra. The northern Sierra also has the largest lode mine of the Sierra gold belt, the Empire Mine at Grass Valley. Other important lode mining areas in the northern Sierra include Nevada City, Allegheny, and the Sierra Buttes.

During the trip to the northern Sierra, you will see the Eocene erosion surface and some of the Tertiary sedimentary and volcanic rocks that were deposited on the Eocene surface. You will also see some of the rocks of the Western Metamorphic Belt that are unique to the northern Sierra and visit the largest hydraulic mine and the largest lode mine in the Sierra Nevada gold belt.

The Eocene Yuba River

If you had flown over the northern Sierra in Eocene time, you would have been impressed by the size of the Eocene Yuba River. The river was much larger than the present-day Yuba River and extended far into Nevada as it drained the low rolling hills of the Eocene erosion surface. The channels of the Eocene river were broad, and the central parts were filled with gravel up to several hundred feet thick.

The accompanying map shows the extent of the Eocene Yuba River. The south fork began east of Foresthill, then went through Yankee Jim, Iowa Hill, Gold Run, You Bet, and joined the middle fork at North Columbia. The north fork began north of La Porte, then passed through Camptonville and joined the central fork east of North San Juan. The middle fork began near Alleghany, then went through North Bloomfield and joined the south fork at North Columbia. From North Columbia, the middle fork flowed through Cherokee and joined the north fork west of Cherokee. The river then flowed through North San Juan, French Corral and Smartville, and into the ocean in the Great Valley.

All three forks of the Eocene Yuba River carried gold, and gold has been mined from Eocene river gravels in all of the above localities. Most of this mining was hydraulic. The gold had come from the gold-bearing veins of the Sierra gold belt and had been concentrated on the Eocene erosion surface during millions of years of weathering. The gold was heavy and indestructible, so most of the gold stayed near the veins until it was swept into the Eocene river. The gold-bearing central channel came to be known as the *blue lead* due to the characteristic blue color of the gravel in the channel. The Eocene river gravel can be seen at a number of places in the Sierra. Two of the best places are at Gold Run on I-80 and at the Malakoff Diggins near North Bloomfield.

This picturesque river setting ended in Oligocene time, when volcanoes began to erupt the huge quantities of volcanic ash of the Valley Springs Formation. The ash rapidly covered the Eocene river gravels and filled the river valleys. Volcanism continued through Miocene time with deposition of the Mehrten Formation, forming a blanket of volcanic rocks over the entire landscape. As the volcanic rocks were deposited, old river courses were filled-in and new river courses were established. Some of the new rivers also contained gold, but only where these rivers cut through gold-bearing Eocene river gravel and picked up the gold from the Eocene gravel.

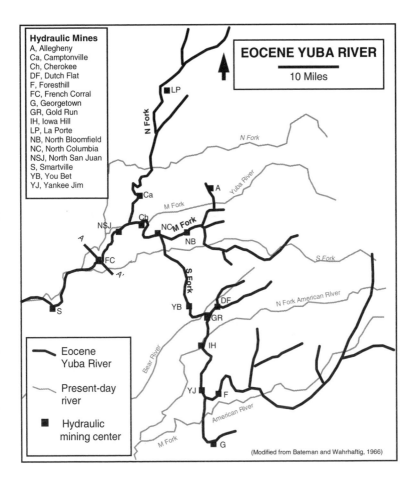

EOCENE YUBA RIVER

10 Miles

Hydraulic Mines
A, Allegheny
Ca, Camptonville
Ch, Cherokee
DF, Dutch Flat
F, Foresthill
FC, French Corral
G, Georgetown
GR, Gold Run
IH, Iowa Hill
LP, La Porte
NB, North Bloomfield
NC, North Columbia
NSJ, North San Juan
S, Smartville
YB, You Bet
YJ, Yankee Jim

— Eocene Yuba River
~ Present-day river
■ Hydraulic mining center

(Modified from Bateman and Wahrhaftig, 1966)

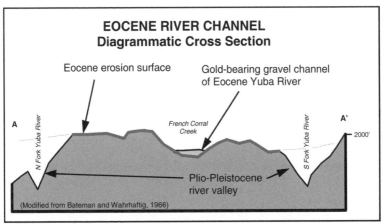

EOCENE RIVER CHANNEL
Diagrammatic Cross Section

Eocene erosion surface

Gold-bearing gravel channel of Eocene Yuba River

French Corral Creek

A

N Fork Yuba River

S Fork Yuba River

A'

2000'

Plio-Pleistocene river valley

(Modified from Bateman and Wahrhaftig, 1966)

Interstate 80

Between Sacramento and Reno, I-80 crosses the Sierra Nevada using Donner Pass. This is the lowest, easiest, and busiest path across the Sierra Nevada. It was used by early Native Americans and by early explorers, pioneers, and gold miners. Later, it was used by the railroad and Highway 40, and now I-80. All of the millions of people who have used this route across the Sierra owe their thanks to the geology of the mountain range.

Most of the major passes across the Sierra Nevada follow deep and torturous river valleys on their way across the Sierra crest. Not so for I-80. From Auburn to Emigrant Gap I-80 stays out of river valleys. Instead, the highway follows the drainage divide between the Bear River and the North Fork of the American River. This flat drainage divide is a remnant of the low rolling Eocene erosion surface that extended over the Sierra during Eocene time. Most of Tertiary sedimentary and volcanic rocks have been eroded from the divide, so the Eocene erosion surface now forms a convenient ramp that goes up the west flank of the Sierra. Since the Eocene erosion surface was formed near sea level, the present incline of the ramp closely reflects the amount of westward tilting of the Sierra during the Plio-Pleistocene uplift.

The Eocene erosion surface can be easily identified by the thick red soil that was formed on the surface during the long humid period of Eocene erosion. This red soil can be seen in many of the roadcuts between Auburn and Emigrant Gap. Near Gold Run, the highway passes through a river channel that was cut into the Eocene erosion surface by the Eocene Yuba River. The gravel that was deposited in this river channel is exposed in the large roadcuts of red gravel along the highway in this area.

The American and Bear rivers have cut deep valleys into the Eocene erosion surface on each side of the drainage divide. To appreciate how far the present-day rivers have cut into the Eocene erosion surface, take the short trip on Highway 49 from Auburn to the south. At Auburn, Highway 49 leaves the Eocene erosion surface and abruptly descends into the steep valley of the North Fork of the American River. Most of the erosion of the valley of the American River occurred during the Plio-Pleistocene uplift and tilting of the Sierra block.

I-80 uses the Eocene erosion surface as a geological bridge across the western slope of the Sierra. Thanks to the long period of Eocene erosion, you can cross the Sierra in comfort at highway speed in less than two hours. You can't do that on any other Sierra pass!

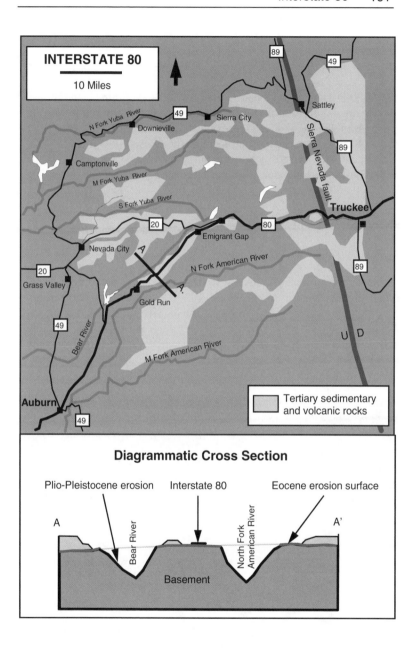

INTERSTATE 80

10 Miles

Tertiary sedimentary and volcanic rocks

Diagrammatic Cross Section

Plio-Pleistocene erosion   Interstate 80   Eocene erosion surface

A   Bear River   North Fork American River   A'

Basement

❶ *Donner Pass*

The best place to see the geology of Donner Pass is along the old Donner Pass Road from Donner Lake to Soda Springs. This road leaves busy I-80 at Donner Lake and rejoins I-80 at Soda Springs, and allows for a more leisurely look at the rocks and scenery along this historic pass. From Donner Lake, Donner Lake Road climbs up the granitic rocks of the steep eastern escarpment of the Sierra Nevada block. This escarpment was formed by faulting along the Sierra Nevada fault zone as the Sierra Nevada block was uplifted several thousand feet during the last five million years. At the summit of Donner Pass, the highway passes over the top of the tilted fault block and then descends gently along the top of the west-tilted fault block.

Several million years ago, prior to uplift of the Sierra, the top of the fault block was covered by thick Tertiary sedimentary and volcanic rocks. During uplift, most of these soft Tertiary rocks were eroded and removed from the top of the block. However, patches of the Tertiary rocks remain, mainly along drainage divides where erosion has not yet reached the rocks. From Donner Ski Ranch to the Sugar Bowl parking area, Donner Pass Road skirts along the southern edge of one of these remnants of Tertiary rocks. Donner Ski Ranch and the Sugar Bowl parking lot are good areas to see these Tertiary rocks.

Springtime view looking west from ice-covered Donner Lake. The steep escarpment of the Sierra Nevada was formed by 1,800 feet of uplift along the Sierra Nevada fault zone.

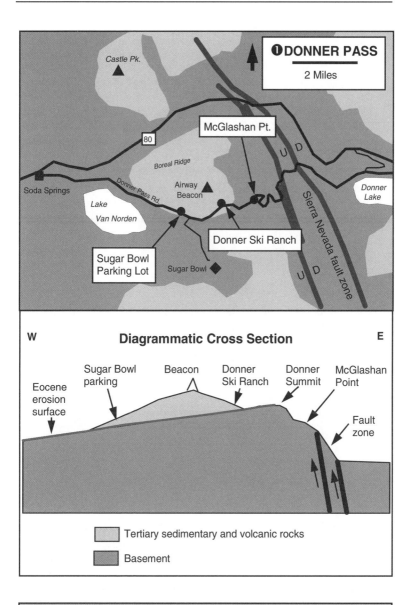

Donner Lake is named for the Donner Party, which camped at the lake during the winter of 1846-47 after being stopped by early snow. During that winter, the snow was 22 feet deep at this locality. Of the original party of 89, 42 perished. Donner Memorial State Park, on Donner Pass Road, at the east end of Donner Lake, is at the site of the camp. The park includes a visitor center, monument, campground and trails (530-582-7892 or www.parks.ca.gov).

McGlashan Point - *From the Donner State Park exit on I-80 drive W on Donner Pass Rd. 6 mi.; turn right at the "Vista Point" sign for the McGlashan Point parking area; walk to the SE end of the overlook wall.*

McGlashan Point is near the top of the steep eastern escarpment of the Sierra Nevada, about 1,000 feet above Donner Lake. This escarpment was formed by faulting along the Sierra Nevada fault zone. The Sierra Nevada was uplifted an estimated 1,800 feet along the fault zone, which lies between McGlashan Point and Donner Lake.

Looking east from McGlashan Point you can see down the U-shaped glacial valley of the Truckee River. During Pleistocene time, glaciers flowed off the steep eastern slope of Donner Pass and then eastward down this river valley. From here, you can see the lateral moraines that were formed by these glaciers on both sides of the valley, and the recessional moraine that forms the dam at the east end of Donner Lake.

The granitic rocks of the Sierra Nevada batholith are well exposed at McGlashan Point, where they were cleaned and polished by the glaciers moving down from Donner Pass. Most of these rocks are granodiorite of mid-Cretaceous age. The granodiorite has many xenoliths, almost giving it the appearance of a boulder conglomerate. The xenoliths probably represent pieces of roof rock that fell into the hot magma and were incorporated into the granodiorite. Judging from the large number of xenoliths, these granodiorites were probably near the top of the magma chamber, and erosion has not cut deeply into this pluton. Xenoliths may also form by segregation of dark minerals in the magma or by intrusion of a mafic magma into a granitic magma.

The granodiorite near the observation area is cut by a white alaskite dike. The dike has the appearance of a white ribbon running down the slope below the overlook. Alaskite consists almost solely of feldspar and quartz and is very hard. It probably represents the last of the magma in the magma chamber and was intruded into granodiorite that had already crystallized. The alaskite is more resistant to weathering than the granodiorite, so the glacial polish is well-preserved on the alaskite dike.

The white alaskite dike in the center of the outcrop cuts though granodiorite at McGlashan Point.

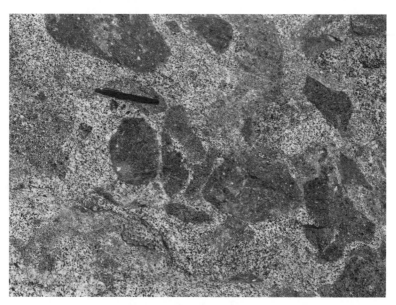

The granodiorite at McGlashan Point has many dark xenoliths. These are probably pieces of roof rock that fell into the granodiorite magma. Note the pen for scale.

Donner Ski Ranch - *Donner Ski Ranch is on Donner Pass Rd. immediately W of Donner Pass.*

The granitic rocks of the Sierra Nevada batholith are exposed at the summit of Donner Pass. Just west of the pass, there is a small hill at the Donner Ski Ranch. The hill has a ski lift and there is an airway beacon at the top of the hill. This hill consists of Tertiary sedimentary and volcanic rocks. These rocks are an erosional remnant of the Tertiary sedimentary and volcanic rocks that once covered the entire northern Sierra Nevada. These Tertiary rocks now sit on top of the granitic rocks of the Sierra batholith like a cupcake on a tilted plate.

The rocks in the lower half of the hill are mainly light-colored tuffs of the Oligocene Valley Springs Formation. We'll see more of these rocks at the Sugar Bowl parking lot. The upper half of the hill consists mainly of andesitic volcanic rocks of the Miocene Mehrten Formation.

The sedimentary and volcanic rocks that make up the hill are layered, and the layers dip gently to the west. This west dip is best seen by following the dark ledge of volcanic rocks in the center of the hill. When deposited, these rocks were near-horizontal. The rocks were tilted westward during uplift of the Sierra Nevada block, and conveniently record the amount of tilting of the Sierra block in this area.

This small hill at Donner Ski Ranch is an erosional remnant of the Tertiary sedimentary and volcanic rocks that once covered the central and northern Sierra.

Sugar Bowl Parking Lot - *From Donner Pass, drive 1 mi. W on Donner Pass Rd. to the large Sugar Bowl parking lot on the N side of the highway.*

The Sugar Bowl parking lot is cut into the light-colored rhyolitic tuffs of the Oligocene Valley Springs Formation. These tuffs were deposited as ash flows and ash falls and once covered much of the northern and central Sierra Nevada and extended eastward into Nevada, where they reached a maximum thickness of 4,000 feet near Pyramid Lake. Throughout the northern and central Sierra, the tuffs formed a thick blanket over the Eocene erosion surface and filled the river valleys that had been cut into the Eocene surface. As the old river valleys were filled by tuff, new river courses were established on the new blanket of tuff. The new rivers also drained west, but did not follow the old river valleys.

By mid-Pliocene time, the rhyolitic tuffs of the Valley Springs Formation and the overlying andesitic volcanic rocks of the Mehrten Formation had accumulated to a thickness of several hundred to several thousand feet over much of the central and northern Sierra Nevada. As the Sierra Nevada was uplifted during Plio-Pleistocene time, most of these soft sedimentary and volcanic rocks were rapidly eroded from the Eocene erosion surface. The rocks at the Sugar Bowl parking lot are a small remnant of this once-extensive blanket of Tertiary rocks.

The light-colored rhyolitic tuffs of the Valley Springs Formation at the Sugar Bowl parking lot record a major period of volcanic activity during Oligocene time. At one time these tuffs completely covered northern and central Sierra.

❷ *Gold Run*

From 1860 to 1880, the town of Gold Run was the center of a major hydraulic gold-mining operation. The gold was removed from gravel that had been deposited in the South Fork of the Eocene Yuba River. The river channel at Gold Run was about a mile wide and 300 feet thick. This river probably had its headwaters in Nevada, and generally flowed westward and northward as it drained the low Eocene hills. The river channel at Gold Run had come north from Iowa Hill. After passing through Gold Run, the river turned northwest toward North Columbia, where it joined the Middle Fork of the river and flowed west into the ocean near Marysville. During the Plio-Pleistocene uplift of the Sierra Nevada, the rejuvenated rivers cut deeply into the old Sierra landscape and Eocene river system. Thus, the Eocene river gravels are now found only in isolated patches, mainly on divides between the present-day rivers. Gold Run lies on one of these drainage divides.

Gold Run Rest Stop (Westbound) - *From the Monte Vista exit drive 1 mi. W on I-80 to the Gold Run rest stop on the north side of I-80.*
The roadcuts along I-80 between the Monte Vista and Gold Run highway exits expose thick layers of red Eocene river gravel. To see this gravel, it is best to get off of I-80. One of the best places to do this is at the Gold Run rest stop on the north side of I-80 westbound. The rest stop is at the site of the old Stewart Mine, one of the major hydraulic gold mining pits in the Gold Run area. From the eastern end of the rest stop you can take a short trail to the working face of the Stewart Mine where there is a monitor in place poised for action. This mine was in operation from 1865 to 1878.

To recover the gold, the miners hosed out the gravel from the channel with powerful jets of water. The water was piped from an uphill location and then carried into the monitors that sprayed the hillside under tremendous pressure. The gold-bearing gravels were then washed through sluices and riffles charged with mercury where the gold was separated.

The gravels exposed at Gold Run are from the upper part of the Eocene river channel. Although these gravels contain some gold, they are not rich. Most of the rich gold was in the coarse gravel in the lower part of the channel. The boulders were mainly greenstone, phyllite, slate, and granodiorite, and some of the boulders were up to several feet in diameter. The rich, coarse, lower unit is called the *blue gravel* or *blue lead*. The gold in the blue lead averaged several dollars per yard. Not surprisingly, all of the blue gravel is now gone.

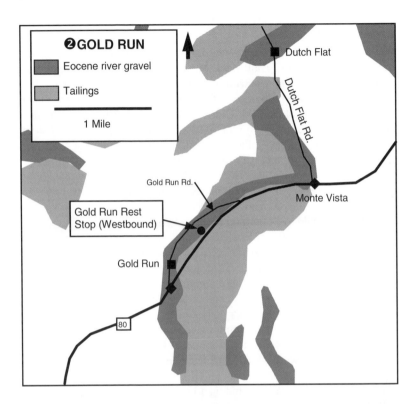

Eocene river gravels are exposed in the large roadcuts near the Gold Run rest stop on I-80. From 1865 to 1878 the Gold Run area was the site of extensive hydraulic mining of these gold-bearing river gravels.

❸ Grass Valley

For many years, Grass Valley was the richest and most famous gold-mining district in all of California. Most of the gold from this area was produced from lode mines with extensive underground workings. The largest of these operations was the Empire-North Star Mine. Other important mines included the Old Brunswick, New Brunswick, Idaho, and Eureka. There was even a mine in the heart of the business district of Grass Valley, fittingly called the Golden Center Mine. By 1956, the Grass Valley area had an estimated 367 underground mines.

Grass Valley began as a small placer mining settlement in 1849. In 1850, a lump of quartz with gold was discovered. This discovery was quickly followed by quartz-gold discoveries at Ophir, Rich, and Massachusetts Hills. By 1851 Grass Valley was a boomtown with over 150 wooden structures. The surface placers were rapidly exhausted and most of the new discoveries were lode deposits. Lode mining was difficult and expensive, and large companies were needed to carry out the operation. These companies combined many of the smaller claims to facilitate development. In order to get experienced miners who would work at low wages under difficult underground mining conditions, they hired Cornish miners from the tin mines of Cornwall, England. The tin mines at Cornwall were nearly depleted, and the Cornish miners needed jobs. The Cornish miners have left their mark on the Grass Valley community in many ways, including a local specialty, Cornish meat pies called pasties. The pasties were carried in a tin box, heated by a candle, and eaten by the miners during their half-hour lunch break. The durable crust enabled the miner to eat the pastie easily by hand.

Most of the gold at Grass Valley occurs in quartz veins that cut igneous and metamorphic rocks of the Western Metamorphic Belt. Some of the ore-bearing quartz veins are in granodiorite, and some occur in greenstone, amphibolite schist, and serpentine.

North Star Mining Museum: *The North Star Mining Museum is at the S end of Mill St. (530-273-4255).*
The North Star Mining Museum occupies the old powerhouse for the North Star Mine. The museum has many mining displays, including pumps, a stamp mill, and other tools. The most impressive item on display, however, is the large Pelton water wheel. This wheel, which is 30 feet in diameter, was used to power an air compressor. The compressed air powered hoists, drills, pumps and other mining machinery. Pelton water wheels were used in many mining operations in the northern Sierra.

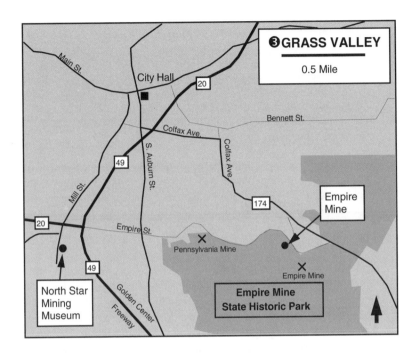

The North Star Mining Museum in Grass Valley is situated in the old powerhouse for North Star Mine.

Empire Mine – *The Empire Mine State Historic Park is at 10791 E. Empire St. (530-273-8522).*

The Empire Mine State Historic Park is on the site of the Empire Mine, the largest of the mines in the Grass Valley area. The park has a museum with models and displays that give a good understanding of the mining operation. The park also has a self-guided tour of the restored mine buildings, workshops, offices, and mining equipment.

The Empire Mine operated from 1851 to 1956, except when it was forced to close during World War II. The combined Empire-North Star Mine had 367 miles of passages and was mined to a vertical depth of over one mile. The mine produced in excess of 5.8 million ounces of gold. At $300/oz. that gold would be worth over 1.7 billion dollars.

The gold in the Empire Mine occurred in many different veins. Most of the veins were in granodiorite, and most dipped at about 35 degrees. The largest and most extensive of these veins was the Empire vein. Other important west-dipping veins included the Pennsylvania and Hanging Wall veins. The large North Star vein was also in granodiorite, but dipped gently to the north. The ore is mainly free gold, with varying amounts of iron, lead, copper, and zinc sulfides. Distribution of the gold in the veins was erratic, but some of the veins extended thousands of feet.

The yard of the Empire Mine is adjacent to the visitor center and museum. The remains of the slanting headframe of the mine are in the center of the photo. Other buildings include a machine shop, blacksmith shop, and compressor building. The mine office, refinery room, and the foundations of the stamp mill and cyanide plant are adjacent to the mine yard.

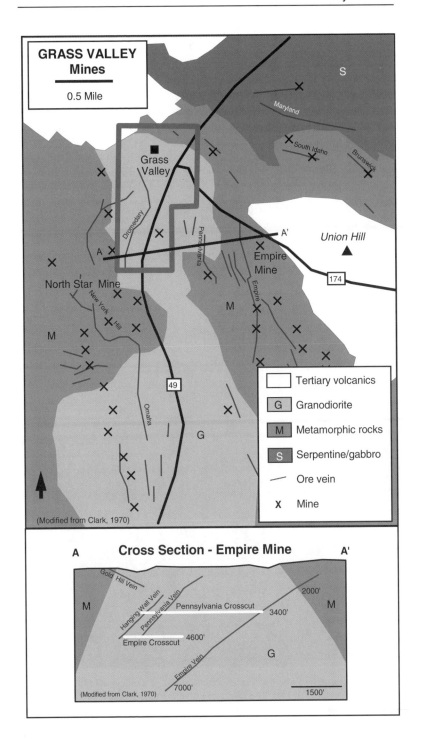

GRASS VALLEY Mines

0.5 Mile

(Modified from Clark, 1970)

Tertiary volcanics

G Granodiorite

M Metamorphic rocks

S Serpentine/gabbro

— Ore vein

X Mine

Cross Section - Empire Mine

(Modified from Clark, 1970)

1500'

❹ *Malakoff Diggins*

During the late 1870's and early 1880's the Malakoff Diggins was one of the largest hydraulic mining operations in the Sierra Nevada. The nearby town of North Bloomfield served as the center for the Malakoff Mine and several nearby hydraulic mines. Other large hydraulic mines in this area included Lake City to the west, Derbec to the north and Relief to the east.

North Bloomfield - *From Nevada City take Hwy. 49 N 11 mi.; turn right on Tyler Foote Crossing Rd.; bear left on Cruzon Grade Rd. and follow the signs 17 miles to Malakoff Diggins State Historic Park.*

In the early 1880's, at the height of the hydraulic mining activity, the town of North Bloomfield had 1,700 residents, including a large settlement of Chinese immigrants. There were eight saloons, two churches, five hotels, and the other business establishments common to gold rush towns. In 1884, hydraulic mining activities abruptly ceased, as a result of a famous court case known as the "Sawyer decision" that prohibited the dumping of hydraulic mining debris into the local rivers. The town was off the beaten track and had little other economy, so it slowly became a ghost town. After years of neglect, most of the buildings had fallen into ruin or disappeared. In 1966, North Bloomfield became a state park. Following this, the few buildings that were still standing were preserved, and other buildings were reconstructed from original plans.

This monitor near the West Point Overlook now lies silent on the floor of the Malakoff Pit. During the 1870's as many as a dozen monitors were used in the hydraulic mining of the pit.

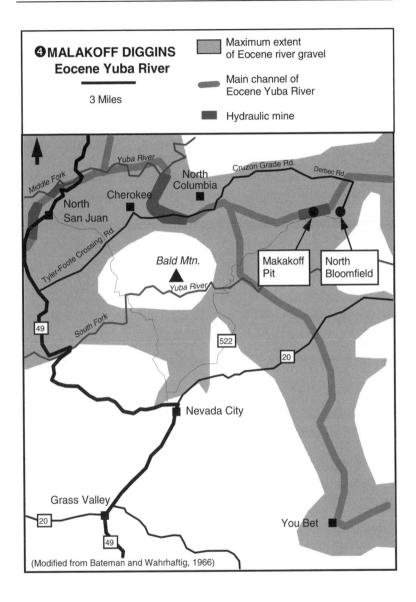

❹MALAKOFF DIGGINS
Eocene Yuba River

3 Miles

Maximum extent of Eocene river gravel

Main channel of Eocene Yuba River

Hydraulic mine

Yuba River

Middle Fork

North San Juan

Cherokee

North Columbia

Cruzon Grade Rd.

Derbec Rd.

Tyler-Foote Crossing Rd.

Bald Mtn.

Yuba River

Makakoff Pit

North Bloomfield

49

South Fork

522

20

Nevada City

Grass Valley

20

49

You Bet

(Modified from Bateman and Wahrhaftig, 1966)

Malakoff Diggins State Historic Park has a museum in a former saloon on Main Street with displays and artifacts from the hydraulic mining era (530-265-2740 or www.parks.ca.gov).

Malakoff Pit - *From North Bloomfield drive N 1 mi. to the Chute Hill Campground; follow the signs in the campground to the Rim Overlook.*
From the Rim Overlook at the Chute Hill Campground, you can see the large Malakoff Pit that was formed by the hydraulic mining of the Eocene river gravel. The pit is over one-and-one-half miles long and a half-mile wide. At the time of the hydraulic mining operations, the pit was 600 feet deep. It has partially filled in since then, and is now about 300 feet deep. The gold occurs in Eocene river gravels that were deposited in the Middle Fork of the Eocene Yuba River. The gravel is up to 600 feet thick in this area. Most of the gold was in the lower 130 feet of blue gravel.

Although the blue gravel at the Malakoff Mine was rich, two things had to be done to reach the gravel. First, several hundred feet of nearly worthless overlying gravel had to be removed. Then, in order to get to the high-grade ore at the bottom of the channel, it was necessary to drain the mining pit. In 1874, work was completed on the 8,000-foot Hiller Tunnel that was dug in hard bedrock and provided drainage from the pit into Humbug Creek. Following completion of the tunnel, operations expanded, and the mine operated seven monitors 24 hours a day, expelling huge amounts of tailings into the Yuba River.

The mining was carried out by the North Bloomfield Gravel Mining Company. An extensive system of ditches and flumes supplied water to the mining operation from Bowman Lake and other reservoirs in the High Sierra. The hydraulic operations continued to expand rapidly during this period. By 1875 tailings from the mine were creating a major environmental problem. The tailings polluted streams and rivers and killed fish. Silt reached into San Francisco Bay and passed into the Pacific through the Golden Gate. The Yuba and Sacramento Rivers were no longer navigable for ocean-going vessels. The bed of the Sacramento River rose and farmland and cities flooded. Finally, because of the ruination of much farmland, farmers filed a lawsuit to stop the hydraulic mining. In 1884, Judge Lorenzo Sawyer issued an injunction against dumping mine debris into the Sacramento and San Joaquin Rivers and their tributaries. The Sawyer decision effectively stopped hydraulic mining in northern California. It is estimated that the North Bloomfield Gravel Mining Company spent three million dollars on capital improvements to carry out their hydraulic mining operation. They recovered about three million dollars in gold before the mining operations were stopped by the Sawyer decision.

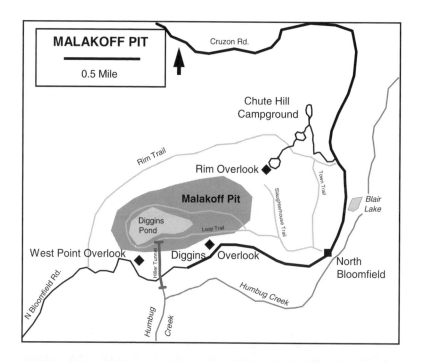

MALAKOFF PIT

0.5 Mile

Cruzon Rd.

Chute Hill Campground

Rim Trail

Rim Overlook ◆

Malakoff Pit

Diggins Pond

Loop Trail

Slaughterhouse Trail

Town Trail

Blair Lake

West Point Overlook ◆

Hiller Tunnel

Diggins ◆ Overlook

North Bloomfield

N Bloomfield Rd.

Humbug Creek

Humbug Creek

This view from the Rim Overlook at the Chute Hill Campground shows the Eocene river gravels that are exposed along the north wall of the Malakoff Pit.

❺ Yuba River

North of Nevada City, Highway 49 travels for 20 miles on top of the Eocene erosion surface. The weathered rocks of the Western Metamorphic Belt and the red soil that was developed on this surface are exposed in many of the roadcuts along the highway. These red soils are especially well developed at Camptonville. Near North San Juan and Camptonville, isolated patches of Eocene gravels that have been preserved on the Eocene erosion surface have been hydraulically mined for their gold.

On the trip north from Nevada City on the Eocene erosion surface, Highway 49 crosses the South, Middle and North Forks of the Yuba River. During the Plio-Pleistocene uplift of the Sierra, these rivers cut deep valleys into the Eocene erosion surface. The rocks of the Western Metamorphic Belt are fresh and well exposed in the bottoms of these river valleys. The best places to see these rocks are in the vicinity of the Highway 49 bridges that cross the rivers.

Erosion of the soft Tertiary sedimentary and volcanic rocks that lie on top of the Eocene erosion surface is rapidly working its way eastward from the foothills toward the crest of the Sierra. From Nevada City to Camptonville, most of the Tertiary rocks west of Highway 49 have been removed from the erosion surface, whereas east of the highway a number of broad ridges are still covered by the Tertiary rocks. These include Harmony Ridge, Washington Ridge, San Juan Ridge, Layfayette Ridge, and Pliocene Ridge. The road from North San Juan to North Bloomfield follows the San Juan Ridge and provides a good look at the Tertiary sedimentary and volcanic rocks.

South Fork Bridge - *From Nevada City, drive N on Hwy. 49 7 mi. to the bridge across the South Fork of the Yuba River; park in the designated parking area; this is a popular swimming area; if the weather is warm bring your bathing suit.*
North of Nevada City, Highway 49 traverses the erosion surface for several miles and then abruptly descends into the deep canyon of the South Fork Yuba River. This canyon cuts into the Sierra basement rocks below the Eocene erosion surface. The rocks exposed along the bottom of the canyon at the highway bridge are granodiorite of Jurassic age. These rocks are part of the large Yuba Rivers Pluton, an outlier pluton of the Sierra Nevada batholith that has been intruded into the rocks of the Western Metamorphic Belt. The pluton is about 20 miles long and four miles wide, and extends across the three major forks of the Yuba River.

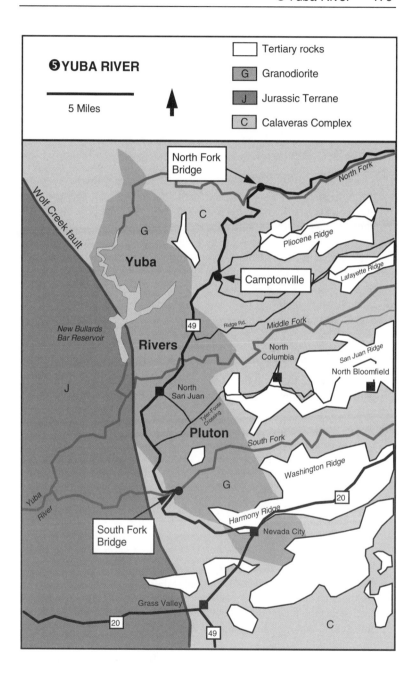

❺**YUBA RIVER**

5 Miles

Tertiary rocks
G Granodiorite
J Jurassic Terrane
C Calaveras Complex

North Fork Bridge
North Fork
C
G
Pliocene Ridge
Lafayette Ridge
Yuba
Wolf Creek fault
Camptonville
49
Ridge Rd.
Middle Fork
New Bullards Bar Reservoir
Rivers
North Columbia
San Juan Ridge
North Bloomfield
J
North San Juan
Tyler Foote Crossing
Pluton
South Fork
Yuba River
Washington Ridge
G
20
Harmony Ridge
South Fork Bridge
Nevada City
Grass Valley
20
49
C

Camptonville - *From the South Fork bridge, drive 14 mi. N on Hwy. 49 to Camptonville; turn right and follow the signs into the town.*

Camptonville lies on the thick red soil of the Eocene erosion surface. In roadcuts near town there are good exposures of the red soil and the deeply weathered basement rocks below the red soil. The basement rocks are metavolcanics of the Western Metamorphic Belt and are so thoroughly decomposed that they can easily be crushed by hand.

The rich blue lead of the north branch of Eocene Yuba River goes through the Camptonville area. Most of the Tertiary sedimentary and volcanic rocks have been eroded from this area, so the gold-bearing river gravels in this area are covered only by a thin layer of dirt and rock. The river gravels were, thus, ideally suited to hydraulic mining, and the town prospered with this activity in the late 1850's. Unfortunately, the original town was situated on one of the Eocene river channels and the hydraulic operations ate away the land that the town had been built on, forcing the town to move to higher ground.

The Pelton water wheel was invented at Camptonville by Lester Pelton in 1878. These water wheels powered many different types of mining machinery in the northern Sierra, and were used for many years in the Empire and North Star Mines of the Grass Valley area.

North Fork Bridge - *From Camptonville drive N 9 mi. on Hwy.49 to the bridge that crosses the North Fork of the Yuba River; park at the bridge.*

North of Camptonville, Highway 49 crosses the North Fork of the Yuba River and then follows the river up the western flank of the Sierra Nevada. Over much of this distance, the river has been incised into the rocks of the Western Metamorphic Belt, and the metamorphic rocks are well exposed along the river and in many roadcuts.

The metamorphic rocks from the North Fork bridge to Goodyears Bar belong to the Calaveras Complex. The rocks near the bridge are partially metamorphosed volcanic rocks, and consist of basalt, agglomerates, and tuffs. Some of the tuffs have been recrystallized into schist, and others are only partly altered.

The Downieville Museum at 330 Main St., Downieville, is located in a former Chinese store and gambling house. The museum has a good display of local gold rush relics.

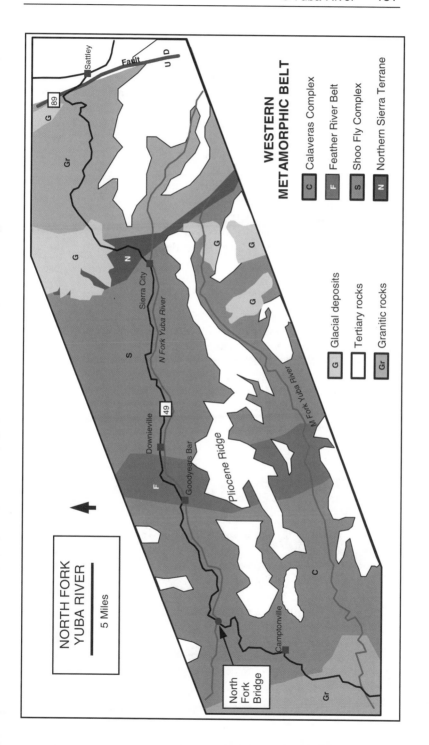

NORTH FORK YUBA RIVER

5 Miles

North Fork Bridge

Camptonville

Downieville

Goodyears Bar

Sierra City

Sattley

Fault

U D

N Fork Yuba River

M Fork Yuba River

Pliocene Ridge

WESTERN METAMORPHIC BELT

C Calaveras Complex
F Feather River Belt
S Shoo Fly Complex
N Northern Sierra Terrane

G Glacial deposits
   Tertiary rocks
Gr Granitic rocks

❻ *Goodyears Bar*

Rich placer gold deposits were discovered at Goodyears Bar in 1849, and the area prospered during the 1850's, until the placer deposits were exhausted. At Goodyears Bar, Highway 49 crosses through a sequence of ultramafic rocks known as the Feather River Belt. These rocks lie between the Calaveras Complex and the Shoo Fly Complex, and represent a slab of oceanic crust that was carried into the Calaveras subduction zone and inserted under the rocks of the Shoo Fly Complex.

The Feather River Belt includes serpentine, metamorphosed sedimentary and volcanic rocks, gabbro, amphibolite gneiss, and blueschist. In the northern Sierra, the belt ranges up to several miles wide. To the south, the belt narrows and becomes the Calaveras-Shoo Fly fault. The rocks of the Feather River Belt near Goodyears Bar are mainly serpentine.

Serpentine – *From Downieville drive 3 mi. W on Hwy. 49 to Goodyear Creek Rd.; the serpentine roadcut is on the N side of the highway immediately E of Goodyear Creek Rd.*
The serpentine of the Feather River Belt can be found in many places near Goodyears Bar. However, the best exposures are in the large roadcuts along Highway 49 just east of the turnoff to Goodyears Bar. There are also good exposures of the serpentine along the South Fork of the Yuba River near the bridge where Goodyear Creek Road crosses the North Fork. Some of this serpentine displays a very intense green hue, and is specimen quality.

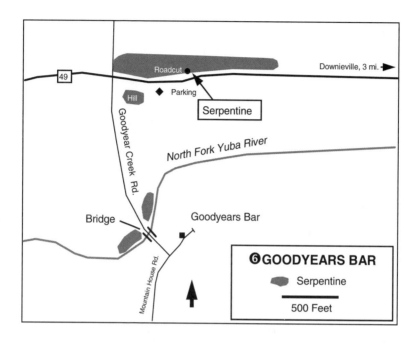

↑This large roadcut on Highway 49 near Goodyear Creek Road has excellent exposures of serpentine from the Feather River Belt.

←The serpentine is also exposed along North Fork of the Yuba River at the bridge for Goodyear Creek Road.

❼ Sierra City

Sierra City was founded in 1850, following discovery of placer gold in the North Fork of the Yuba River. A short time later, lode deposits were discovered in the mountains north of town. The large Sierra Buttes Mine was opened in 1850 and was followed by many other discoveries, including the nearby Kentucky Mine. The district was highly productive from 1870 to 1914, but was only intermittently productive thereafter. There is little mining at present.

The placer deposits at Sierra City contained many large gold nuggets, and the mines were known for their very rich high-grade surface pockets of gold. The gold occurs as free gold in a series of north-trending quartz veins that range up to 40 feet in thickness. Some of the veins are several hundred feet long and several thousand feet deep. Most of the quartz veins are in slate and metamorphosed rhyolite, but veins also occur in many other igneous and metamorphic rocks in this area.

This part of the Western Metamorphic Belt includes two very different types of metamorphic rocks, the Shoo Fly Complex and the Northern Sierra Terrane. The rocks of the Shoo Fly Complex are of Cambrian to early Devonian age and consist mainly of metamorphosed slate, schist and chert. These rocks are well exposed in the roadcuts along Highway 49 near Ladies Canyon west of Sierra City. During mid-Devonian time, the rocks of the Shoo Fly Complex were subjected to a major period of mountain building, referred to as the Antler orogeny. During this orogeny, the rocks of the Shoo Fly Complex were folded, faulted, metamorphosed, uplifted, and eroded. As a result of the Antler orogeny, the Shoo Fly Complex was added to the western margin of North America.

The Northern Sierra Terrane consists of great thicknesses of volcanic rocks of late Devonian to Permian age. These rocks were deposited on top of the Shoo Fly Complex, and are separated from the Shoo Fly Complex by a major unconformity. This unconformity represents the mid-Devonian interval of geologic time during which the Antler orogeny was in progress. The rocks below the unconformity were affected by the Antler orogeny, and the rocks above the unconformity were not affected. The Sierra Buttes, north of Sierra City, are formed from rocks of the Northern Sierra Terrane, and these rocks extend north from the Sierra Buttes for about 30 miles, passing through the Gold Lake and Big Bear Lake areas. Some of the best exposures of these volcanic rocks are at Big Bear Lake where the rocks have been cleaned off and polished by glaciers.

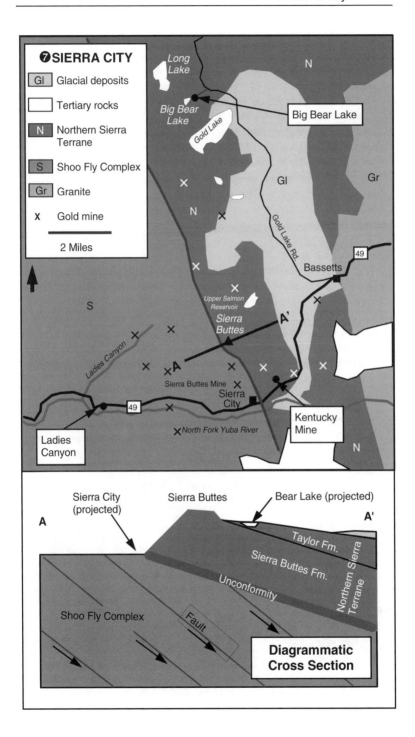

❼SIERRA CITY

Gl	Glacial deposits
	Tertiary rocks
N	Northern Sierra Terrane
S	Shoo Fly Complex
Gr	Granite
X	Gold mine

2 Miles

Long Lake

Big Bear Lake

Gold Lake

Big Bear Lake

N

Gl

Gr

Gold Lake Rd

49

Bassetts

Upper Salmon Reservoir

Sierra Buttes

A'

S

Ladies Canyon

A

Sierra Buttes Mine

Sierra City

49

North Fork Yuba River

Kentucky Mine

N

Ladies Canyon

Diagrammatic Cross Section

A

Sierra City (projected)

Sierra Buttes

Bear Lake (projected)

A'

Taylor Fm.

Sierra Buttes Fm.

Northern Sierra Terrane

Unconformity

Shoo Fly Complex

Fault

Ladies Canyon — *From Sierra City drive 5 mi. S on Hwy. 49; park in the pullout near milepost 24.27, 300 feet N of the Ladies Canyon Bridge.*

The metamorphosed sedimentary rocks of the Shoo Fly Complex are exposed in many places between Downieville and Sierra City. One of the best places to examine these rocks is in the roadcuts near Ladies Canyon. The rocks in this area are mainly slate, phyllite, and schist, and occur in thin, steeply dipping layers. The rocks of the Shoo Fly Complex are of Cambrian to early Devonian age and were derived from the North American continent when the continent lay far to the east of the present-day Sierra. The rocks were folded, faulted and metamorphosed during the mid-Devonian Antler orogeny.

Kentucky Mine - *From Sierra City drive 1 mi. E on Hwy. 49 to the Sierra City Historical Park and Museum (530-862-1310).*

The Sierra City Historical Park and Museum is on the grounds of the Kentucky Mine, one of early lode mines in the Sierra Buttes area. The six-story Kentucky Mine operated from the 1850s to 1953. The portal to the mine's 1500-foot horizontal mineshaft is on the side of the mountain just above the museum. The park also has an operational 10-stamp mill, blacksmith shop, and miner's cabin. There are guided daily tours of the mill, with stops to explain the milling and extraction process.

The craggy Sierra Buttes, which lie north of Sierra City, are formed from volcanic rocks of the Northern Sierra Terrane. These rocks were deposited along an island arc during late Devonian time along what was then the western border of the North American continent.

The metasedimentary rocks of the Shoo Fly Complex in this roadcut near Ladies Canyon dip steeply and are mainly thinly layered phyllite and schist. These are some of the oldest rocks of the Western Metamorphic Belt.

Gold ore from the Kentucky Mine was carried in small ore cars across this trestle to the mill where the gold was processed. The mill is open for tours and is typical of the mills of the Sierra Nevada gold belt.

Big Bear Lake - *From Sierra City go 5 mi. N on Hwy. 49; at Bassetts turn left on Gold Lake Rd. and drive 9 mi. to the turnoff to Lakes Basin Campground; take the Big Bear Lake trail from the campground and hike 0.5 mi. to the S shore of the lake.*

The volcanic rocks of the Northern Sierra Terrane are about three miles thick and were deposited by a series of island arcs that existed along the western margin of North America during late Devonian to Permian time. Deposition of these rocks began immediately after the end of the Antler orogeny. Most of these rocks were deposited under water. After the volcanic material was ejected from the volcanoes along the arcs, it accumulated on the slopes of the volcanoes and then slumped and flowed into the ocean basins between the arcs. The rocks of the Northern Sierra Terrane have been divided into several different formations, depending on the age of the deposits and compositional differences of the units. From oldest to youngest, these include the Sierra Buttes, Elwell, Taylor, Peale, Goodhue and Reeve formations.

The Sierra Buttes Formation is the oldest, lowermost, and one of the best-known rock units in the Northern Sierra Terrane. These rocks lie directly on the Shoo Fly Complex, and represent the earliest volcanic activity that took place after the Antler orogeny. The Sierra Buttes, which lie immediately north of Sierra City and rise 3,000 feet above the city, are formed from these rocks. The Sierra Buttes Formation is also well-exposed at Jamison Lake, about ten miles north of Sierra City.

One of the best places to see the volcanic rocks of the Northern Sierra Terrane, however, is at Big Bear Lake, about 15 miles north of Sierra City. The volcanic rocks of the Taylor Formation have been cleaned and polished by glaciers and are well exposed along the shoreline of this scenic lake. As described by Brooks (2000), these rocks are mainly basaltic in composition, and consist of pillow lavas, turbidites, and debris flows. The pillow lavas appear as rounded blobs a foot or so across, and some have margins that are brick red. The turbidites are fine to very coarse-grained and stratified. Some strata show graded bedding.

Along the road to the Lakes Basin Campground, there are several small rounded outcrops of the Taylor Formation that were cleaned and polished by Pleistocene glaciers and have been used as a drawing board by early inhabitants of this area. The petroglyphs on these rocks include pictures of humans, animals, mystical beings and geometric designs. The drawings were made by pounding or pecking the pictures in the rocks.

The volcanic rocks of the Northern Sierra Terrane are well-exposed along the shore of Big Bear Lake where Pleistocene glaciers cleaned and polished the rocks. The rocks at the lake include pillow basalts, turbidities, and debris flows that were deposited along island arcs in late Devonian time.

This small roche moutonnée near the Lakes Basin Campground is inscribed with a number of petroglyphs made by early inhabitants of the area. This rock is part of the Taylor Formation, and is similar to the volcaniclastic rocks at Big Bear Lake.

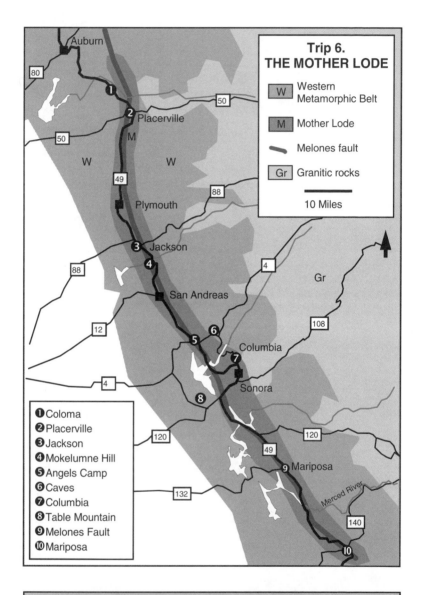

Trip 6.
THE MOTHER LODE

W Western Metamorphic Belt

M Mother Lode

━ Melones fault

Gr Granitic rocks

10 Miles

❶ Coloma
❷ Placerville
❸ Jackson
❹ Mokelumne Hill
❺ Angels Camp
❻ Caves
❼ Columbia
❽ Table Mountain
❾ Melones Fault
❿ Mariposa

The Placer County Department of Museums operates six museums that cover different aspects of Placer County's gold mining activity. For information, contact Placer County Museums, 101 Maple St., Auburn, CA 95603 (530-889-6500).

Trip 6
THE MOTHER LODE
The Gold Rush

This trip begins in Coloma, on the bank of the South Fork of the American River, where the gold rush began. From there, the trip follows Highway 49 to Mariposa, passing through the heart of the Mother Lode. As the highway makes it way along the Mother Lode, it closely follows the Melones fault, weaving from side to side, but seldom leaving the fault for long. The Melones fault is one of the major faults within the Western Metamorphic Belt, and fluids generated in the deep parts of the Franciscan subduction zone left deposits of gold in the shattered and broken rocks along the fault. Most of the large gold mines of the Mother Lode lie within a mile or so of the fault, and Highway 49 follows the gold mines.

One hundred and fifty years ago, in the early days of the gold rush, this area was mobbed by thousands of prospectors and miners looking for gold in rivers and creeks. Dozens of gold mining towns were settled, and more towns would be founded in the next few years. There is almost no gold mining now, and most of the mines, miners, and towns have faded and left little trace. However, some towns have lingered on, and some have even prospered, based mainly on tourism and agriculture.

The emphasis in this book will be on the geology and mines of the Mother Lode. Unfortunately, there is little space or time for the other fascinating aspects of the gold rush. Many excellent books have been written about the gold rush, and you should take some of these books with you on your trip. For a very readable account of the history and geology of California gold, get a copy of *Gold, The California Story* by Hill (1999), and for descriptions of the gold rush towns see *The California Gold Country* by Koeppel (1996).

During this trip, you'll visit several famous mining towns of the Mother Lode—Coloma, Placerville, Jackson, Angels Camp, Columbia, and Mariposa—and get a good understanding of life during the gold rush. You'll also examine the rocks along the Melones fault zone, see some caves, and learn how Table Mountain got its flat top.

191

❶ Coloma

Gold was discovered at Coloma by James Marshall in January of 1848. At the time of discovery, Coloma was a small town on the South Fork of the American River. Within four months of the discovery, nearly the entire population of San Francisco had departed to prospect in the gold fields. Many of these new prospectors first headed for Coloma. Within a few months after the discovery, 2,000 miners had arrived in the town. By the end of 1848, news of the gold had spread throughout the United States and the gold rush was on. By the end of 1849, the population of Coloma was 10,000. Despite the efforts of all of these prospectors, little gold was found at Coloma. By 1852, the population had moved on, and the town declined. The town is now a state park, and 70% of the town is in the park. The park includes a visitor center and many historic exhibits, sites, and buildings from the gold rush era. Several of the buildings in Coloma date from the early and mid 1850's, before the gold rush began.

Considering the many rich gold deposits waiting to be discovered in the Sierra foothills, Coloma was an unlikely place for the first discovery. Coloma is not on the Mother Lode and there are no significant lode mines nearby to provide a source for the placer gold in the river. Ironically, because the prospectors moved on rapidly to better pickings, the town of Coloma is a remarkably well-preserved piece of gold rush history.

It is also somewhat ironic that the gold was discovered while Marshall was correcting a mistake in construction of a sawmill. The foundation for the sawmill had been built too low, and the water was not flowing through the tailrace fast enough to turn the mill wheel. In order to increase the flow of water, Marshall dug a ditch in the gravel under the mill. He had inadvertently created a natural sluice. Some small nuggets of gold were separated from the river gravel along the sluice, and one of these nuggets caught Marshall's eye. You can see a replica of this small nugget at the park visitor center in Coloma.

Visitor Center - *From Placerville drive N 8 mi. on Hwy. 49 to Coloma; park at the visitor center for the Marshall Gold Discovery State Historic Park at Bridge St.; for park information phone 530-622-3470.*
Begin at the excellent visitor center and bring yourself up to speed on the history of the gold rush. Then get a copy of the park map and take the self-guided Discovery Tour. This tour includes a mining exhibit, a replica of Sutter's sawmill, the site of the original sawmill, and the gold discovery site along the original tailrace for the sawmill. You can also pan for gold on the American River across the bridge from the visitor center.

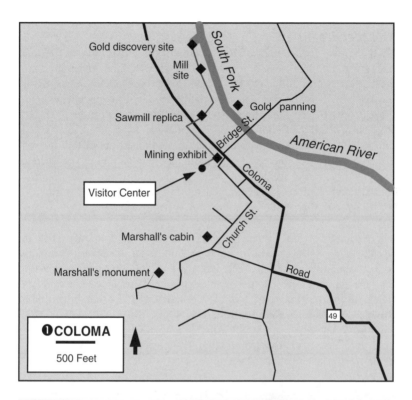

Gold discovery site

Mill site

South Fork

Gold panning

Sawmill replica

American River

Bridge St.

Mining exhibit

Visitor Center

Coloma

Church St.

Marshall's cabin

Marshall's monument

Road

49

❶COLOMA

500 Feet

This replica of Sutter's Mill lies along the South Fork of the American River in Marshall Gold Discovery State Historic Park. The site of the original mill lies about 500 feet north of the replica.

❷ *Placerville*

By the spring and summer of 1848, many of the prospectors at Coloma had given up their search for gold in that area, and began to look elsewhere. Some followed the South Fork of the American River upstream to Big Canyon and then followed Big Canyon upstream to what is now Placerville. The prospectors didn't know it at the time, but Big Canyon and the South Fork of the American River had been incised into the Eocene erosion surface. When they climbed out of this incised drainage, they encountered the more subdued topography of the Eocene erosion surface. For millions of years, great quantities of gold from the Mother Lode had been concentrated on this erosion surface, waiting to be discovered. Placerville is built on this erosion surface.

The first gold in the Placerville area was discovered in July 1848 in stream deposits at Spanish Ravine. Additional discoveries rapidly followed along Hangtown Creek and many of the other ravines that fed into Hangtown Creek. Some of these placer deposits were extremely rich. During the first year, a million dollars in gold came from Cedar Ravine and another million from Log Cabin Ravine, which is now Bedford Road. One pan of gold from Hangtown Creek had 75 ounces of gold dust recovered from white clay. The placer deposits were rapidly depleted in a just a couple of years.

By late 1849, as the placer deposits were being depleted, gold was discovered in the upper parts of Spanish Ravine and several other ravines along Hangtown Creek. This gold came from Eocene river gravels exposed on the sides of Spanish Hill and Texas Hill. The miners dug into the sides of these hills to follow the gold deposits as far as they could. Some of the larger channels were later developed into drift mines, with larger and better tunnels. The river gravels in these mines had been deposited in various channels of the Eocene American River as it flowed across the Eocene erosion surface.

During the early years of the gold rush, water was scarce in the Placerville area. The placer deposits could be worked only in the wet season or by transporting the gold-bearing deposits to flowing streams. However, because the deposits were rich, water flumes were soon built. The gold deposits could then be worked year-round. In 1855, hydraulic mining began. The hydraulic mining was directed mainly at the gold-bearing Eocene river gravels on Spanish Hill, Texas Hill, and at Coon Hollow. Most of the drift and hydraulic mining occurred from the mid-1850's to the 1870's. Hydraulic mining stopped abruptly in 1884 with the Sawyer decision, which is discussed in more detail during the trip to the Malakoff Diggins.

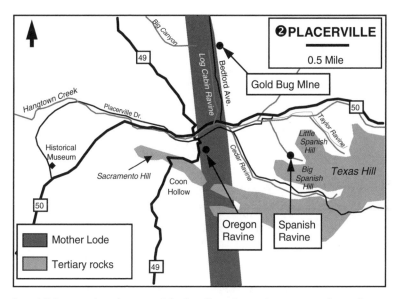

In addition to the placer and hydraulic mines, there were also a large number of lode mines in the Placerville area. Most of the lode mines occur along the Mother Lode. Conveniently, the Mother Lode passes directly under the County Courthouse in downtown Placerville, and the largest of the lode mines, the Pacific Mine, was in the center of Placerville. Mining began at the Pacific Mine in 1852, but the main period of lode mining was from the 1880's to 1915. The gold in these mines mainly occurs in massive quartz veins in slate, and the ore is typically low to moderate grade. Some mines were developed to depths up to 2,000 feet.

The scars of the early mining activity have largely healed. Tunnels, and mine shafts have caved in. The headframe of the Pacific Mine was unceremoniously shoved down its own mineshaft a few years ago and the opening closed. Rotary Park now occupies the site of the large Atlantic Mine. Old roads, trails, and hydraulic mines have become overgrown. The streets of Placerville wind along the old gold-bearing creeks and ravines with little but the street names—Cedar Ravine, Spanish Ravine, Taylor Ravine, Log Cabin Ravine—to recall past mining activity. Houses and buildings now follow the ravines and cling to hillsides where fortunes were once made in gold. You have to look hard to see the work of the early miners.

The El Dorado County Historical Museum at 100 Placerville Drive on the El Dorado County Fairgrounds has historical exhibits of gold rush times and displays of old mining equipment (530-621-5865).

Oregon Ravine - *From Hwy. 49 and Main St. go S on Pacific St. three blocks to Benham St.; City Park is on the E side of Benham St.*

During the early gold rush, Oregon Ravine had the richest placer deposits in Placerville. City Park now lies within the old ravine. The ravine had the good fortune of lying directly on a rich gold-bearing section of the Mother Lode, and a great amount of placer gold was concentrated in this small area. There was little or no water in the ravine, so the gold-bearing dirt was carried to nearby creeks to process. Many large bean-sized nuggets were found.

Spanish Ravine - *From Main St. drive S on Spanish Ravine Rd. to the end of the road.*

Spanish Ravine is one of several ravines on the north side of Texas Hill that had rich placer deposits that were mined in the early days of the gold rush. As the placer gold in Spanish Ravine was depleted, prospectors found gold in the Eocene river gravels that were exposed along the sides of Texas Hill. The Eocene river gravel, which had a distinctive blue color, was especially rich where it rested on bedrock. This same blue stratum was found all the way through the surrounding hills. The miners found that the blue gravel drifted in channels that trended west-southwest under the hill and gave names to these channels, such as "deep blue lead." Miners dug into the hillside and followed these channels. Later, some of the channels were developed into drift mines with horizontal tunnels up to a mile long. By 1854, water flumes had been brought into the area and hydraulic mining began. With hydraulic mining, it was no longer necessary to tunnel into the hillside—the entire hillside could simply be washed down. By 1855, the whole top of Spanish Hill had been washed out to a depth of 60 feet. By 1859, the ridge between Spanish and Taylor Ravines was also gone. None of this mining activity is apparent today, but with some imagination you can appreciate the hectic activity at that time.

Gold Bug Mine - *From Hwy. 50 drive N on Bedford Ave.; follow the signs 1 mi. to Gold Bug Park; opening hours change seasonally; owned by City of Placerville; small entrance charge (530-642-5238).*

The Gold Bug Mine was opened in 1888, and is typical of the small gold mines of that time. It is the only underground mine in California on public property that visitors can enter. The mine has a 352-foot tunnel and provides a self-guided tour where visitors can get a good look at how hardrock mining was done. While at the park, also see the Joshua Hendy Stamp Mill. The mill is on its original site, and has an operating scale model that demonstrates how gold is separated from the ore.

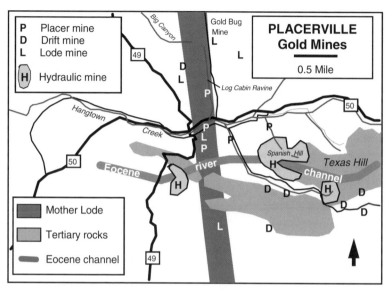

Gold in the Placerville area was found in many different types of deposits. Placer gold was found in Spanish Ravine, Cedar Ravine, Oregon Ravine, Log Cabin Ravine, and Hangtown Creek. Drift mines followed gold-bearing Eocene river channels under Texas Hill. Hydraulic mines were located where the Eocene gravels were exposed on the flanks of Texas Hill. Lode mines occurred in the vicinity of the Mother Lode, which goes through the center of Placerville.

The entrance to the Gold Bug Mine is on the hillside immediately in back of the Hattie Museum at Gold Bug Park. The mine is open for self-guided tours.

❸ Jackson

The ten miles of Highway 49 between Jackson and Plymouth goes through the heart of the Mother Lode, and many of the most famous and productive mines of the Mother Lode lie within a mile of this part of the highway. These mines have produced over seven million ounces of gold, valued at over two billion dollars at today's prices. This is more gold than was produced from any other part of the Sierra Nevada gold belt, with the exception of the Grass Valley area.

Placer mining began in the Jackson area in 1848. The placer deposits were rapidly depleted, but by that time, rich gold-bearing quartz veins had been found. The first lode mine, the Argonaut, opened in 1850. This was followed by many other lode mines through the 1850's and 60's. Gold mining provided a stable industry for the area for nearly 100 years, until the mines were closed during World War II. Few mines reopened after the war because the mines had deteriorated and filled with water while they were closed. The last major mining operation was the Central Eureka Mine, which reopened in 1945 and then closed again in 1953.

Most of the gold mines are concentrated in a mile-wide zone along a splay of the Melones fault. The main fault lies about a mile to the east. The gold typically occurs as fine-grained native gold in quartz veins that dip steeply east and cut slate and greenstone. Some of the quartz veins are several tens of feet thick. One of the veins at the Keystone Mine was 200 feet thick. The quartz veins generally occur in areas of abundant fault gouge. Although much of the ore was low to moderate grade, some of the mines had rich high-grade pockets with grains, wires, and plates of gold.

The largest mines in this area were the Kennedy and Argonaut. Other major mines included the Plymouth Consolidated, Original Amador, Lincoln, Wildman, Mahony, Old Eureka, Central Eureka, South Eureka, Oneida, and Zelia. Dozens of other mines also contributed to the production of this gold mining district from time to time.

Vista Point - *From Hwy. 49 and N. Main St. in Jackson drive N 1.2 mi. to the Jackson vista point; the best overlook is the one on the W side of the highway.*
From this vista point, you can get a good view of the Jackson area and also see the headframe to the Kennedy Mine, which lies east of the viewpoint. The Argonaut Mine lies immediately west of the viewpoint, but is difficult to see from the viewpoint. The Argonaut and Kennedy Mines were connected at one time by underground workings.

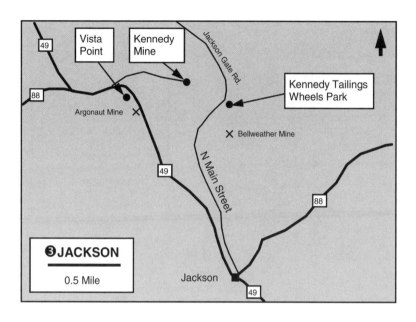

The headframe of the now quiet Kennedy mine can be seen from the vista point on Highway 49 at the north end of Jackson. This was one of the richest gold mines ever worked along the Mother Lode.

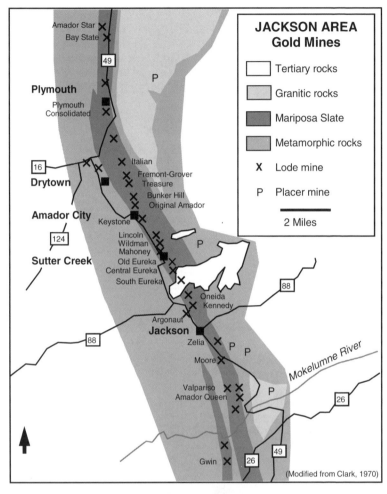

Gold Mines - Jackson Area
(Based on Clark, 1970)

Alma: located next to the Argonaut Mine; active prior to 1900; 1,000-foot shaft.

Alpine: opened in the 1860's, active in the 1890's and from 1910 to 1914; 600-foot shaft and a 10-stamp mill.

Amador Gold: active prior to 1900; minor prospecting in the 1960's; 800-foot shaft.

Amador Queen: worked in the early days and in the 30's, 40's and 60's; 1,200-foot adit; 900-foot winze; 20-stamp mill.

Amador Star: active prior to 1900 and from 1917-1935; adit and 900-foot shaft.

Argonaut: first opened in 1850; extensively developed from 1893 to 1942; underground fires in 1919 and again in 1922 in which 47 lives were lost; 5,700-foot inclined shaft with a winze down to 6,300 feet; 60-stamp mill; later ore was treated with ball mills, flotation, and cyanidation; headframe and buildings remain.

Ballard: active in the 1870's and the 1930's; prospected again in the 1940's and 1950's; 285-foot shaft.

Bay State: opened in 1896; active until 1909; minor development during the 1930's; 1,065-foot shaft; 10-stamp mill.

Bellweather: active in the 1890's; purchased by Kennedy Mine; 320-foot shaft.

Bunker Hill: opened in 1853; active until 1888 and again from 1893 to 1922; 2,800-foot shaft with a winze down to 3,440 feet; connected underground to the Treasure Mine; 40-stamp mill; headframe remains.

Central Eureka: opened in 1853; active until 1875; reopened in 1895; combined with the Old Eureka in 1924; active until 1942 and again from 1945 to 1953; 4,855-foot shaft; 30-stamp mill; headframe remains.

Crown: active in the 1930's; 485-foot shaft.

Fremont-Grover: active in the 1860's, from the 1880's to 1918, and in the 1930's; fire in 1910 took 11 lives; 40-stamp mill; 2,950-foot shaft called the Fremont shaft and a 1,500-foot shaft called the Grover shaft; Fremont shaft headframe remains.

Hardenbergh: active during the early days and from the 1890's to 1918; 1,500-foot shaft; 20-stamp mill.

Italian: worked in the 1860's, 1890's, and from 1932 to the 1940's; prospected recently; adit; 5-stamp mill.

Kennedy: first worked in 1850's, active in 1860's and from 1885 to 1942; fires in 1920 and in 1928 and 1929; 4,764-foot vertical shaft with a winze to 5,912 feet; 100-stamp mill; tailings delivered to a reservoir by four 68-foot diameter wheels; headframe, buildings, and wheels remain; wheels preserved as landmarks.

Keystone: discovered in 1851; active until 1919 and from 1933 to 1942; 2,680-foot shaft; old mine office now a motel.

Lincoln: first worked in 1851; active until the early 1900s; combined with the Wildman Mine and the Mahoney Mine to form Lincoln Consolidated Mines; 2,000-foot shaft.

Mahoney: opened in 1861; active from the 1870's to 1906; combined with the Wildman Mine and later the Lincoln Mine; 1,200-foot shaft connected underground to the Wildman Mine; 40-stamp mill.

Moore: active in the 1880's and from 1921 to 1934; 2,290-foot shaft; 20-stamp mill.

New London: active prior to 1894; 1,340-foot shaft; 40-stamp mill.

North Star: opened in the early days; again active in 1890's and from 1917 to 1927; 1,340-foot shaft; 40-stamp mill.

Old Eureka: opened in 1852 and in production until 1881; reopened in 1916; combined with the Central Eureka Mine in 1924; 3,500-foot shaft with winze to 4,150 feet.

Oneida: active in 1860's and again from the 1890's to 1914; 2,280- and 1,350-foot shafts; connected underground to the South Eureka; 60-stamp mill.

Original Amador: opened in 1852; active until the 1870's, from 1898 to 1918, and in the 1930's; 1,240-foot shaft; 20-stamp mill.

Pioneer: active in the 1890's; 550-foot shaft.

Plymouth Consolidated: located in 1852; active until the 1880's and from 1911 to the 1930's; 4 shafts; deepest shaft 4,600 feet; 30-stamp mill.

Pocahontas: active prior to and during the 1890's; 620-foot shaft; 10-stamp mill.

Seaton: active in the 1860's and 1880's; 950- and 500-foot shafts; 40-stamp mill.

South Eureka: active from 1891 to 1917; 2,785-foot shaft with winzes to 2,900 feet; connected to the Oneida Mine; 80-stamp mill.

South Jackson: active from 1912 to 1915; 577-foot shaft.

South Spring Hill: opened in 1851; active until 1902 and again in 1934; 3 shafts; deepest shaft 1,200 feet.

Treasure: active in the 1860's and from 1907 to 1922; 1,600-foot shaft with winzes to 3,030 feet; connected underground to the Bunker Hill Mine; headframe remains.

Valpariso: active in 1850's and 1860's; intermittently active from the 1880's to the 1930's; 1,300-foot adit.

Wildman: opened in 1851; active from 1887 to 1906; combined with the Mahoney Mine and later the Lincoln Mine; 1,400-foot shaft; 40-stamp mill.

Zeila: active from the 1860's to 1914; 1,700-foot shaft; old mine office is now a private home.

Kennedy Mine – *From the Jackson vista point drive N on Hwy. 49 0.1 mi. to Kennedy Mine Rd.; turn E and drive 0.5 mi. to the Kennedy Mine; surface tours of the mine are available on weekends seasonally; for information phone 209-223-9542.*
The Kennedy Mine is one of the richest mines ever worked in the Sierra Nevada gold belt. It was discovered in 1856 and was in operation from 1860 to 1942. There were over 150 miles of underground workings in the mine, and these extended to a vertical depth of 5,912 feet. It was the deepest mine in North America when it closed in 1942.

Mining at the Kennedy Mine was difficult because the gold-bearing quartz veins were in fault zones where the rocks were shattered and filled with water. The rocks caved easily so that heavy timbering and backfilling were required. For this reason, shafts and tunnels were mainly cut in hard rock where less timbering was required.

The gold occurs in steeply dipping quartz veins that cut across Mariposa Slate and greenstone. Some of the veins are several tens of feet thick. The gold often occurs in areas with abundant fault gouge. Most of the gold is free and in small grains. Much of the ore was low grade.

The Kennedy Mine had a 100-stamp mill. Ore was processed by crushing in this mill, then passing the finely ground product over amalgamating plates with mercury, shaking tables, and other processes. The final product was a gold-rich concentrate that was shipped to smelters for refining.

In 1922, the nearby Argonaut Mine was the site of one of California's worst mining disasters. Fire broke out at the 4,200 foot level of the mine while work was going on at deeper levels. A shift of 47 men were trapped by the fire and could not be reached through the Argonaut mineshaft. The Kennedy Mine was already connected underground to the Argonaut Mine, but there was no direct access to the trapped men. Tunneling from the Kennedy Mine began as soon as possible, but it was three weeks before the tunnel finally broke through to the lower levels of the Argonaut Mine. Unfortunately, there were no survivors. The miners had perished from poisonous gas about five hours after the fire had started.

The Amador County Museum on 225 Church St. in Jackson is in the historic Brown House, built in 1859. The museum has gold rush artifacts, antique mining equipment, and a detailed working model of the Kennedy Mine, stamp mill, and tailings wheels (209-223-6386).

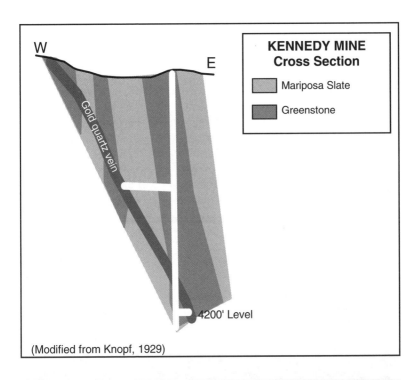

W

E

**KENNEDY MINE
Cross Section**

Mariposa Slate

Greenstone

Gold quartz vein

4200' Level

(Modified from Knopf, 1929)

This mining equipment on display at the Empire Mine at Grass Valley is typical of the equipment that was used in working the lode mines of the Sierra Nevada.

Kennedy Tailings Wheels Park - *From North Main St. and Hwy.49 in Jackson drive N on Main St. 1 mi. to Kennedy Tailings Wheels Park.*

Kennedy Tailings Wheels Park has the remains of four large tailings wheels that were built in 1914 in response to federal anti-debris laws. The wheels were connected by flumes and were used to transport tailings from the Kennedy mill to a dam one-half mile away where the tailings were impounded. The tailings dam was higher than the mill, and the wheels were used to lift the tailings 58 feet on their way to the dam. The wheels are 68 feet in diameter and were driven by electric motors. The wheels were in operation until the Kennedy Mine shut down in 1942. Two of the wheels have been reconstructed, and two lie where they toppled some years ago.

This is one of the four large tailings wheels at Kennedy Tailings Wheels Park. The headframe of the Kennedy Mine can be seen in the distance through the spokes in the wheel.

❹ *Mokelumne Hill*

Mokelumne Hill is one of the few areas south of Placerville where significant gold production has come from Tertiary river gravels. These river gravels were deposited in a complex system of at least eight different channels of the Tertiary Mokelumne River, and occur in an erosional remnant of the Tertiary rocks that once blanketed this area. The gravels were mined extensively in 1850's and 1860's by both drift and hydraulic methods, and production declined in 1870's. The hydraulic pits and drift mines that were used to mine the gravels are not visible from Highway 49. In some places, the Tertiary gravels contain large well-formed quartz crystals of optical grade. These crystals were mined for electronics during World War I and World War II at the nearby Calaveras Crystal Drift Mine, located in Chile Gulch.

Chile Gulch - *From Hwy. 49 and Main St. in Mokelumne Hill drive 1.4 mi. S on Hwy. 49 to the historic marker for Chili Gulch.*

In 1848 and 1849, this part of Chile Gulch was the site of intensive placer mining activity. This placer gold probably was derived from the Tertiary river gravels that were extensively mined in this area. The roadcuts between Mokelumne Hill and this historic marker have large exposures of yellowish gray tuffs of the Valley Springs Formation. The gold-bearing Tertiary gravels lie below these rocks. The Mehrten Formation is exposed in roadcuts along Highway 26 immediately west of Mokelumne Hill.

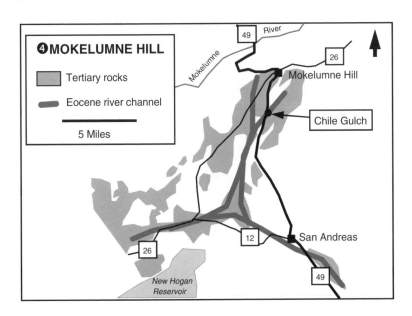

❺ *Angels Camp*

Angels Camp was founded in 1848 as a trading post for nearby placer mines. The placers did not last long. However, gold-bearing quartz veins were soon discovered under the main street of the town. These veins were worked by several mines. The largest of these was the Utica, the most famous mine between Carson Hill and Jackson. Angels Camp also served as the mining center for several of other mines in the vicinity, including the large Carson Hill Mine to the south. Gold mining ended in this area in 1918.

> **Utica Mine** - *From Valecito Rd. and Main St. in Angels Camp, go N on Main St. four blocks to Sams Way; turn left and park at Utica Park.*
>
> The north shaft of the Utica Mine was located in what is now Utica Park. This shaft collapsed in 1889, and 17 men were buried by the collapse. It was 12 years before all of the bodies were recovered. The park is in a depressed area that subsided when the shaft caved in. The Utica Mine is located along a spur of the Melones fault, about a half-mile east of the main fault zone. The gold occurs mainly as finely divided native gold in quartz veins, schist, and greenstone in the fault zone. The veins are nearly vertical, and have been worked to a depth of 3,050 feet below the surface. The ore-bearing veins are faulted off on the south side of town. Many efforts to find their continuation have been in vain. The Utica Mining Company was organized in the 1850's, and peak production was in the1880's and 1890's.

This monument at Utica Park is dedicated to the 17 miners that were lost in the 1889 collapse of the north shaft.

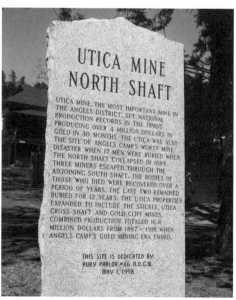

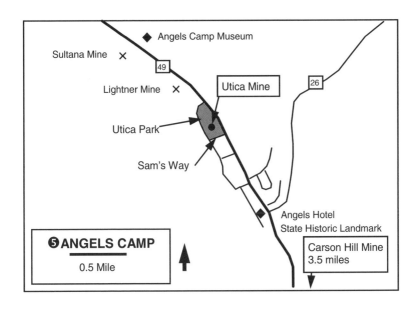

Angels Camp Museum

Sultana Mine ✕

49

Lightner Mine ✕

Utica Mine

26

Utica Park

Sam's Way

Angels Hotel
State Historic Landmark

❺ANGELS CAMP
0.5 Mile

Carson Hill Mine
3.5 miles

Utica Park in Angels Camp is at the site of the North Shaft of the Utica Mine. The park is in a depressed area that was formed by a major collapse of the underground workings at the North Shaft.

Carson Hill Mine - *From Angels Camp drive 3.5 mi. S on Hwy. 49 to the historical marker for the Carson Hill Mine; park in the pullout at the marker.*

From this pullout on Highway 49, you can see a large open pit that has been carved out of Carson Hill. The pit is the remains of the large Carson Hill Gold Mine, the last of many mines that have intermittently extracted gold from Carson Hill for nearly 150 years. The hill is named for James Carson, a sergeant in the U.S. Artillery. In 1848, Carson and his partners took 180 ounces of gold from a creek on the northwest side of the hill. However, it would be two more years before gold was discovered on Carson Hill. Legend has it that, in 1850, John Hance found a 14-pound lump of gold at the top of Carson Hill while chasing his runaway mule. This may well have been the most significant gold discovery ever made by a mule.

Most of the early gold came from rich surface pockets, where the gold had been concentrated by surface weathering. The gold was produced from a number of different mining claims on the hill. A 195-pound nugget was found in one of these early mines. Gold production declined in the late 1850's as the rich pockets were depleted.

Most of the later mining was of low-grade ore and was carried out by a number of separate underground mines that operated until 1942, when production stopped during World War II. The Carson Hill Gold Mining Corporation began open pit mining and leaching operations in 1986. This activity ended in 1989 as a result of low gold recoveries and low gold prices. In 1991, the Morgan Mine began open pit mining on Carson Hill after consolidating the Carson Hill, Morgan, and many other claims and mines on the hill. After extensive open pit mining, the top of the hill is now gone, and there is a large pit on the side of the hill. Leaching operations of the mine tailing were also carried out at the mine. The gold was recovered by leaching heaps of ore with cyanide. At present, there is no mining, but the mine is being operated for aggregate and decorative rock.

Carson Hill lies east of the Melones fault, along a shear zone that cuts through serpentine and metamorphosed rocks of Jurassic age. The rocks along the shear zone have been intensely altered by hydrothermal solutions, and are cut by numerous quartz veins. The gold occurs in these altered rocks. The shearing, alteration, and gold mineralization are particularly intense in the bend of the shear zone.

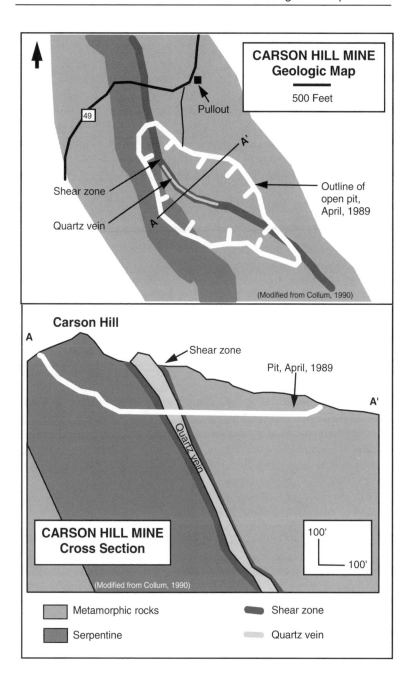

CARSON HILL MINE
Geologic Map

500 Feet

Pullout

49

Shear zone

Quartz vein

A'

A

Outline of
open pit,
April, 1989

(Modified from Collum, 1990)

Carson Hill

A

Shear zone

Pit, April, 1989

A'

Quartz vein

CARSON HILL MINE
Cross Section

100'

100'

(Modified from Collum, 1990)

Metamorphic rocks

Serpentine

Shear zone

Quartz vein

❻ Caves

There are dozens of limestone caves scattered along the foothills of the Sierra Nevada. Three of these caves are open to the public and can be easily visited during your trip to the Mother Lode: California Caverns east of San Andreas, the Mercer Caverns near Murphys, and Moaning Caverns east of Angels Camp. Two other caves are open to the public in the southern Sierra Nevada, Crystal Cave in Sequoia National Park, and Boyden Cavern in Kings Canyon National Forest. These caves are described on the trip to Sequoia and Kings Canyon National Parks.

California, Mercer, and Moaning Caverns occur in large outcrops of limestone that lie within the Calaveras Complex of the Western Metamorphic Belt. This limestone was formed in some distant shallow warm sea, probably hundreds of miles southwest of California and probably during Permian time. The limestone was carried to the margin of North America by plate movement, swept into the Nevadan subduction zone, and altered to marble under the high temperatures and pressures in the subduction zone.

When you build a house, first you make the rooms, and then you decorate the rooms. Mother Nature builds a cave in much the same way. The rooms of the cave are made when limestone lies below the water table and weak acidic groundwater moves through the fractures, joints, and bedding surfaces of the limestone. As the water flows along these surfaces, it dissolves the limestone and forms a series of rooms, chambers, and passageways that follow the fractures, joints, and bedding surfaces. This process is interrupted when the water table drops and the limestone is no longer filled with water. When this happens, dissolution of the limestone stops and the rooms are ready to decorate.

The decoration takes place when water from the surface seeps downward along the joints and cracks in the limestone and becomes saturated with $CaCO_3$ as it flows through the limestone. When the $CaCO_3$-rich water reaches the open chambers and passageways of the cave, the water evaporates and calcite is precipitated as stalactites, stalagmites, draperies, and countless other forms of cave decorations.

California Caverns - *From Mokelumne Hill go S 8 mi. on Hwy. 49; turn E on Mountain Ranch Rd. and go 7 mi.; turn S on Cave City Rd. and drive 2 mi. to California Caverns (209-736-2708).*
This cavern has been open to the public since 1850. In addition to the one-hour tour along lighted trails, trips are available to other parts of the extensive cavern with professional guides.

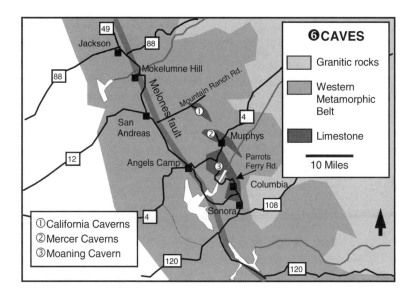

Mercer Caverns - *From the junction of Hwy. 49 and Hwy. 4 (Vallecito Rd.) in Angels Camp, go E 8 mi. on Hwy. 4 to Murphys; turn N on Sheep Ranch Rd.; Mercer Caverns is at 1665 Sheep Ranch Rd.; open daily (209-728-2101).*

Mercer Caverns was discovered in 1885 by Walter Mercer while prospecting for gold. The cave consists of a number of rooms and chambers that extend to a depth of nearly 200 feet. The rooms follow steeply-dipping joints and faults in the limestone, and are accessed by a series of staircases that go from room to room down the joint system. Mercer Cavern has been designated as a State Historic Site.

Moaning Cavern - *From the junction of Hwy. 49 and Hwy. 4 (Vallecito Rd.) in Angels Camp go E 4.5 mi. on Vallecito Rd.; turn S on Parrotts Ferry Rd. and drive 1.5 mi. to the turnoff to Moaning Cave; drive 1 mi. to Moaning Cavern; open to the public (209-736-2708).*

Moaning Cavern has California's largest single chamber underground room. The room is reached by an historic 100-foot spiral staircase, and extends for another hundred feet or so below the spiral staircase. Among the many cave decorations are a 14-foot long stalactite, and several huge stalagmites.

Moaning Cavern is located in a large outcrop belt of marble that lies within the Calaveras Complex. This belt of marble extends from Moaning Cavern southeast as far as Columbia. At Columbia, the marble provides the rough karst surface that trapped much of the placer gold that was found in that area.

❼ Columbia

Placer deposits of gold were discovered at Columbia in 1850. Although the deposits were rich, there was little water in the immediate area and the placers were therefore difficult to work. To alleviate this problem, a 60-mile aqueduct was constructed and hydraulic mining began in 1856. During the late 1850's and early 1860's Columbia was one of the largest, richest, and most famous towns in California.

The early town grew rapidly. In 1852, there were over 150 stores, saloons, and other buildings. Many of these early buildings were destroyed by fire in 1854. The town was rebuilt after the fire, including 30 brick buildings. In 1857, there was another fire, and this fire destroyed 13 blocks and several of the new brick buildings. The mines began to play out in the late 1860's, but minor mining activity continued for many years. The central part of the town became a State Park in 1945. Many historic buildings in the town have been restored, and provide good insight into life in an 1850's mining town.

The city lies in a flat valley underlain by a bed of marble that lies within the Calaveras Complex. During the long Eocene erosion period, the marble had weathered to form a highly irregular karst surface, pitted by numerous deep potholes and cavities. At the time of the gold rush, this irregular limestone surface was covered by about ten feet of rich gold-bearing gravel. The gold was concentrated in the potholes and cavities in the marble. The town was built on this gold-bearing gravel, and the buildings and streets of the town were continually under siege by ambitious miners. You can see the results of their efforts to get at the gold-bearing gravel at many places in and around the town, such as at the miner's cabin and the Donnell and Parsons Building site.

It is likely that this placer gold came from quartz veins that occur in slate and schist of the Calaveras Complex east of Columbia. The quartz veins in that area were famous for having small extremely rich pockets of gold. During Eocene time, gold from these veins was transported by streams to the limestone of the Columbia area where the gold was trapped in the potholes on the karst surface. Nature had devised a remarkably efficient way to concentrate the gold.

Some very large nuggets of gold have been recovered from the Columbia area. The largest was a slab-shaped mass that weighed more than 50 pounds. Another nugget weighed 23 pounds. The placer gold production within a one-mile radius of Columbia from 1853-70 has been estimated at $860,000,000, valued at $300 per ounce.

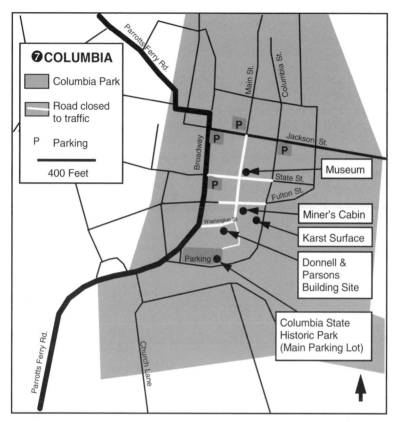

❼COLUMBIA

Columbia Park

Road closed to traffic

P   Parking

400 Feet

Parrotts Ferry Rd.

Main St.

Columbia St.

Broadway

Jackson St.

State St.

Fulton St.

Washington St.

Parking

Parrotts Ferry Rd.

Church Lane

Museum

Miner's Cabin

Karst Surface

Donnell & Parsons Building Site

Columbia State Historic Park (Main Parking Lot)

Many of the old buildings along Main Street in Columbia have been restored and the street is closed to traffic. Columbia was one of the most famous placer mining towns along the entire Mother Lode.

Columbia State Historic Park – *The main parking lot for the Columbia State Historic Park is at Broadway (Parrots Ferry Rd.) and Columbia St. For information on the park phone 209-532-0150 or visit the website www.parks.ca.gov.*
The gold discovery site is marked by a plaque in the picnic area at the east end of the parking lot. Here, gold was discovered by the Hildreth party on March 27, 1850. This group consisted of Dr. Thaddeus Hildreth, his brother George, and several other prospectors. Within one month several thousand miners had flocked to this site, first known as Hildreth's Diggins. The town was soon named Columbia, to give the town a sense of permanency.

Museum – *In Columbia at Main St. and State St. (209-532-0150).*
The museum is in a former miner's supply store that was erected in 1854. The museum has many relics of Columbia from the gold rush days and is operated by the Columbia State Historic Park.

Miner's Cabin - *Main and Washington Streets, Columbia (209-532-9693).*
The Matelot Gulch Mine Supply Store occupies an old miner's cabin. The store sells mining supplies, minerals, and pans of sand and gravel that you can pan for gold. It also has tours to an operating gold mine. Just outside the cabin is a long tom, used for separating gold in placer mining. The cabin sits more than ten feet below the original ground surface, and shows how much ground was washed away by hydraulic mining in this area.

Karst Surface - *Main and Washington Streets, Columbia.*
Just east of the miner's cabin, toward Columbia Street, you can see the smooth white marble of the Calaveras Complex. The surface of the marble is very irregular, with a relief of five to ten feet and lots of potholes and crevices. The gold-bearing gravels were trapped in low spots on this irregular *karst* surface. The gravel was removed from the holes and crevices by monitors using high-pressure water.

Donnell & Parsons Building Site - *The site the Donnell & Parsons Building is on S side of Washington St. near Main St.; an historical marker identifies the site.*
This vacant lot is the site of the Donnell & Parsons Building, built in 1853, and Columbia's first brick building. The building was torn down in 1866 and the site was mined in 1867. After the lot was mined, it left Washington St. at the top of the steep ten-foot slope that abruptly descends to the main parking area for Columbia. The parking area is low because the gold-bearing gravel was removed from this area by the hydraulic mining.

Long toms, like these near the miner's cabin in Columbia, were used for recovering gold from placer deposits during the gold rush.

Ten feet of gold-bearing gravel once covered this irregular karst erosion surface near the miner's cabin. The gravel was removed by hydraulic mining, and the gold recovered from the gravel. Most of the rich gold was trapped in the crevasses and pits in the marble.

❽ *Table Mountain*

Table Mountain is one of the best examples of inverted topography in the Sierra Nevada. This long, sinuous, flat-topped mountain can be traced for over 50 miles across the Sierra foothills from Hathaway Pines to Knights Ferry. The flat top of the mountain is formed by lava that flowed down a valley of the Miocene Stanislaus River. The bottom of that Miocene river valley now forms the top of the mountain. Let's take a look at how Table Mountain got inverted.

Table Mountain consists entirely of Tertiary sedimentary and volcanic rocks. These rocks lie on top of the hard Eocene erosion surface, and the erosion surface forms most of the low-relief landscape in the vicinity of the mountain. Below the Eocene erosion surface are the basement rocks of the Western Metamorphic Belt. The Tertiary rocks of Table Mountain sit on the Eocene erosion much like a Twinkie on a plate.

At the base of Table Mountain are Eocene river gravels, which lie directly on the Eocene erosion surface. The Eocene gravels are overlain by the Tertiary sedimentary and volcanic rocks of the Valley Springs and Mehrten Formations. At the end of Miocene time, the Tertiary rocks formed a thick blanket that covered most of the Sierra Nevada. About ten million years ago, before uplift of the present-day Sierra, lava erupted from an active volcanic center area near Sonora Pass. The lava was very fluid. Some of the lava flowed east toward Nevada and some flowed west into a channel of the Miocene Stanislaus River that had been cut into the soft Tertiary rocks. The lava filled the river channel to a thickness of about 200 feet and flowed down the channel for 60 miles to Knights Ferry. After the flow, the lava cooled slowly, and columnar joints formed as the lava contracted.

In early Pliocene time, several million years after the Miocene lava flow, the Sierra Nevada began to be uplifted and eroded. The renewed erosion rapidly removed the Tertiary rocks from most of the Sierra foothills and exposed the Eocene erosion surface over much of this area. However, at Table Mountain, the lava that had filled the Miocene Stanislaus river channel was hard and protected the underlying Tertiary rocks from erosion. Because of this protective cap, Table Mountain now traces the course of the Miocene Stanislaus River. The present day Stanislaus River lies nearby, but follows a different course.

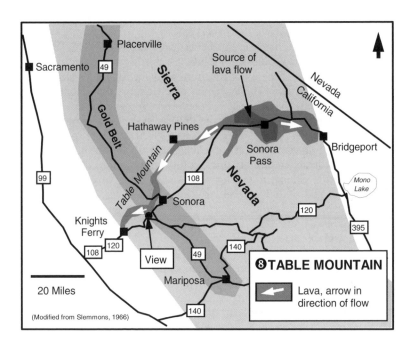

Placerville

Sacramento 49

Sierra

Gold Belt

Source of lava flow

Nevada
California

Hathaway Pines

Table Mountain

Sonora
Pass

Bridgeport

Nevada

Mono
Lake

99

108

Sonora

120

Knights
Ferry

View

49

140

395

108 120

Mariposa

❽TABLE MOUNTAIN

Lava, arrow in
direction of flow

20 Miles

(Modified from Slemmons, 1966)

140

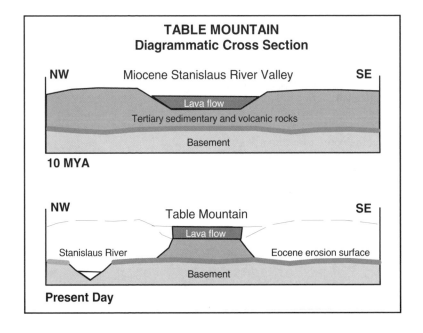

TABLE MOUNTAIN
Diagrammatic Cross Section

NW   Miocene Stanislaus River Valley   SE

Lava flow

Tertiary sedimentary and volcanic rocks

Basement

10 MYA

NW   Table Mountain   SE

Lava flow

Stanislaus River   Eocene erosion surface

Basement

Present Day

View - *Hwy. 108 1 mi. N of Yosemite Junction.*
From Yosemite Junction to Jamestown, Highways 108 and 49
follow along the southeastern flank of Table Mountain and you can
get good views of the mountain from a number of places along this
part of the highway. However, the best views of the mountain are
from Highway 108 between Yosemite Junction and the intersection
of Highway 108 and Highway 49. Pull out along the highway where
convenient and safe. Note the vertical cliffs of the dark gray
columnar-jointed lava that form that cap of Table Mountain. The
lava flow is about 200 feet thick in this area and the columns are a
foot or so in diameter. The lava consists of latite, which is between
andesite and basalt in composition. If you examine a hand
specimen, you'll see that the lava has a very fine-grained matrix and
phenocrysts of feldspar and augite. The feldspar phenocrysts are
white and the augite is dark green.

It is difficult to see the Tertiary sedimentary and volcanic rocks that
make up the flanks of Table Mountain, since these rocks are soft
and generally covered by vegetation. However, some of these
Tertiary rocks are gold-bearing in the portion of Table Mountain
that lies northwest of Sonora and Jamestown. This part of Table
Mountain crosses the Mother Lode. As the Eocene streams flowed
across the bedrock in this area, they followed joints and cracks on
the Eocene erosion surface. Gold from the Mother Lode
accumulated in these joints and cracks in the deeper parts of the
Eocene stream channels. Some of the stream gravels in the Mehrten
Formation also contain gold, but only where the Mehrten channels
had cut into the underlying gold-bearing Eocene gravels and
captured the gold from the Eocene gravels.

Typically, the Eocene gravels and the younger Mehrten stream
channels were mined by drift mines that cut into the base and flanks
of Table Mountain and followed the channels. Few of the drift
mines in the Mehrten Formation were successful because the placer
gold deposits were sparse and spotty.

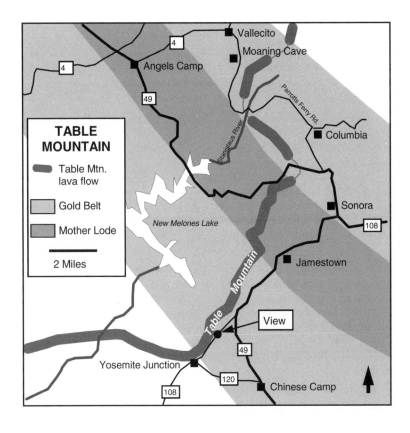

Table Mountain is a classic example of inverted topography. The flat top of the mountain is formed from lava that flowed down the Miocene Stanislaus River. The lava flow now forms the steep cliff at the top of the mountain. The columnar joints that developed in the flow can be seen in the photo.

❾ *Melones Fault*

The Melones fault is one of the best-known faults in the Western Metamorphic Belt. It extends for over 200 miles from Mariposa to north of Sierra City and is closely associated with gold deposits over much of this distance. The fault was formed during Jurassic time, and is one of the main faults along which subduction took place in the Nevadan subduction zone. During this subduction, the Jurassic rocks west of the fault were carried eastward into the subduction zone and thrust under the rocks that were already in the subduction zone. The rocks in the vicinity of the fault were sheared and shattered during this subduction process. In early Cretaceous time, subduction was transferred from the Nevadan subduction zone to the Franciscan subduction zone. When this occurred, there was no more faulting along the Melones fault. However, mineral-rich fluids expelled from the Franciscan subduction zone were forced into the sheared rocks along the Melones fault zone. Gold, copper, zinc, quartz and many other minerals were deposited along the fault zone as temperatures, pressures, and the chemistry of the fluids and wall rocks changed during ascent of the fluids. One of the best places to see the Melones fault is along Highway 49 between Coulterville and Bagby, where the Highway closely follows the fault. This part of the fault zone is marked by extensive bodies of serpentine that can be seen in the roadcuts along the highway.

Mariposite - *From Hwy. 49 in Coulterville turn W on Hwy. 132; drive W 0.2 mi.; park on the S side of Hwy. 132 along old Highway 49; the mariposite roadcut is across the road; cross Hwy. 132 with care.*

This roadcut is one of the best exposures of mariposite rock along the entire Mother Lode. The outcrop marks the trace of the Melones fault zone and the Mother Lode in this area. The rock in the outcrop is green and white and consists of massive white quartz veins that cut green-colored quartz-ankerite-mariposite rock. The green color comes from the mineral mariposite, which is a bright apple-green chromium-rich mica. This mica usually occurs in a groundmass of white fine-grained quartz, and this rock is referred to as mariposite rock. Mariposite is formed from serpentine that has been altered under pressure by mineral-laden hot water. The water, containing potassium, silica, carbon, oxygen, and other elements, reacts with the serpentine and forms deposits of quartz, chromium-rich mica, sulfides, and carbonates such as ankerite (magnesium, iron, manganese carbonate). Mariposite was first described from a specimen collected at the Josephine Mine, just south of Bagby. Most of the workings at the Mary Harrison Mine, two miles south of Coulterville, were in dolomite-ankerite-mariposite-quartz rock. The mine is now closed and not accessible.

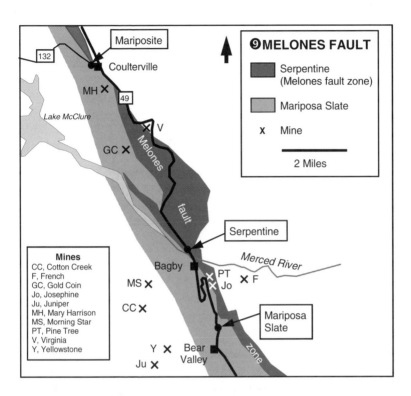

❾MELONES FAULT

- Serpentine (Melones fault zone)
- Mariposa Slate
- X Mine
- 2 Miles

Mines
CC, Cotton Creek
F, French
GC, Gold Coin
Jo, Josephine
Ju, Juniper
MH, Mary Harrison
MS, Morning Star
PT, Pine Tree
V, Virginia
Y, Yellowstone

The mariposite in this roadcut along highway 132 near Coulterville marks the trace of the Melones fault in this area. The mariposite is cut by veins of white quartz and ankerite. This is one of the best exposures of mariposite along the Mother Lode.

Serpentine - *From Coulterville drive S on Hwy. 49 10 mi. to the vista point on the N side of the bridge across the Merced River; park at the vista point.*
This vista point is at the north end of the bridge where Highway 49 crosses the Merced River. The old town of Bagby lies nearby, but is now flooded, following building of the dam for Lake McClure. Bagby began as a ferry crossing for the Merced River. Later, the town became an important stop on the Yosemite Valley Railroad, which took visitors up the Merced River Canyon to El Portal.

The green rocks in the large roadcut on the north side of the bridge are serpentine. There are also many other exposures of serpentine along Highway 49 from Bagby to Coulterville, where the road closely follows the Melones fault zone. The serpentine outcrops along the fault zone represent chunks of oceanic crust that were broken off in the Nevadan subduction zone and forced upward along the fault zone. The blocks of serpentine traveled upward along the fault zone like watermelon seeds squeezed between fingers. The serpentine is green, breaks into irregular curved fragments, and has a waxy luster and feel. Many pieces have grooves along smooth curved surfaces. The grooves formed as the slippery serpentine mass moved along the Melones fault zone.

Serpentine is formed at spreading centers. As basalt flows onto the sea floor at the spreading center, seawater enters cracks along the spreading center and alters the ultramafic rocks in the upper part of the mantle into hydrated iron-magnesium silicates. The serpentine is then carried away from the spreading center along with the overlying basalt as new rocks are formed at the spreading center.

Mariposa Slate - *From the Merced River bridge go S 2 mi. on Hwy. 49 to the Frémont historic marker.*
The Mariposa Slate is well exposed in the roadcut across the highway from the Frémont historic marker. This slate is one of the best-known rock units of the Foothills Terrane, and was the host rock for many of the gold-quartz veins of the Mother Lode. The slate was formed from shale that was deposited in the Nevadan subduction zone during Jurassic time and then metamorphosed during the late Jurassic Nevadan orogeny. In many parts of the Sierra foothills, the steep-dipping platy black slate sticks out of the ground like a crop of black tombstones growing in a field of grass (see the photo on page 227).

The serpentine in this roadcut on the north side of the Merced River bridge lies within the Melones fault zone. Highway 49 follows the fault zone from here north to Coulterville.

The Mariposa Slate, seen in this roadcut along Highway 49 near the Frémont historic marker, is the host rock for many gold-bearing quartz veins along the Mother Lode.

⑩ Mariposa

Although Mariposa is best-known as the gateway to Yosemite, you don't have to scratch the surface hard to find that it was born at the beginning of the gold rush and had a lively and exciting gold mining history. The earliest mining activity was in the spring of 1849 when placer gold was discovered along Mariposa Creek just below the bridge across Highway 140. Later that year, the townsite was laid out.

Mariposa was situated on the large Mariposa Land Grant, which was owned by famed explorer John Frémont. Many of the streets in town are named for members of Frémont's family: Charles Street for himself, Jessie Street for his wife, Bullion Street for his father-in-law, Senator Thomas "Old Bullion" Benton, and Jones Street for his brother-in-law. Despite disastrous fires in 1858 and 1866, the city prospered for many years as a supply center for mines at the south end of the Mother Lode. The city has the Mariposa Mine, one of the oldest gold mines along the Mother Lode, and many historic buildings and artifacts from the gold rush days.

The Mariposa County Courthouse has been in continuous use since 1854, and was the site of many famous mining law court cases.

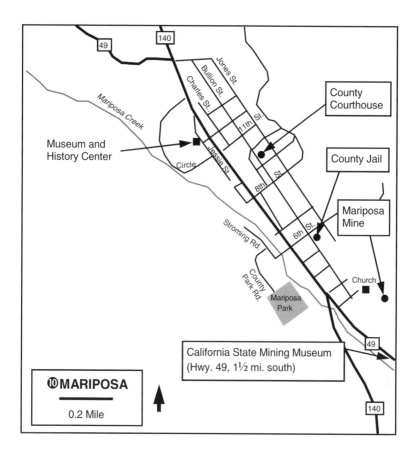

Mariposa Mine - *The Mariposa Mine is in back of St. Joseph's Catholic Church near the S end of Bullion St., Mariposa.*

The old Mariposa Mine is not accessible, but the headframe can be seen from Mariposa Park on the west side of Mariposa Creek. The mine was discovered in 1849 by Kit Carson and Alex Goody, and is the first lode mine in California. The discovery was made when gold from Mariposa Creek was followed up the hillside to gold-bearing quartz veins. The gold occurs in veins of milky quartz up to four feet wide. The mineshaft is 1,550 feet deep. Peak production of the mine was from 1900 to 1915, and the mine produced 116,000 oz. of gold. The mine had a 40-stamp mill.

The Mariposa Museum and History Center at 12th and Jessie Streets in Mariposa has Gold Rush memorabilia, mining equipment and mining exhibits (209-966-2924).

County Courthouse – *In Mariposa on Bullion St. between 9th St. and 10th St.*
The Mariposa County Courthouse is the oldest county courthouse in continuous use west of the Rocky Mountains. It was constructed in 1854 at a cost of $9,000 using local timber and pegs. This courthouse was the site of many noted civil and mining cases, including a famous case concerning the title to Frémont's Land Grant.

County Jail – *In Mariposa on Bullion St. between 5th St. and 6th St.*
The old County Jail was built in 1858 for $14,770 and was in use until 1960. It was constructed of large granite blocks from a quarry at Mormon Bar, two miles south of Mariposa. The walls are 2½ feet thick. You can see the quarry marks on the granite blocks.

California State Mining Museum - *The California State Mining and Mineral Museum is on the Mariposa County Fairgrounds on Hwy. 49 2 mi. S of Mariposa (209-742-7625; www.parks.ca.gov).*
The mining museum has a 150-foot long mine tunnel, a stamp mill, a replica of 1890's mining complex, and an excellent collection of California gems, minerals, rocks, and fossils.

The old County Jail in Mariposa, constructed of large blocks of granite, was in use until 1960.

The California State Mining and Mineral Museum at the Mariposa County Fairgrounds near Mariposa.

These "tombstones" are formed from the Mariposa Slate and are characteristic of outcrops of the slate. The layering of the slate dips steeply east, as shown by the eastward tilt of the tombstones.

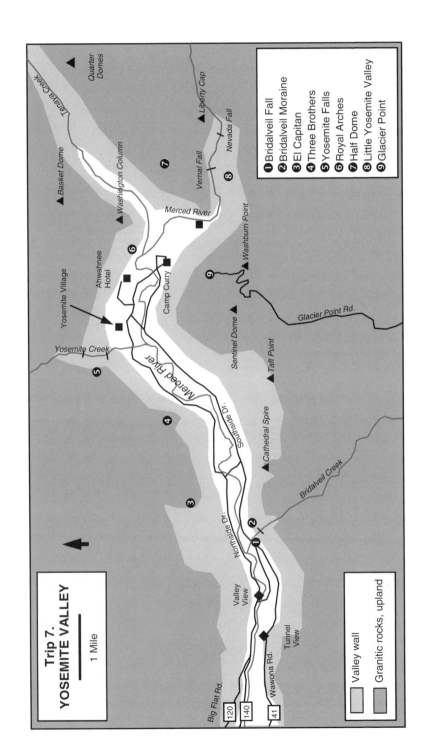

Trip 7.
YOSEMITE VALLEY

1 Mile

❶ Bridalveil Fall
❷ Bridalveil Moraine
❸ El Capitan
❹ Three Brothers
❺ Yosemite Falls
❻ Royal Arches
❼ Half Dome
❽ Little Yosemite Valley
❾ Glacier Point

Valley wall

Granitic rocks, upland

Quarter Domes

Tenaya Creek

Basket Dome

Washington Column

Liberty Cap

Nevada Fall

Vernal Fall

❼

Merced River

❽

Ahwahnee Hotel

❻

Washburn Point

Yosemite Village

Camp Curry

❾

Yosemite Creek

Glacier Point Rd.

❺

Sentinel Dome

Merced River

Taft Point

❹

Southside Dr.

Cathedral Spire

❸

Northside Dr.

Bridalveil Creek

❷
❶

Valley View

Tunnel View

Big Flat Rd.

120
140

Wawona Rd.

41

YOSEMITE VALLEY
A Sculpture in Granite

The spectacular scenery in Yosemite Valley didn't just happen. Creation of the cliffs, waterfalls, spires, columns, arches, and domes of Yosemite required just the right type of rock and the right combination of geologic tools to shape the rock. The granitic rocks of the Sierra Nevada batholith were the perfect rocks to use in the sculpture of the valley. Granite is known for its hardness, beauty and enduring qualities. Among all of the rocks of the earth's crust, only granite would produce the scenery of Yosemite. The geologic tools that were used to shape the granite included jointing, exfoliation, river erosion, and glacial erosion. Each tool worked in its own special way on the granite, and it is the combination of these tools that have produced the magnificent scenery of the valley. During the trip to Yosemite, we'll visit many of its best-known scenic features, see examples of the different types of granitic rocks, and examine the tools that were used to form the scenery.

The Granite
At first glance, all of the granitic rocks in Yosemite Valley look alike. However, if you look at the rocks in more detail, you will see that there are several different types of granite. Each type represents a different pluton intruded at a different time and at a different depth, and has its own composition, cooling history, and characteristic minerals. Once you know what to look for, you can easily identify the different plutons. The accompanying table summarizes characteristics of the more important plutons in Yosemite Valley.

Each pluton weathers and erodes in a different manner. Granite that contains relatively large amounts of quartz, like the El Capitan Granite, tends to be massive, and has wide-spaced joints. In contrast, diorite, which has little or no quartz, tends to break into small blocks. The Half Dome Granodiorite tends to be massive with few joints, and is especially prone to developing exfoliation joints. The variety of cliffs, waterfalls, points, and domes that you see along the walls of Yosemite Valley are in large part due to the many variations of the granitic bedrock.

GRANITIC ROCKS Yosemite Valley			
Name	**Age**	**Description**	**Location**
Half Dome Granodiorite	Cret. 87 MYA	Medium to coarse grained, contains well-formed platesof biotite and rods of hornblende.	Half Dome Royal Arches North Dome Nevada Falls Vernal Falls Olmstead Point
Granodiorite of Kuna Crest	Cret. 91 MYA	Darker than Sentinel Granodiorite, streaky appearance, parallel flakes of biotite and hornblende; disc-shaped inclusions.	Glacier Point Washburn Point
Sentinel Granodiorite	Cret.	Medium gray, medium grained, contains poorly formed biotite and hornblende crystals.	Sentinel Rock Sentinel Fall
Taft Granite	Cret.	Similar to El Capitan, but lighter, finer, and no phenocrysts.	Brow of El Capitan Fissures
El Capitan Granite	Cret. 108 MYA	Massive, contains phenocrysts.	El Capitan Three Brothers Cathedral Rocks Leaning Tower Sentinel Dome
Diorite		Mostly plagioclase and dark minerals, little quartz and potassium feldspar.	Rockslides "North America" wall of El Capitan

The Valley Visitor Center in Yosemite Village has maps, books, and excellent displays explaining the scenery, glaciers, and rocks of Yosemite.

For general information about Yosemite, visit the official Yosemite National Park website www.nps.gov/yose. For recorded park information phone 209-372-0200. For information about roads and lodging in the surrounding area go to website www.yosemite.com

If you are interested in the distribution of the different types of granitic rocks of Yosemite, get a copy of U.S. Geological Survey Map I-1635 *Bedrock Geologic Map of Yosemite Valley*. Also, get the excellent publication *The Geologic Story of Yosemite National Park* by Huber, Both of these publications are available at the visitor center.

Joints

Joints are simply surfaces along which rocks have cracked. Joints may be formed by tectonic stresses or by contraction or expansion of the rocks. When granite solidifies from magma, it is buried at a depth of several miles and is under high pressure. Following uplift and erosion of the overburden, joints typically form in the granite as the rock expands because of release from the pressure of the overlying rocks.

Most joints are flat and parallel and most are nearly vertical. However, joints may also be inclined or even horizontal. Some joints are spaced just a few inches apart. Others are spaced hundreds of feet apart and extend for several miles. There may also be more that one set of joints. Where three sets of joints intersect, the granite is broken into blocks of various sizes, depending on the spacing of the joints.

Joints represent zones of weakness in the rock, and the rocks tend to break, weather, and erode along the joints. Rivers tend to follow joints. Cliffs and ledges are formed by large joints. Sloping ledges are formed by sloping joints. Joints play an important role in shaping all of the major landforms in Yosemite Valley. Where there are few joints, massive features such as El Capitan, Half Dome, and the Royal Arches are formed. Other features, such as Yosemite Falls, Three Brothers and Glacier Point are sculptured by two or three sets of intersecting joints.

Joints are breaking this granite into large blocks. The blocks at the right side of the roadcut are being rounded into boulders by weathering along the joints.

Exfoliation Domes

Yosemite has a number of large, rounded domes such as Sentinel Dome, Half Dome, and North Dome. These domes were formed by a process referred to as exfoliation. Exfoliation occurs in large masses of homogeneous granite that are unjointed. As the overlying rocks are stripped by erosion, the granite expands. If the granite is jointed, then the expansion is accommodated along the joints. If the granite is not jointed, or has few joints, then the exposed surface of the granite tends to expand faster than the underlying granite. The surface layer of granite, typically a couple of feet thick, separates from the underlying granite along an expansion joint and forms a shell. As the process continues, several concentric shells may form to depths of a hundred feet or more.

Most of the massive chunks of granite that form domes began as large pieces of homogeneous granite that were bounded by large joints. During exfoliation, the sharp corners and flat surfaces along the joints were rounded and the granite was shaped into domes and elongated domes. Most of Yosemite Valley's domes are formed in the Half Dome Granodiorite. This rock is especially homogeneous and has few joints. The sparsity of jointing is probably related to the abundant quartz in the rock.

Some of the more important domes and exfoliation features that formed in the Half Dome Granodiorite include Half Dome, North Dome, Basket Dome, Liberty Cap, and Mt. Starr King. Since these domes were formed from unjointed rocks, they have resisted weathering and protrude above the surrounding landscape.

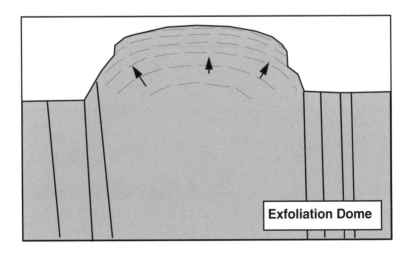

Exfoliation Dome

The Work of the Rivers

Although glaciers often get top billing for the formation of Yosemite Valley, the glaciers could not have done their job without the earlier work done by rivers. Rivers had a huge job to accomplish. During Cretaceous and early Tertiary time, they removed several miles of Tertiary rocks and metamorphic rocks from the top of the granite, and then cut deeply into the granite. By late Miocene time, the granite in the Yosemite area had been worn down to a landscape of low rolling hills with broad river valleys. The river valleys followed the joints in the granitic rocks. The unjointed granitic rocks resisted erosion and formed exfoliating domes that stood above the general landscape. If you want to see what this erosion surface looked like, take the short hike to Taft Point or Sentinel Dome. These trails lie on the Miocene landscape, and this upland surface has probably changed little since Miocene time.

At the beginning of Pliocene time, the Sierra Nevada began to be uplifted and tilted to the west along the Frontal fault system. The gradients of the west-flowing rivers, like the Merced River, were increased by the tilting, and these rivers began to cut deep valleys into the Miocene landscape. However, much of the Miocene landscape was unaffected by the westward tilting. Many of the tributary creeks to the Merced River, such as Yosemite Creek and Bridalveil Creek, flowed north or south. The west tilt of the uplifted Sierra block did not significantly steepen the gradient of these rivers, so there was no extra downcutting. However, when these tributaries reached the lip of the incised Merced River valley, the tributaries suddenly descended into the valley by waterfalls and cascades and then joined the Merced River at the bottom of the valley.

By the beginning of the Pleistocene time, the Merced River had cut a 1,500-foot-deep valley into the Miocene landscape. The valley was V-shaped, with a narrow bottom and steep slopes, and took several jogs as it followed large northeast- and northwest-trending joints. The valley was now ready to receive the glaciers that would apply the final carving and polishing to the granite sculpture.

Pleistocene Glaciation

About two million years ago, at the beginning of Pleistocene time, a series of glaciers began their work on Yosemite Valley and profoundly changed the narrow V-shaped valley of the Merced River. The glaciers scooped out the bottom of the valley and removed as much as 2,000 feet of granite. They also excavated the sides of the valley so that the valley had a broad bottom and steep cliffs along the sides. Some of these cliffs were up to 3,000 feet high. Not yet satisfied, the glaciers carved these cliffs into arches, spires, and columns. The glaciers also cut off the lower parts of many of the tributaries to the Merced River so that these tributaries now flowed over the steep sides of the valley as waterfalls and cascades. These truncated tributaries, like Yosemite Falls and Bridalveil Fall, now form some of the highest and most spectacular waterfalls in the world. Enormous quantities of rock were excavated and removed from Yosemite Valley by these glaciers, and the glaciers did a major part of sculpturing nearly all of the scenic features that are characteristic of Yosemite Valley.

Each of the four major Pleistocene glacial episodes started with formation of a thick icefield that covered the Tuolumne Meadows area. From this icefield, glaciers descended down many of the valleys along the east and west slopes of the Sierra. One of these glaciers went down Tenaya Creek and another went down Little Yosemite Valley. These two glaciers joined at the head of Yosemite Valley and formed the Yosemite Valley glacier. The Yosemite Valley glacier then continued west through Yosemite Valley as far as El Portal.

Each glacial episode produced glaciers of different sizes and characteristics. The largest glacier was formed during the Sherwin glacial episode, about one million years ago. This glacier spilled over the sides of Yosemite Valley and covered Glacier Point, Washington Column, the Royal Arches, Bridalveil Fall, and the Cathedral Rocks. However, the tops of Half Dome, El Capitan, and Sentinel Dome were never covered by this or any other glacier. The Sherwin glacier was nearly 4,000 feet deep at the head of the valley north of Glacier Point. Imagine the tremendous pressure on the underlying rocks and on the rocks along the sides of the valley.

The last of the glacial episodes, the Tioga, reached its maximum about 20,000 years ago. This glacier was much smaller than the Sherwin, and extended west only as far Bridalveil Meadow, where it left a small terminal moraine.

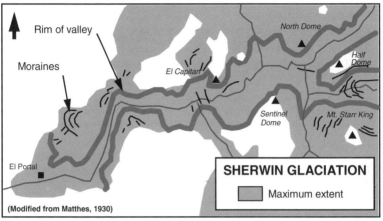

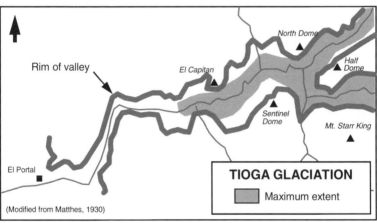

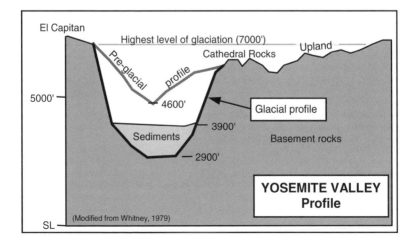

❶ *Bridalveil Fall*

Bridalveil Fall is a classic example of a hanging valley. The valley of Bridalveil Creek lies 850 feet above the floor of Yosemite Valley and the fall leaps over a 650-foot near-vertical cliff where the creek enters the valley. The valley of Bridalveil Creek above the fall slopes very steeply so that the water in the creek is propelled over the edge of the cliff with great force. This large stream of water forms a beautiful parabolic curve if not broken by the wind. If the wind does take hold of the spray, it spreads the water into a beautiful shimmering veil.

Prior to the Pleistocene glaciation, Bridalveil Creek flowed down a steep slope and joined the Merced River in the bottom of the valley. During the Pleistocene glacial episodes, glaciers deepened and widened Yosemite Valley and cut off the lower part of the creek. When the ice melted, Bridalveil Creek was left hanging high on the side of the valley.

Viewpoint - *Park at the Bridalveil picnic area, located on Hwy. 41 (Wawona Rd.) 100 feet S of Southside Dr.; take the short paved trail to the viewpoint at the base of Bridalveil Fall.*

From the Bridalveil viewpoint, you can get a close look at the waterfall. In the spring, when the water is flowing at full force, you can get quite wet here. Along the cliff face at the tip of Bridalveil Fall is a thick horizontal sheet of smooth-weathering Bridalveil Granodiorite. This rock is fine-grained and consists of evenly distributed light and dark minerals, which give the rock a salt-and-pepper appearance. Much of the remainder of the cliff is made up of the Granodiorite of Illilouette Creek.

The vertical face of the cliff is formed by a major north-trending joint that cuts the granodiorite. Moisture from the spray of the falls has accelerated weathering of the granitic rocks at the base of fall, forming a recess in the cliff. Because of this, Bridalveil Fall is steeper now than at the end of the Tioga glacial episode.

Yosemite has many hanging valleys. Almost all of the creeks that entered the valley from the sides are now hanging valleys. Among the most prominent of these are Yosemite Creek with Yosemite Falls, Sentinel Creek with Sentinel Fall, and Ribbon Creek with Ribbon Fall.

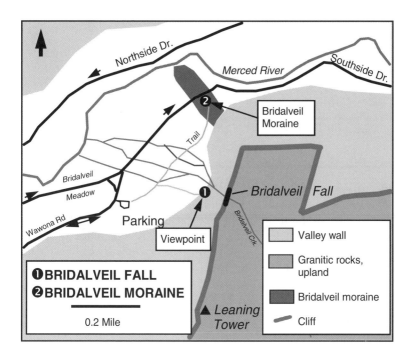

Bridalveil Fall is a classic example of a hanging valley. The lower part of
Bridalveil Creek was cut off by the Yosemite Valley glacier.

❷ Bridalveil Moraine

During Pleistocene time, glaciers periodically plowed down Yosemite Valley and left moraines and other glacial deposits on the valley floor as they retreated. Because the valley walls are steep, each glacier swept away the moraines that had been deposited on the valley floor by the previous glacier. Thus, all of the moraines on the present valley floor were deposited during the latest glacial episode, the Tioga.

You can see these moraines in several places on the valley floor. A small terminal moraine along the east side of Bridalveil Meadow marks the furthest westward extent of the Tioga glacier. Another moraine can be found along the south wall of the valley near Bridalveil Fall and is described below. Further east, the El Capitan moraine crosses the valley on the west side of El Capitan Meadow. This recessional moraine served as a dam for Lake Yosemite, which at one time covered much of the valley floor east of the moraine. The lake, which held the waters of the melting Tioga glacier, was rapidly filled by sediments from the re-treating glacier and evolved into the meadow that now forms the flat floor of Yosemite Valley.

Another moraine occurs at the head of Yosemite Valley just north of the Pines Campground. This is a medial moraine that was formed where the Tenaya and Little Yosemite Valley glaciers joined at the head of Yosemite Valley. The moraine forms a hummocky ridge 50 to 60 feet high and about half-a-mile long. The road from Happy Isles to Mirror Lake passes through a saddle in this moraine.

Bridalveil Moraine - *From the Bridalveil parking area, go E on Southside Drive 0.3 miles and park near the roadcut on the S side of the road.*
The Bridalveil moraine forms a wooded ridge about 40 feet high that extends northwest from the south wall of the valley across Southside Drive to the bank of the Merced River. The materials that make up the moraine can best be seen in the roadcut on Southside Drive. In this roadcut, you will see many large smooth rounded boulders. Some of these granitic boulders have large feldspar phenocrysts which identify them as the Cathedral Peak Granodio-rite. These boulders came from the Tuolumne Meadows area where there are extensive exposures of the Cathedral Peak Granodiorite. The granite boulders are mixed with many angular rock fragments of various sizes and abundant sand and mud. Many of the boulders and cobbles were scratched and grooved during transportation by the glacier.

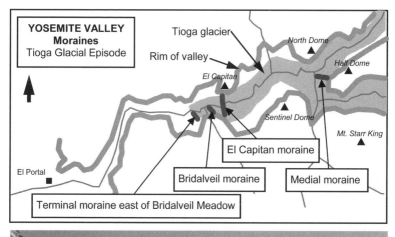

YOSEMITE VALLEY
Moraines
Tioga Glacial Episode

Tioga glacier
Rim of valley
North Dome
Hall Dome
El Capitan
Sentinel Dome
Mt. Starr King

El Capitan moraine

El Portal

Bridalveil moraine

Medial moraine

Terminal moraine east of Bridalveil Meadow

Glacial outwash exposed along the bank of the Merced River at Bridalveil
Meadow. Bridalveil Fall and the Leaning Tower are in the background.

❸ El Capitan

The huge granite monolith of El Capitan is the tallest unbroken cliff in the world, measuring 3,593 feet from base to summit. Although El Capitan stood directly in the path of the many Pleistocene glaciers that carved out Yosemite Valley, the monolith consists of hard unjointed granite and withstood the repeated onslaught of these powerful glaciers.

Most of El Capitan consists of the El Capitan Granite. This granite was ofrmed 108 million years ago and is one of the oldest granites in Yosemite Valley. The grains in the granite are large, and include quartz (30%), potassium feldspar (30%), plagioclase feldspar (30%), and dark grains of biotite and hornblende (10%). Coarse-grained granitic rocks with a high percentage of quartz, such as the El Capitan Granite, tend to be resistant to fracturing and jointing. This resistance to jointing enabled El Capitan to withstand the quarrying action of the glaciers.

Shortly after the El Capitan Granite solidified deep in the earth's crust, it was intruded by the Taft Granite, which is lighter gray, finer grained, and has no phenocrysts. The Taft Granite forms the summit brow of El Capitan. The east face of El Capitan is known as the North American Wall. This wall got its name came from a large irregular mass of dark rock that is exposed on the wall. This dark mass of rock is roughly the shape of North America and consists of diorite that has intruded the El Capitan Granite. Diorite is finer-grained and more mafic in composition than granite, and gives "North America" its dark color. Detailed studies have shown that the granite and diorite magmas mixed along their contacts, forming rocks of intermediate composition. This indicates that the intrusion of the diorite took place when the diorite was extremely hot and before the El Capitan Granite had completely solidified.

View - *Park on Northside Drive, immediately W of El Capitan Bridge.*
From El Capitan Bridge, there are excellent views of the steep face of El Capitan. If you want to get to the base of El Capitan, take the short trail that leaves from the parking area near marker V7. At the base of the cliff, you will see the large rocks that have broken from the cliff. These rocks give a good representation of the rocks that make up the cliff. You may even find some rocks that show the contact between the granite and the dark diorite that intruded the granite. Considering the height of the cliff, there are relatively few rocks at the base, indicating that the cliff is eroding more slowly than most of the other cliffs along the valley. Looking at the rocks at the base of the cliff is a good alternative to climbing the North American Wall.

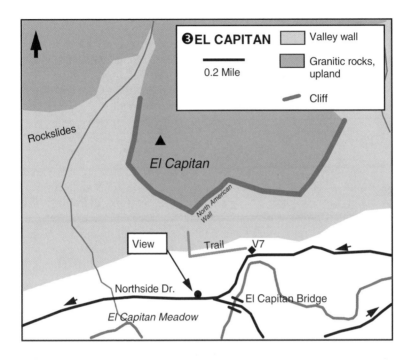

The North American Wall on the southeast face of El Capitan has a large dark area shaped like North America. The dark patch is formed from diorite that intruded the El Capitan Granodiorite during crystallization of the granodiorite.

❹ Three Brothers

The Three Brothers are a series of three peaks that lie on the north side of Yosemite Valley between El Capitan and Yosemite Falls. The three peaks have similar sloping surfaces, and are obviously related. The Three Brothers were formed by jointing and provide one of the finest examples of jointing that can be seen in Yosemite Valley.

View - *On Southside Dr. 2 mi. E of Bridalveil Fall; marker V16.*
Looking north from this viewpoint you can get a good view of the three successively higher rocky peaks that make up the Three Brothers. The highest point is Eagle Peak. Next are Middle Brother and Lower Brother. The Three Brothers are formed from the El Capitan Granite. The granite is cut by three intersecting sets of wide-spaced joints, and these joints form the outline of each of the three peaks. The most prominent set of joints dips steeply to the west and forms the steep west-sloping roof of each brother. On each roof you can see many thinner parallel slabs of granite formed by the same set of west-sloping joints. Another set of joints forms the near-vertical south face of each peak. The third set of joints is less

The Three Brothers are formed by three sets of intersecting joints and are one of the finest examples of jointing in Yosemite Valley.

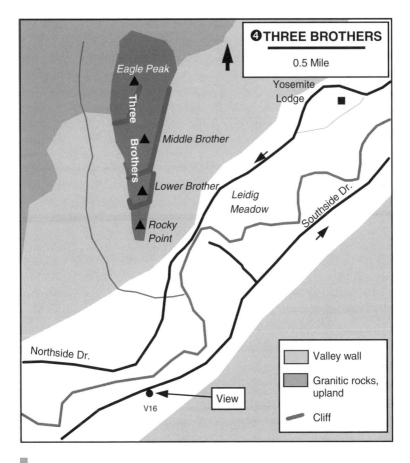

regular, but forms the steep east slope of each brother. Ledges and broken rocks follow smaller joints along all three sets of joints.

During Pleistocene glaciation, the glaciers that moved west down the valley covered much of the Three Brothers from time to time, although they never covered the top of Eagle Peak. As the glaciers moved down the valley they removed large blocks of granite from the three sets of joints. The quarry action of the glaciers worked especially well on the west sides of the peaks and the glaciers were very efficient at removing the flat slabs of rock that form the roofs of the Three Brothers.

The same three sets of joints that are responsible for the Three Brothers can be seen on the south side of the valley, where they form asymmetric spurs and slanting rock surfaces near Taft Point.

❺ *Yosemite Falls*

Yosemite Falls are one of the main scenic attractions of Yosemite Valley. At the top of the Upper Fall, the water from Yosemite Creek descends 70 feet through a chute worn in the top of the cliff. When the water leaves the chute, it leaps clear of the cliff and descends 1,430 feet in a broad parabolic curve to the base of the Upper Fall. This is reportedly the highest leaping waterfall in the world. After collecting itself at the base of the Upper Fall, the water descends 675 feet through a chain of cascades to the top of the Lower Fall. The water then drops another 320 feet over the Lower Fall. The combined drop of the falls and cascades is 2,425 feet.

The Upper Fall, like Bridalveil Fall, is a hanging valley. During the Plio-Pleistocene uplift and west tilting of the Sierra Nevada, Yosemite Creek was unable to keep pace with the rapid downcutting of the Merced River and the creek descended into the Merced River Valley in a series of cascades. During Pleistocene glaciation, the wall of Yosemite Valley was steepened by glacial erosion. This erosion removed the cascades and left the valley of Yosemite Creek hanging high above the valley floor.

The steep cliff at Upper Yosemite Fall was formed by a major west-trending vertical joint. The Lost Arrow, to the right of the Upper Fall, is a remnant of a slab of granite that is breaking away from the cliff along the same set of vertical joints. The base of the Upper Fall is on a ledge formed by a near-horizontal joint. The top of the Lower Fall lies on a ledge formed by another horizontal joint. See the cover photo for a closer view of the Lost Arrow.

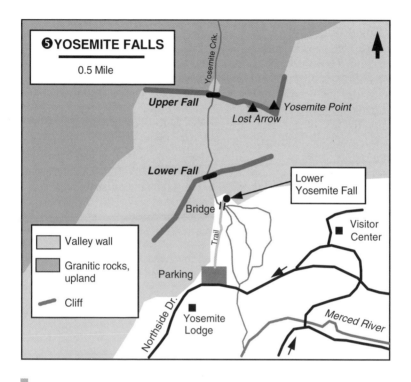

Lower Yosemite Fall - *Park at the Yosemite Falls parking area 0.5 mi. W of Yosemite Valley Visitor Center; walk N on the paved trail 0.25 mi. to the viewing area and bridge at the base of Lower Yosemite Fall.*

You can get a good view of the Upper and Lower Falls from the trailhead near the parking lot for Yosemite Falls. The Yosemite Falls cliff is made up of light gray El Capitan Granite, which has been intruded by medium to dark gray Sentinel Granodiorite. These rocks are very hard and are sparsely jointed.

The falls are formed by two sets of wide-spaced joints. When the glaciers went through Yosemite Valley, they excavated the granite along these two joint trends. One set of joints is nearly vertical and trends east-west. The steep cliff that supports the Upper Fall was formed along a major joint in this trend. The Lower Fall plunges over still another joint in this trend. The other important set of joints is nearly horizontal. The large, sloping, vegetation-covered ledges at the base of the Upper Fall and the top of the Lower Fall are formed by joints in this trend. Near the bridge at the base of the Lower Fall, there are many granite boulders that have broken from the cliff. Most of these rocks are light gray El Capitan Granite, but you may also find some boulders of dark gray Sentinel Granodiorite.

❻ Royal Arches

The Royal Arches are a set of large, thick, concentric granite arches that occur on the north wall of Yosemite Valley between the Ahwahnee Hotel and Washington Column. The arches are part of a large exfoliation dome that lies on the north wall of Yosemite Valley. The top of this exfoliation dome is represented by North Dome, and the Royal Arches are on the side of this dome. During the Pleistocene glaciation, glaciers pealed away the outer exfoliation shells along the side of the dome, leaving this series of arches. Since the granite was very homogeneous and very strong, it gave rise to exceptionally smooth, thick, high, and broad arches, and allowed these arches to stand rather than to collapse in a pile of rubble.

View - *Park at the Ahwahnee Hotel; hike 0.5 mi. E on the Mirror Lake Trail to the base of the Royal Arches.*

The Mirror Lake trail from the Ahwahnee Hotel to Mirror Lake follows along the base of the Royal Arches, and from this trail you can appreciate the size of the arches. The main outer arch of the Royal Arches is 1,000 feet high, spans a distance of 1,800 feet, and is about 200 feet thick. Below this arch are a number of smaller arches from 10 to 80 feet thick.

The Royal Arches are formed from the Half Dome Granodiorite. This is one of the youngest granitic rocks in Yosemite Valley and covers much of the head of the valley east of the Ahwahnee Hotel and Curry Village. The Half Dome Granodiorite is coarse-grained and can be distinguished from the other granitic rocks in Yosemite Valley by its well-formed plates of shiny biotite and long rods of black hornblende. This particular rock is especially good at making exfoliation domes. Among its offspring are Half Dome, North Dome, Basket Dome, Liberty Cap, Mount Broderick, Mount Starr King, and Mount Watkins.

The right side of the Royal Arches is abruptly terminated in a steep gully and the Washington Column lies to the right of the gully. Since the Washington Column and Royal Arches are formed from the same rock, the gully does not represent a contact between two different types of rock. Instead, the gully was formed along a major joint within the Half Dome Granodiorite. The stresses that formed the exfoliation slabs at the Royal Arches were apparently relieved along this joint.

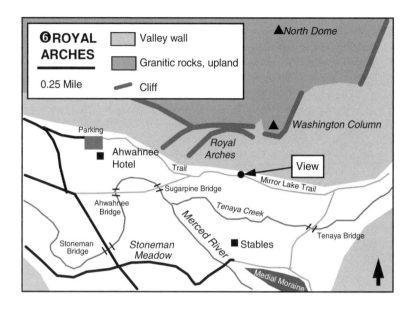

- ❻**ROYAL ARCHES**
- 0.25 Mile
- ☐ Valley wall
- ▰ Granitic rocks, upland
- ⌁ Cliff

▲*North Dome*

Parking

■ Ahwahnee Hotel

Royal Arches

▲ *Washington Column*

View

Trail

Mirror Lake Trail

‖ Sugarpine Bridge

Ahwahnee Bridge

Tenaya Creek

Merced River

Tenaya Bridge ‖

Stoneman Bridge ‖

Stoneman Meadow

■ Stables

Medial Moraine

The Royal Arches were formed when thick slabs of exfoliating granite were quarried by glaciers that moved down Yosemite Valley. North Dome is seen above the arches and Washington Column lies to the right.

❼ Half Dome

Half Dome, with its sheer northwest face and rounded summit, dominates the head of Yosemite Valley. This is one of the best known and best loved features of Yosemite, and also one of the least understood. From the valley floor, it appears that the dome has been cut in half, and that the missing half has disappeared. Read on if you've ever wondered where it went.

Tenaya Bridge - *From Shuttle Stop 17 follow the trail to Tenaya Bridge.*
From Tenaya Bridge you can get a good view of the steep glaciated northwest face of Half Dome. Half Dome is formed from a large block of unjointed Half Dome Granodiorite that is bounded on the northwest and southeast sides by major joints. This block of granite was extremely resistant to erosion, and stood above the general landscape during most of mid- to late-Tertiary time. During this period, the sharp corners of the block were rounded by exfoliation to form a steep-sided elongated dome.

During the Pleistocene glacial episodes, the largest of the glaciers that flowed down Tenaya Canyon reached to within 700 feet of the summit of the dome, but none of the glaciers ever covered Half Dome. The glaciers did, however, remove the exfoliating rock on the northwest flank of the dome and then began to remove the rock along the existing joint surfaces. The jointed granite above the glacier ice was quarried by the freeze and thaw action of ice along the joints. By the end of the Pleistocene, the joint zone on the northwest flank of the dome had become a steep cliff. The crest and backside of the dome were unaffected by the glaciation, and retained the curved surfaces of the exfoliated granite. The trail to the summit of Half Dome goes up the steep slope of exfoliated granite on the northeast end of the dome.

The exfoliating granite shells on the southeast flank of Half Dome are eroding at a very slow rate. They have been in place so long that furrows several feet deep have been worn into the rock where rain has carried decomposed granite down the side of the dome. The exfoliation shells at the top of Half Dome have also eroded slowly. These shells have accumulated to a depth of 100 feet, since they have not been carried away by gravity. Most of the shells on the top are six to ten feet thick. Some of these exfoliation shells overhang the steep northwest face, forming a visor for the dome. The jointed rock on the precipitous northwest face of the dome was quarried out from under the visor during Pleistocene glaciation.

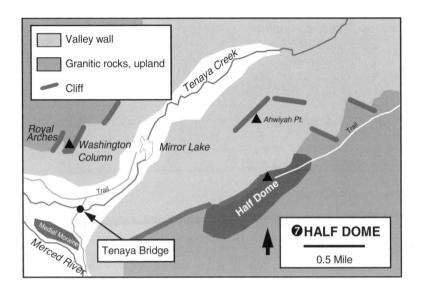

The steep northwest face of Half Dome is formed by vertical joints. The granite along the joints was removed by glaciers that flowed down Tenaya Canyon. The visor at the top of Half Dome is formed from exfoliated slabs of granite that were undercut by the vertical joints.

❸ Little Yosemite Valley

As the Merced River enters Yosemite Valley from Little Yosemite Valley, the river drops 2,000 feet in a series of foaming cascades, rapids, and waterfalls. This turbulent mile-and-a-half stretch of the river begins at Nevada Fall, then passes through the Emerald Pool, across the Silver Apron, over Vernal Fall, and then steeply descends to Happy Isles on the floor of Yosemite Valley. This section of the river crosses the Half Dome Granodiorite where there are few joints in the granite. The Pleistocene glaciers had a hard job cutting into this rock, and left the series of ledges, cliffs, and chutes over which the water now tumbles.

Vernal Fall - *From Happy Isles (Shuttle Stop 16) hike up Little Yosemite Valley to the viewpoint just beyond the bridge over the Merced River; for a closer look, take the 500-step Mist Trail to the top of Vernal Fall, but be prepared to get wet; 3 mi. RT.* Vernal Fall (317') flows over a cliff formed by a major northwest-trending joint in the Half Dome Granodiorite. When the Merced glacier encountered this joint, it quarried the jointed rock and carried it downstream, leaving behind the cliff for Vernal Fall. The cliff extends across the entire valley because the glacier covered the entire valley.

Emerald Pool, at the top of Vernal Fall, was formed in unjointed resistant granite that was scoured out and polished by the Merced glacier. From the pool, the Merced River flows across the Silver Apron, then plunges over Vernal Fall. Some of the granite at the Silver Apron still has glacial polish and striations. The granite at the top of Vernal Fall has not been notched by the water flowing over the cliff during the 15,000 years since the glaciers melted because there is little sediment in the Merced River at this point. Most of the sediment dropped out in Merced Lake, eight miles upstream. Without sediment, the water has little cutting power. Further up the valley you can see Nevada Fall (594'). The cliff that forms Nevada Fall trends northeast and was formed along the same set of joints that formed Half Dome. These joints are in a different direction from the joints that formed Vernal Fall.

During the glacial episodes, the Little Yosemite glacier covered much of Little Yosemite Valley, but never covered the top of Half Dome. Liberty Cap, immediately north of Nevada Fall, is a large roche moutonnée and was covered by the larger glaciers that flowed down Little Yosemite Valley.

→This photo of Little Yosemite Valley, taken from Glacier Point, shows Vernal Fall in the lower center and Nevada Fall to the right.

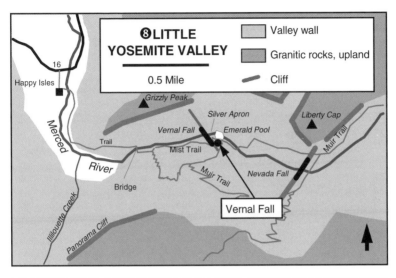

❽ LITTLE YOSEMITE VALLEY

0.5 Mile

Valley wall

Granitic rocks, upland

Cliff

Happy Isles

16

Merced River

Illilouette Creek

Grizzly Peak

Trail

Mist Trail

Bridge

Panorama Cliff

Silver Apron

Vernal Fall

Emerald Pool

Muir Trail

Nevada Fall

Liberty Cap

Muir Trail

Vernal Fall

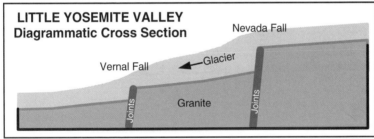

LITTLE YOSEMITE VALLEY
Diagrammatic Cross Section

Nevada Fall

Vernal Fall

Glacier

Joints

Granite

Joints

Nevada Fall

Vernal Fall

❾ *Glacier Point*

The trip to Glacier Point provides excellent views of Yosemite Valley from several places along the rim of the valley. On this trip you can also see and walk on the old Miocene land surface that existed prior to the Plio-Pleistocene uplift of the Sierra.

Sentinel Dome - *From the junction of Hwy. 41 and Glacier Point Rd. go 13 mi. E on Glacier Point Rd. to the parking area for Sentinel Dome and Taft Point; take the trail to Sentinel Dome; 2 mi. RT.*

Sentinel Dome is one of many domes that protrude above the High Sierra landscape. These domes are all made of hard, unjointed granite and have a rounded shape formed by exfoliation of the granite. Sentinel Dome is formed from the El Capitan Granite. Glacier ice covered some of the domes in Yosemite, but Sentinel Dome was always above the glaciers. Moraines from the highest Yosemite glacial stages lap up onto the edge of the dome.

When you hike to the top of Sentinel Dome, you are walking on a land surface that has not changed much since Miocene time. Although the Sierra Nevada block was uplifted about 4,000 feet in this area during Plio-Pleistocene time, Sentinel Dome and the surrounding area looks today much as it did several million years ago. From the top of the dome you will have a 360^0 panoramic view of the park and this highland area.

Taft Point - *From the parking area take the trail to Taft Point; 2 mi. RT.*

The first part of the trail to Taft Point goes across the gray weakly foliated Sentinel Granodiorite. This granodiorite forms Sentinel Rock and Sentinel Fall, which lie on the steep wall of Yosemite Valley between Taft Point and Glacier Point.

On the way to Taft Point, you will pass the Fissures. The Fissures were formed from weathering of joints in the granite along the rim of Yosemite Valley. Some of these joints are several feet wide and tens of feet deep and testify to the importance of joints in promoting weathering in granite.

Near Taft Point, the trail crosses into the El Capitan Granite. The outcrops at Taft Point are coarse-grained El Capitan Granite, which is cut by the younger fine-grained light colored Taft Granite, the same granite that forms the summit brow of El Capitan. From Taft Point there are excellent views of El Capitan and the Three Brothers on the opposite side of Yosemite Valley.

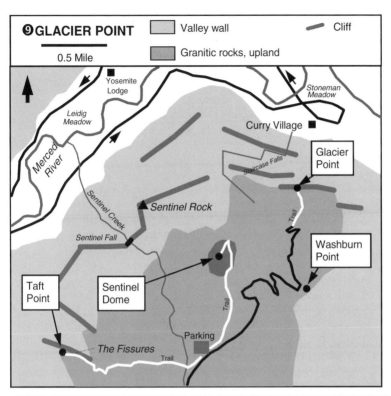

View from Taft Point, left, across Yosemite Valley to El Capitan, right center. Note the low relief of the old Miocene land surface above the rim of the valley.

Washburn Point - *From the Taft Point/Sentinel Dome parking area drive N on Glacier Point Rd. 2 mi. to the Washburn Point parking area.*

From Washburn Point, there are excellent views of the High Sierra. Almost all of the rocks east of Washburn Point are granite. From here you can also see how Vernal and Nevada Falls were formed along two different joint trends in Little Yosemite Valley. To the northeast, note the steep sides of Half Dome. The exfoliated backside is nearly as steep as the cliff that faces Yosemite Valley.

Glacier Point - *From the Washburn Point parking area drive N on Glacier Point Rd. 0.5 mi. to Glacier Point; take the short trail to Glacier Point. While at Glacier Point, visit the hut with exhibits explaining the formation of the Yosemite landscape.*

Both Glacier Point and Washburn Point are formed from the Granodiorite of Kuna Crest. This rock has a streaky appearance, with flakes of biotite and rods of hornblende. The rocks at Glacier Point are moderately jointed, and have three prominent sets of intersecting joints. These joints are responsible for many of the interesting features that can be seen on the steep cliff below Glacier Point. Some of the joints are inclined, and have formed a number of sloping ledges. Staircase Falls step down and move eastward along a series of these ledges. Glacier Point and Washburn Point were both covered at the time of maximum glaciation, so glacial erratics can be found in this area. At the maximum glacial stage, Glacier Point was covered by about 700 feet of ice.

The overhanging ledge at Glacier Point is at the left. Yosemite Falls, on the far side of Yosemite Valley, are dry. Note the long cascade between the Upper Fall and Lower Fall.

The Royal Arches (RA), Washington Column (WC), and North Dome (ND), as seen from Glacier Point. North Dome is an exfoliation dome that was overridden by the largest Pleistocene glaciers.

View of Half Dome from Glacier Point. During Pleistocene glaciation, glaciers that flowed down Tenaya valley (left) did not override Half Dome, but undercut and removed jointed rocks on the northwest side of the dome, leaving the steep cliff that we see today.

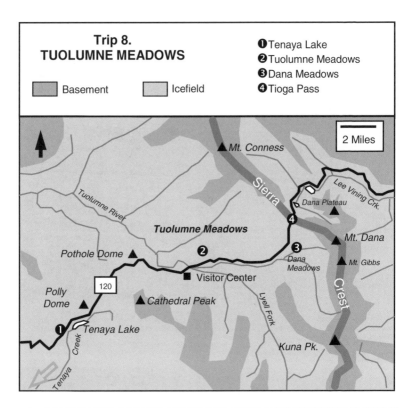

Trip 8.
TUOLUMNE MEADOWS

❶ Tenaya Lake
❷ Tuolumne Meadows
❸ Dana Meadows
❹ Tioga Pass

Basement   Icefield

2 Miles

▲ Mt. Conness

Sierra

Lee Vining Crk.

Tuolumne River

Dana Plateau

❹

Tuolumne Meadows

▲ Mt. Dana

Pothole Dome ▲

❷

❸

Dana
Meadows

▲ Mt. Gibbs

■ Visitor Center

Crest

Polly
Dome ▲

120

▲ Cathedral Peak

Lyell Fork

❶ Tenaya Lake

Kuna Pk. ▲

Tenaya Creek

In this view from Pothole Dome, Tuolumne Meadows is the low grassy area in the middle ground. The boulders in the foreground are glacial erratics, stranded on Pothole Dome when the Tuolumne icefield melted.

TUOLUMNE MEADOWS
The Tuolumne Icefield

During the Pleistocene glacial episodes, the Tuolumne Meadows area was covered by a huge icefield. Only the tops of the highest mountains rose above the ice. From this icefield, glaciers extended down many valleys on the eastern and western slopes of the Sierra. Among these, the Lee Vining glacier flowed down Lee Vining Canyon to Lake Russell, the Merced glacier flowed through Yosemite to El Portal, and the Tenaya glacier followed Tenaya Creek where it joined the Merced glacier at the head of Yosemite Valley. As the ice moved from the icefield down the glacial valleys, the ice was continually replenished by new snowfall over the icefield.

The Tuolumne icefield was about 2,000 feet thick, and the thick ice exerted a tremendous pressure on the underlying rocks. As the ice moved across Tuolumne Meadows and into the glacial valleys, it removed the soil and weathered rocks that had covered the High Sierra surface in pre-glacial times. The ice also gouged out the underlying granitic rocks where they were jointed and weak. Where the underlying rocks were hard, the glacial ice smoothed and polished the bedrock with rocks that were carried in the ice, as if the icefield were a huge sheet of sandpaper.

When the icefield melted, about 15,000 years ago, it left a blanket of sand, silt, clay, and boulders littering the surface of the ground. Much of this glacial debris collected in the lower parts of Tuolumne Meadows, where it formed a flat land surface with poor drainage that was covered by marshes, ponds, and shallow lakes. Over time, many of the bodies of water on that land surface were filled in to form meadows. The meadows have remained largely open, because trees find it difficult to grow in the shallow water table with poor drainage. Although Tuolumne Meadows is the largest of these alpine meadows, Dana Meadows and a number of other smaller meadows were formed the same way.

On the geologic trip to the Tuolumne Meadows, you'll see examples of the handiwork of the icefield: polished granite, scoured-out lakes, roche moutonnée, nunataks, exotic rocks, alpine meadows, and glacial till left behind when the icefield melted.

The Tuolumne Intrusive Suite

One of the great benefits of glaciation – for a geologist – is that the glaciers scrape away all of the soil and decomposed rock and leave the underlying bedrock clean and well-exposed. For this reason, the Tuolumne Meadows area is an excellent place to study the granitic rocks of the Sierra Nevada batholith. Detailed studies have shown that most of the granitic rocks in this area are related and are part of the same pluton. The rocks in different parts of the pluton appear different because they crystallized at different times and the composition of the magma changed as the rocks crystallized.

These related granitic rocks, referred to as the Tuolumne Intrusive Suite, were intruded into the Sierra Nevada batholith during Cretaceous time, about 86 to 91 million years ago. The oldest member of the suite, the Granodiorite of Kuna Crest, forms the outer edges of the pluton and is rich in biotite and hornblende. Biotite and hornblende crystallize at high temperatures and are among the first minerals to crystallize from magma. The Granodiorite of Kuna Crest is exposed at Glacier Point on the west side of the pluton and near Tioga Pass on the east side of the pluton.

The next rock to crystallize was the Half Dome Granodiorite, which contains more quartz and potassium feldspar than the earlier rocks. Quartz and feldspar crystallize at lower temperatures than biotite and hornblende and thus crystallize later in the sequence. The Half Dome Granodiorite is exposed from Half Dome to Olmstead Point.

The next rock to crystallize was the Cathedral Peak Granodiorite. This rock is readily identified by its large phenocrysts of potassium feldspar, and forms most of the core of the pluton. The Cathedral Peak Granodiorite is very widespread in Tuolumne Meadows and there are excellent exposures of these rocks at Lembert Dome and Pothole Dome.

The last rock to crystallize was the Johnson Granite Porphyry. This rock occurs in the central part of the pluton and can be seen in a small outcrop near the Tuolumne Meadows store. The Johnson Granite Porphyry has large phenocrysts of potassium feldspar, like the Cathedral Peak Granodiorite, but the matrix is fine-grained. The fine matrix probably formed when the rock chilled quickly, perhaps from release of pressure during volcanism. This rock may represent the roots of a volcano that erupted on the surface above the Tuolumne Intrusive Suite while the granitic rocks were crystallizing at depth.

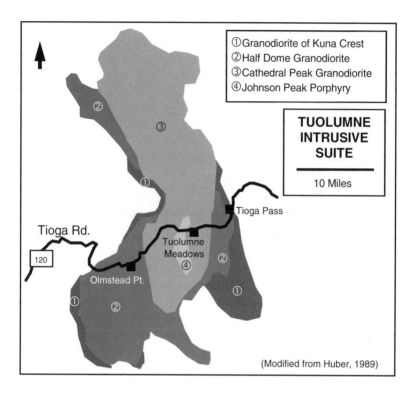

① Granodiorite of Kuna Crest
② Half Dome Granodiorite
③ Cathedral Peak Granodiorite
④ Johnson Peak Porphyry

**TUOLUMNE
INTRUSIVE
SUITE**

10 Miles

Tioga Pass

Tioga Rd.

Tuolumne
Meadows

120

Olmstead Pt.

(Modified from Huber, 1989)

TUOLUMNE INTRUSIVE SUITE

Name	Age	Description	Location
Johnson Granite Porphyry	Cret.	Porphyry; light colored, few large phenocrysts in fine grained matrix.	Tuolumne River, across from store
Cathedral Peak Granodiorite	Cret. 86 MYA	Potassium feldspar phenocrysts 2 to 3" long, medium grained background.	Pothole Dome Lembert Dome
Half Dome Granodiorite	Cret. 87 MYA	Medium to coarse grained, well-formed plates of biotite and rods of hornblende.	Olmstead Point Half Dome Royal Arches North Dome Nevada Fall Vernal Fall
Granodiorite of Kuna Crest	Cret. 91 MYA	Darker than Sentinel Granodiorite, streaky appearance, parallel flakes of biotite and hornblende; disc-shaped inclusions.	Glacier Point Washburn Point Tioga Pass

❶ Tenaya Lake

Part of the ice from the large Tuolumne icefield flowed south down the Tenaya Creek drainage between Mt. Hoffman on the west and Tresidder Peak on the east. In route, the glacier scooped out a 114-foot deep depression from fractured Half Dome Granodiorite west of Tresidder Peak. This depression is now filled by Tenaya Lake. Glacial polish and erratic boulders found along the walls of the valley indicate that the ice was 2,460 feet deep in this area and covered Polly Dome and Pwiack Dome. These domes are roche moutonnée, similar to Lembert Dome.

Tenaya Lake - *From the Tuolumne Meadows Visitor Center go W on Tioga Rd. 8 mi.; park at the picnic area.*
Tenaya Lake (8,149') is partly dammed by glacial till left at the southwest end of the lake by the Tenaya glacier as it melted and retreated toward the icefield in Tuolumne Meadows. The lake is slowly being filled by sediments that are accumulating where Tenaya Creek enters the east end of the lake. In time, the lake will become a meadow, as is the fate of most mountain lakes.

The contact between the Half Dome Granodiorite and the Cathedral Peak Granodiorite lies immediately west of Tenaya Lake. The rocks at Tenaya Lake appear to be a mixture of these two rock units in that the Half Dome Granodiorite contains potassium feldspar phenocrysts like those in the Cathedral Peak Granodiorite.

The granodiorite in the roadcuts near the lake is broken into large exfoliation slabs a foot or so thick that are parallel to the wall of the valley. Exfoliation slabs are formed when massive unjointed granite expands as it is exposed at the surface. Thus, exfoliation slabs on steep slopes and valley walls, like these at Tenaya Lake, are usually parallel to the valley wall.

Olmstead Point - *From the Tenaya Lake picnic area drive W on Tioga Rd. 2 mi. to the parking area for Olmstead Point.*
The bedrock at Olmstead Point consists of the Half Dome Granodiorite. These rocks stood in the path of the Tenaya glacier and were smoothed and polished by the glacier as it rode over the rocks. When the glacier melted, it left numerous glacial erratics lying on the surface of the granite. You can see good examples of glacial polish and erratics by taking the 1/4-mile nature trail from the parking area to Olmstead Point.

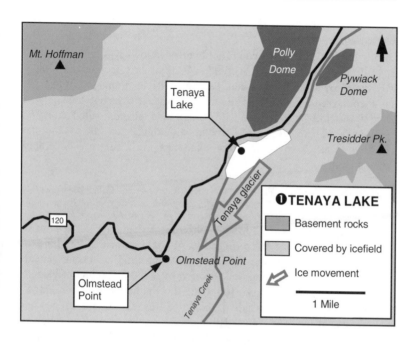

Mt. Hoffman ▲

Polly Dome

Pywiack Dome

Tenaya Lake

Tresidder Pk. ▲

120

Tenaya glacier

Olmstead Point

Olmstead Point

Tenaya Creek

❶TENAYA LAKE

⬛ Basement rocks

⬜ Covered by icefield

⬅ Ice movement

1 Mile

At Olmstead Point, glacial erratics rest on granite that was polished by glaciers moving down Tenaya valley.

❷ *Tuolumne Meadows*

During the last glacial episode, Tuolumne Meadows was covered by the 2,000-foot thick Tuolumne icefield. Much of this ice moved slowly westward down the Tenaya and Tuolumne River drainages. When the ice encountered a low hill of resistant granite, it overrode the hill and ground the hill into a rounded, streamlined shape, called a *roche moutonnée*. There are many roche moutonnée in the Tuolumne Meadows area. Two of the best examples are Lembert Dome and Pothole Dome.

> **Lembert Dome** - *From the Tuolumne Meadows Visitor Center take Tioga Rd. 1.2 mi. E to the Dog Lake parking area; take the Dog Lake trail for 0.9 mi. then follow the primitive trail to the top of Lembert Dome; 2.8 mi. RT; moderate.*
>
> Lembert Dome is a 500-foot high elongated granite dome with a gentle east side and steep rugged west side. Fortunately, the hike to the summit goes up the gentle side. During the Pleistocene glacial episodes, Lembert Dome was covered by about 1,500 feet of glacial ice that was moving west, following the Tuolumne River drainage. The eastward upstream side of the dome was pushed and scraped by this glacial ice. The force of the glacier on this flank was roughly equal to dragging a block of granite the height of Lembert Dome over the dome. When the ice reached the west side of the dome, it was no longer pushing, scraping, and polishing the granite. Instead, it pulled, broke, and quarried the granite, and then removed the quarried blocks, leaving the granite on the west side of the dome steep and jagged.
>
> The dome is formed from the Cathedral Peak Granodiorite, which is easily identified by its large feldspar phenocrysts. These crystals of feldspar are about two inches long, have a pinkish tinge, and break along flat cleavage surfaces. Each phenocryst is twinned, and consists of two halves that have cleavage at opposing angles. The Cathedral Peak Granodiorite is cut by a number of white aplite dikes that are a few inches thick. These dikes intruded the granodiorite at a very late stage of crystallization when no dark minerals remained in the magma.
>
> On the hike to the summit, look for patches of granite that have been polished by the glacier. In places, the aplite dikes retain the polish and the adjacent granodiorite has no polish. This occurs because aplite is more resistant to weathering than the granodiorite. Also, note the many exotic blocks left on the dome when the glacier melted. Some of these blocks are composed of Cathedral Peak Granodiorite and some are composed of other intrusives.

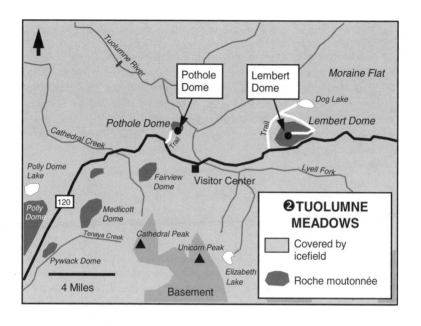

Lembert Dome is a classic roche moutonnée, formed when the Tuolumne icefield covered the dome. The ice, which was moving west, rode up the smooth east flank of the dome and plucked the jointed granite from the steep west flank.

Pothole Dome - *From the Tuolumne Meadows Visitor Center take Tioga Rd. 1 mi. W to the parking lot for Pothole Dome; take the short trail to the dome.*

It is a nice easy hike to the summit of the Pothole Dome. On the hike you'll see that the dome is a roche moutonnée formed from the Cathedral Peak Granodiorite and that the dome has good examples of the same geologic and glacial features described at Lembert Dome. However, Pothole Dome also has potholes and flutes, features that are common in rivers but rarely found on roche moutonnée.

The potholes, which occur on the south side of the dome, are circular steep-sided holes several feet in diameter. Potholes are formed by cobbles or boulders being spun around continuously by a circular turbulent eddy of water. The spinning rocks, called grinders, drill holes into the rock by abrasion. Potholes mostly occur in the beds of turbulent mountain rivers or streams. However, at Pothole Dome the potholes were formed by meltwater from the Tuolumne icefield. The meltwater collected on the surface of the icefield and then flowed into vertical shafts in the ice, called *moulins*. The moulins were scoured out by the swirling meltwater as it poured down from the surface. At the base of the glacier, the water from the moulins collected into rivers that flowed beneath the glacier. The turbulent water in these rivers formed the potholes. The grinders for the potholes were conveniently supplied by rocks carried in the glacier. The force and grinding action of the turbulent water pouring down a shaft in a glacier that is 1,000 to 2,000 feet thick must have been enormous. Some of the granite near the potholes has been shaped into a wavy, fluted surface by the water flowing beneath the glacier. Where fresh, the fluted surfaces are polished. The polish appears similar to glacial polish, but glacial polish forms flat surfaces.

This fluted granite surface on Pothole Dome was polished by meltwater that was running below the Tuolumne icefield.

↑This pothole on Pothole Dome was formed when turbulent meltwater flowing below the ice formed an eddy. Rocks taken from the glacier and caught in the eddy were used as grinders.

←Pothole Dome is similar to Lembert Dome, but also has flutes and potholes formed by water flowing under the icefield.

❸ Dana Meadows

The ice in the Tuolumne icefield picked up a large amount of rock debris as it moved across the granitic basement rocks of the Tuolumne landscape during the glacial episodes. This debris consisted of boulders plucked from the mountains and hills that were encountered by the ice, as wells as sand, silt, clay, and smaller rocks ground up by the glacier. When the icefield melted at the end of the Tioga glacial episode, about 15,000 years ago, large quantities of glacial till were left behind in many of the low-lying areas of Tuolumne Meadows and Dana Meadows. East of Lembert Dome, Highway 120 travels across thick deposits of this glacial till as it follows the Dana Fork of the Tuolumne River to Tioga Pass.

Glacial Till – *From the Tuolumne Meadows Visitor Center go 3 mi. E on Tioga Rd.; park in the pullout at marker T33.*
This roadcut is one of the best places in Tuolumne Meadows to see the glacial till that was left behind at the end of the last glacial episode. The till consists of piles of unsorted and unstratified boulders, sand, silt and clay.

Mt. Dana View – *From marker T33 go E on Tioga Rd. 3.5 mi. to marker T36.*
This viewpoint lies at the south end of Dana Meadows. From here, the Sierra crest and the west side of Mt. Dana (13,053') appear as a subdued rolling landscape tilted to the west. This land surface is probably a remnant of the Miocene landscape that existed prior to the Plio-Pleistocene uplift of the Sierra. When the Sierra block was uplifted, erosion of the western slope began in the foothills to the west, and is slowly working its way eastward toward the crest of the Sierra. This erosion has not yet reached the western side of Mt. Dana, so the gentle Miocene landscape is still preserved.

Dana Meadows View: *From marker T36 go E on Tioga Rd. 1.5 mi. to marker T38.*
This viewpoint is just west of Tioga Pass and is a good place to see Dana Meadows. The meadows lie in the low, poorly-drained area west of Mt. Dana and are dotted with many small ponds and lakes. This was one of the last areas where the Tuolumne icefield lingered at the end of the last glacial episode. The small ponds and lakes in Dana Meadows are referred to as *kettles* and were formed where large blocks of ice were deposited in the till. When the ice melted, the depressions were filled with water in the poorly drained till.

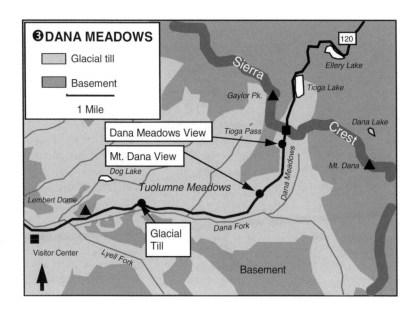

The west slope of Mt. Dana, seen in the far center, is relatively gentle. This surface is a relic of the old Miocene pre-uplift land surface.

❹ Tioga Pass

At Tioga Pass, Highway 120 abruptly leaves Tuolumne Meadows and begins its descent down the steep eastern escarpment of the Sierra Nevada as it follows Lee Vining Creek to the town of Lee Vining. Large glaciers flowed down this canyon during the Pleistocene glacial episodes and the results of this glaciation can be seen in many places. At Tioga Pass, Highway 120 also begins to cut through two large roof pendants that lie within the Sierra Nevada batholith. The first of these roof pendants consists of Mesozoic volcanic rocks. These rocks are exposed in the vicinity of Tioga Lake. The next roof pendant consists of Paleozoic metasedimentary rocks, and these rocks are exposed at Ellery Lake.

Tioga Lake - *From the Tioga Pass Entrance Station drive E on Hwy. 120 1 mi. to the Tioga Lake overlook at the W end of the lake.*

From here, you can look southeast across Tioga Lake and up Glacier Canyon. Mt. Dana lies on the crest of the Sierra to the right, and Dana Plateau is on the left. During the Pleistocene glacial episodes, Glacier Canyon was filled by a large glacier that had its origin along the east flank of Mt. Dana. This canyon cuts deeply into the old Miocene land surface that existed prior the Plio-Pleistocene uplift of the Sierra. Part of the old Miocene land surface is preserved as the flat top of Dana Plateau and another part is preserved on the west flank of Mt. Dana. Prior to the erosion of Glacier Canyon, the Miocene land surface extended from the Dana Plateau to Mt. Dana. Although you cannot see it from here, the small Dana Glacier lies in a cirque on the steep north face of Mt. Dana near the head of Glacier Canyon. This is one of about 100 active glaciers in the Sierra Nevada. Most of these glaciers have been decreasing in size over the last several decades. All of these glaciers completely melted during several warm spells over the last 15,000 years. The present glaciers are not small remnants of Pleistocene glaciers, but have formed during cool periods since the end of the Pleistocene.

Nunatak Nature Trail - *The trailhead for the Nunatak Nature Trail is just E of Tioga Lake, on the N side of Hwy. 120.*

During the Pleistocene glacial episodes, the Tuolumne icefield covered everything in the high country, except for the tops of the highest peaks. These *nunataks* served as refuges for plants and wildlife, and speeded reclamation of barren areas after the ice melted. This quarter-mile nature trail has a number of descriptive plaques about the nunataks and other natural features of this area.

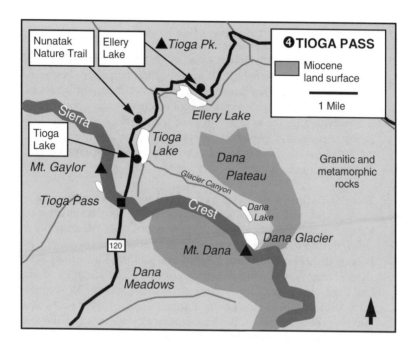

❹ TIOGA PASS

Nunatak Nature Trail

Ellery Lake

▲ Tioga Pk.

Ellery Lake

Miocene land surface

1 Mile

Sierra

Tioga Lake

Tioga Lake

Dana Plateau

Granitic and metamorphic rocks

Mt. Gaylor ▲

Glacier Canyon

Tioga Pass

Crest

Dana Lake

Dana Glacier

120

Mt. Dana ▲

Dana Meadows

In this view looking southeast across Tioga Lake, Glacier Canyon separates Dana Plateau on the left from the Sierra Crest on the right. The flat top of Dana Plateau and the gentle west flank of the Sierra Crest are remnants of the low-relief surface of the Sierra Nevada that existed prior to the Plio-Pleistocene uplift of the range. Glacier Canyon was cut into this gentle land surface mainly by glaciers during the Pleistocene glacial episodes.

Ellery Lake – *From Tioga Lake go E 2 mi. on Hwy 120; park in the large parking area immediately west of the Ellery Lake dam.*

Most of the rocks in Tuolumne Meadows are granitic and are part of the Sierra Nevada batholith. However, along the eastern border of Yosemite National Park there are large areas of metamorphic rocks. These metamorphic rocks occur as roof pendants and are surrounded and underlain by the granitic rocks of the Sierra Nevada batholith. The roof pendants represent older rocks that were part of the roof of the batholith, and were intruded, heated, and metamorphosed during intrusion of the batholith.

There are two main types of roof pendants in this area— metamorphosed Paleozoic sedimentary rocks, and metamorphosed Mesozoic volcanic rocks. Most of the Mesozoic roof pendants occur along the crest of the Sierra from near Bridgeport to south of Mammoth Lakes. Mt. Dana, Tioga Lake, and the Ritter Range are on this trend. Many of these rocks are reddish, and provide a lively landscape. You saw some of these rocks at Tioga Lake. Most of the Paleozoic roof pendants lie in a trend immediately east of the Mesozoic roof pendants. The Paleozoic rocks are mostly dark and somber. Ellery Lake and the Mt. Morrison Roof Pendant are on this trend. The Mt. Morrison Roof Pendant is of special interest because it has a nearly complete sequence of Paleozoic rocks, from Cambrian to Permian.

In the roadcuts across from the Ellery Lake parking area, there are good exposures of the dark metasedimentary rocks of the Paleozoic roof pendant. Most of these rocks are hornfels, a fine-grained rock composed of a mosaic of equidimensional grains. Hornfels is formed when sedimentary and volcanic rocks of various compositions have been heated by nearby granite intrusions. The heat from the intrusion encourages recrystallization of the intruded rock. Other metamorphic rocks found here include quartzite, metaconglomerate, and marble. Prior to metamorphism, these rocks were sandstone, conglomerate and limestone.

Just east of Ellery Lake, Highway 120 leaves the Paleozoic roof pendant and again enters into the granitic rocks of the Sierra Nevada batholith. However, for several miles east of Ellery Lake you can see small roof pendants in many places on the walls of Lee Vining Canyon. The roof pendants appear as dark-colored rocks surrounded by the light-colored granitic rocks of the Sierra batholith.

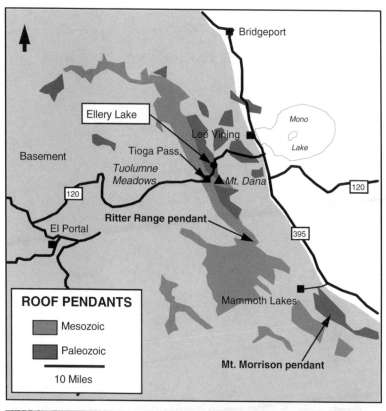

Four miles east of Ellery Lake, this roadcut on Highway 120 exposes a small
roof pendant of dark metamorphic rocks surrounded by light-colored
granitic rocks. This is one of many roof pendants of metamorphic rocks exposed
along the walls of Lee Vining Canyon.

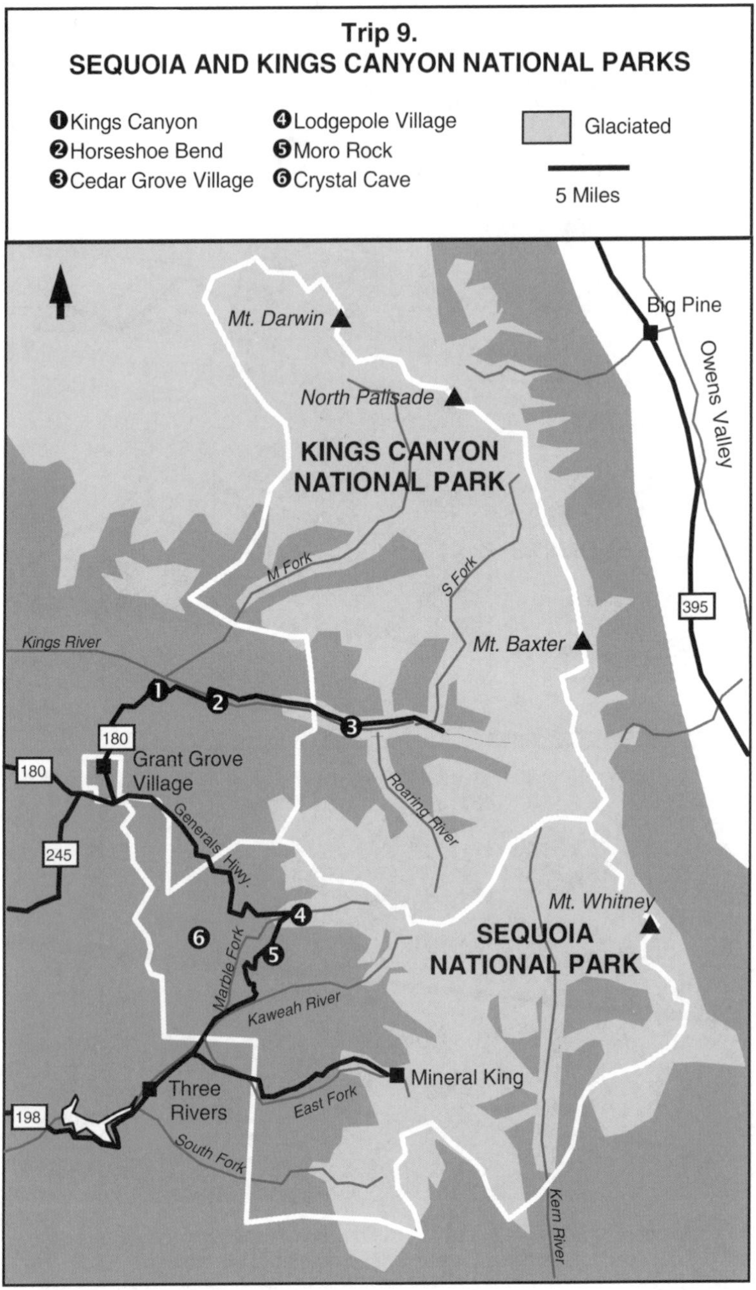

Trip 9.
SEQUOIA AND KINGS CANYON NATIONAL PARKS

❶ Kings Canyon   ❹ Lodgepole Village
❷ Horseshoe Bend   ❺ Moro Rock
❸ Cedar Grove Village   ❻ Crystal Cave

Glaciated

5 Miles

Mt. Darwin ▲

Big Pine

Owens Valley

North Palisade ▲

**KINGS CANYON
NATIONAL PARK**

M Fork

S Fork

395

Kings River

Mt. Baxter ▲

180

❶ ❷

❸

180

Grant Grove
Village

Roaring River

245

Generals Hwy.

Mt. Whitney ▲

❻

❹

Marble Fork

❺

**SEQUOIA
NATIONAL PARK**

Kaweah River

Three
Rivers

Mineral King

East Fork

198

South Fork

Kern River

SEQUOIA AND KINGS CANYON NATIONAL PARKS
The Southern Sierra

Sequoia and Kings Canyon National Parks have the highest and most rugged relief in the entire Sierra Nevada. The area includes Mt. Whitney, the highest mountain in the lower 48 States, and Kings Canyon, one of the deepest canyons in North America. For over 150 miles, there are no roads that cross this part of the Sierra, and the trails that cross the range are rigorous and difficult. This high and harsh topography was formed because the southern part of the Sierra block was uplifted over 8,000 feet during Plio-Pleistocene time, about twice as high as the northern Sierra.

Geologically, the southern Sierra differs from the central and northern Sierra in several other ways as well. Pleistocene glaciation was not extensive in the southern Sierra, compared to the central and northern Sierra. Most of the glaciation in the southern Sierra was confined to the canyons, and the icefield was thin and limited in extent. Thus, glaciers did not remove the thick soil cover from many upland areas. Some of these upland areas now have large groves of giant sequoia. These gigantic trees could not have grown if the soil had been removed by glaciation. Another important difference is that the Western Metamorphic Belt does not extend into the southern Sierra. Instead, the metamorphic rocks in the southern Sierra occur as large roof pendants that lie within the granitic rocks of the Sierra Nevada batholith.

During this geologic trip, you'll drive down into Kings Canyon and gain an appreciation of the work that the rivers and glaciers did in cutting the canyon. You'll also see a large roof pendant of metamorphic rocks exposed in the walls of the canyon. In Sequoia National Park, you'll visit Tokopah Falls, Moro Rock and Crystal Cave, some of the top scenic attractions of the park. Most of the geologic sites on this trip are not accessible in the winter. To see the geology, it is best to visit the area in late spring, summer, or early fall.

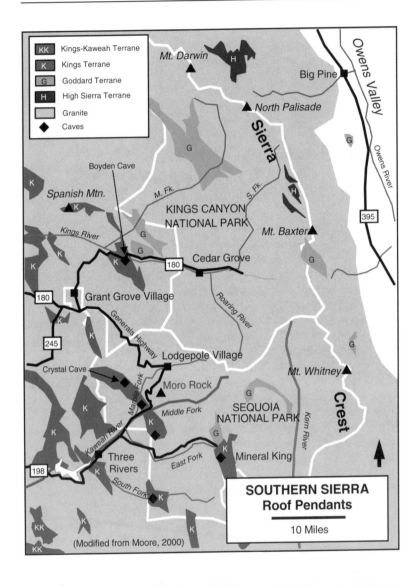

Sequoia and Kings Canyon National Parks are administered together. For park information, visit the parks' website, www.nps.gov/seki or phone 559-565-3341. Some other phone numbers are: Lodgepole Visitor Center, 559-565-3782; Cedar Grove Visitor Center, 559-565-3793; Foothills Visitor Center, 559-565-3135. For more information on the geology of Sequoia and Kings Canyon National Parks, get a copy of *Exploring the Highest Sierra*, by Moore (2000).

Roof Pendants

Although most of the rocks in the southern Sierra are granitic, there are many roof pendants of metamorphic rocks scattered through the granite. Most of the roof pendants are of irregular shape, but in general they are elongated to the northwest. Some are over ten miles long and several miles wide. Although the roof pendants occur in separate patches scattered in the granite, some of the pendants have similar rocks and are obviously related. Based on these similarities, the pendants have been grouped into four terranes:

1) The Kings-Kaweah Terrane occurs in the western foothills of the Sierra and is characterized by ophiolites - ultramafic rocks that were once oceanic crust.

2) The Kings Terrane is mainly metamorphosed shale, but also includes quartzite and marble. Crystal Cave, Boyden Cavern and many other caves in the southern Sierra are in beds of marble that occur within this terrane.

3) The Goddard Terrane is composed largely of metamorphosed volcanic rocks. These are the same metamorphic rocks that occur in the northeastern part of the Alabama Hills.

4) The High Sierra Terrane is found along the east side of the Sierra, and includes metamorphosed Paleozoic rocks, mainly schist and marble.

This photo is from Crystal Cave, which occurs in a marble bed in the Sequoia Roof Pendant of the Kings Terrane. There are over 100 caves in the southern Sierra that occur in similar roof pendants.

❶ *Kings Canyon*

Kings Canyon is one of the deepest canyons on the North American continent. The bottom of the canyon lies from 4,000 to 8,000 feet below the surrounding topography, compared to 4,000 to 6,000 feet for the Grand Canyon. Kings Canyon attained this great depth due to the very high uplift of the southern Sierra during the Plio-Pleistocene. This rapid and high uplift gave the Kings River the power to cut its deep valley.

> ***Junction View*** - *From Grant Village go 14 mi. E on Hwy. 180 to the turnout for Junction View.*
>
> From Junction View, you can see where the Middle and South Forks join to form the Kings River. These rivers are in the steep, rugged, V-shaped canyons that were cut during the Plio-Pleistocene uplift of the Sierra Nevada. The bottom of the canyon is 8,000 feet below the top of Spanish Mountain, which lies five miles northwest of the river junction. Pleistocene glaciers did not reach this part of Kings Canyon, so all of the canyon downcutting was by rivers.
>
> Three miles further east on Highway 180, Yucca Point provides a closer view of this same river junction. The rocks from Grant Grove to Yucca Point are granite and are part of the Sierra Nevada batholith. However, immediately east of Yucca Point, Highway 180 begins to traverse through the metamorphic rocks of the Boyden Cave Roof Pendant. These metamorphic rocks provide some dramatic scenery in the vicinity of Horseshoe Bend, where the South Fork of the Kings River slices through the roof pendant, and exposes the roof pendant in the steep walls of the canyon.

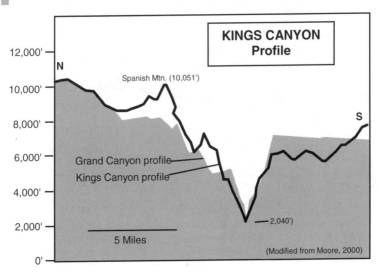

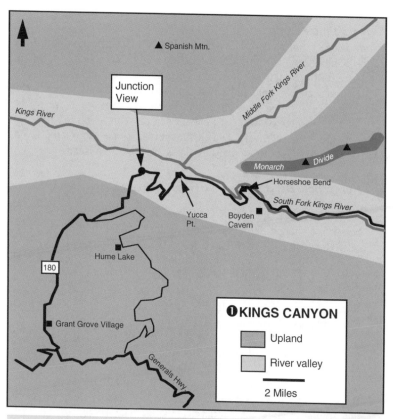

View from Yucca Point looking northwest across Kings Canyon. The Kings River is in the bottom center of the photo. This part of the Kings Canyon is V-shaped, and has not been modified by glaciers.

❷ Horseshoe Bend

From Yucca Point to two miles east of Boyden Cavern, the South Fork of the Kings River cuts through the Boyden Cave Roof Pendant, one of the large roof pendants of the Kings Terrane. The roof pendant consists of slate, quartzite, marble and schist. Sparse fossils, mainly crinoids and ammonites of Jurassic age, have been found in some of these rocks. Excellent exposures of the roof pendant can be seen along the river, in roadcuts along the highway, and in the canyon slopes above the river. One of the best places to see these rocks is at Horseshoe Bend.

Horseshoe Bend – *From Junction View go 8 mi. E on Hwy. 180 to the pullout for Horseshoe Bend.*

At Horseshoe Bend, the South Fork of the Kings River makes a horseshoe-shaped detour as it cuts across a thick bed of very hard quartzite in the Boyden Cave Roof Pendant. The quartzite bed is about 3,600 feet thick, is layered, and the layers are near-vertical. The quartzite was formed by metamorphism of a thick bed of quartz sandstone. Faint cross bedding and graded bedding can be seen in some of the sandstone beds. The sandstone is thought to have been formed in a shallow water tidal environment or perhaps as a channel in a deeper water fan system. Age dating from zircons in the sandstone indicates that the sandstone was sourced from a pre-Cambrian continental mass. The location of this continent is unknown. Looking northwest from the turnout, the rocks of the Boyden Cave Roof Pendant are exposed in several steep ridges on the southern slope of Monarch Divide. The ridges of quartzite appear as dark reddish-brown cliffs. The gray cliffs and spires are formed from beds of marble, and the brown areas of subdued relief are schist.

Boyden Cavern - *From Horseshoe Bend, continue 1 mi. E on Hwy. 180; park in the Boyden Cavern parking area just E of the bridge across the S. Fork of the Kings River. Private; open May through Oct.; visit by guided tour (45 min); 209-736-2708.*

Boyden Cavern is in a thick layer of marble that lies within the Boyden Cave Roof Pendant. This blue-gray marble is exposed in the parking area for Boyden Cavern and in the channel of the South Fork of the Kings River in the vicinity of the bridge. The marble is a massive, vertically-layered unit about 2,000 feet thick. The entrance to Boyden Cavern is in a cliff in the lower part of the river canyon on the south side of the river. The cave has many of the decorations normally associated with limestone caves, including draperies, stalactites, and stalagmites. Boyden Cavern is one of many small-to-moderate-sized caves that occur within the limestone and marble of the Kings Terrane.

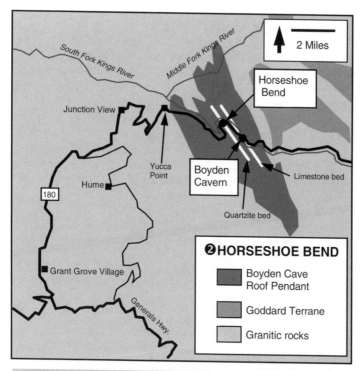

South Fork Kings River

Middle Fork Kings River

↑ 2 Miles

Horseshoe
Bend

Junction View

Yucca
Point

Boyden
Cavern

Limestone bed

Hume

180

Quartzite bed

Grant Grove Village

Generals Hwy.

❷HORSESHOE BEND

Boyden Cave
Roof Pendant

Goddard Terrane

Granitic rocks

At Horseshoe Bend, Highway 180 bends around a thick bed of quartzite in the Boyden Cave Roof Pendant. The highway is in the notch in the shadow at the lower right. The quartzite bed forms a steep cliff on the opposite wall of the valley. The ridge at the upper right is marble.

❸ *Cedar Grove Village*

During the Pleistocene glacial episodes, glaciers extended down the South Fork of the Kings River as far as Cedar Grove Village. These glaciers modified the upper portion of the Kings Canyon to form a typical U-shaped glacial valley, similar to Yosemite Valley. The glaciated part of the Kings Canyon is wide and has steep walls, waterfalls, and meadows. The granitic rocks along the sides of the valley were scraped, plucked and polished by the glaciers, forming a variety of waterfalls, steep cliffs, and granitic domes and spires. The glaciers, however, were neither as thick nor extensive as the glaciers in Yosemite Valley. Thus, the glacial features in Kings Canyon, although impressive, are not quite as spectacular as those in Yosemite Valley.

Roaring River Falls - *From Cedar Grove Village drive 3 mi. E on Hwy. 180; park in the Roaring River Falls turnout on the E side of Roaring River across the bridge; hike 200 yards to the viewpoint.*
Roaring River is a hanging valley that tumbles down a steep narrow granite gorge and then drops 80 feet into a deep pool. This granite is part of the North Mountain unit, a small pluton about three miles in diameter.

Zumwalt Meadow - *The parking area for Zumwalt Meadow is 2 mi. E of Roaring River Falls; take the self-guided 1.5 mi. loop tour.*
Zumwalt Meadow was formed in the same way as the flat floor of Yosemite Valley. The process began when the South Fork was dammed by a glacial moraine, causing a lake to form behind the dam. Over time, the lake was filled with sediment and then plants grew on the sediments. Take the short Zumwalt Meadow Trail for information on the plant life of the meadow and for excellent views of the river, meadow, North Dome, and Grand Sentinel. Part of the trail crosses a talus slope on the south side of the valley and provides a good opportunity to see the granitic rocks that make up the valley wall. This granite has many dark, sharp-edged xenoliths, which are probably pieces of the roof rock that fell into the granite magma.

Grand Sentinel (8,504') is on the south side of the valley, and rises 3,500 feet above Zumwalt Meadows. The rock that forms Grand Sentinel is part of the Lookout Peak Granodiorite, and is characterized by large twinned potassium feldspar crystals. The spires and ledges that give Grand Sentinel its unique character are shaped by vertical and sloping joints that cut through the granite. The sheer face of North Dome (8,717'), across the valley from Grand Sentinel, was shaped by the valley glaciers. The top of the dome lies back from the valley wall.

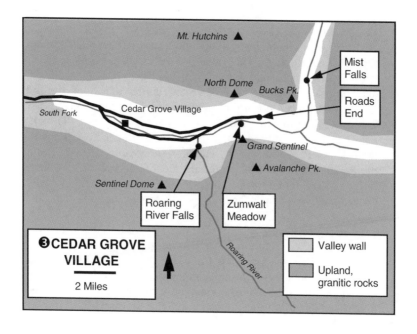

Mt. Hutchins ▲

North Dome
▲
Bucks Pk.
▲

Mist
Falls

Roads
End

South Fork
Cedar Grove Village

Grand Sentinel

▲ Avalanche Pk.

Sentinel Dome ▲

Roaring
River Falls

Zumwalt
Meadow

❸ CEDAR GROVE
VILLAGE

2 Miles

Roaring River

Valley wall

Upland,
granitic rocks

The giant granitic monolith of Grand Sentinel (8,504') dominates the east end of
Kings Canyon as it rises nearly 3,500 feet above Zumwalt Meadow.

Roads End - *From Zumwalt Meadows go 1 mi. E on Hwy. 180 to Roads End.*
At Roads End, the highway splits into a one-way loop and crosses through a small ridge. This ridge is a recessional moraine, and is composed of unconsolidated and non-stratified boulders, sand, silt, and clay. The moraine was deposited during retreat of the last glacier that flowed down the South Fork of the Kings River. The boulders in the moraine provide a convenient sample of the rocks that the glacier passed through on its trip to Roads End. Many of these boulders came from the Paradise Granodiorite. The rocks of the Paradise Granodiorite are easily identified because they have large potassium-feldspar phenocrysts that are filled with concentrically arranged inclusions of biotite, hornblende, and plagioclase.

The Paradise Granodiorite is a part of the very large Whitney Intrusive Suite, which extends from here to the southeast for fifty miles. Mt. Whitney lies in the Whitney Granodiorite in the core of the pluton. This suite of rocks is similar in composition, size and age to the Tuolumne Intrusive Suite at Tuolumne Meadows.

The Whitney Intrusive Suite is thought to have formed from a single very large granodiorite intrusion. The edges of the pluton cooled and crystallized first, forming the Lone Pine and Sugarloaf Granodiorites. Next, the Paradise Granodiorite, which was still hot and molten, rose through the solidified wall rocks of the Lone Pine and Sugarloaf Granodiorites. After the Paradise Granodiorite solidified, the still-hot Whitney Granodiorite, in the core of the pluton, rose through the Paradise Granodiorite. The Whitney Granodiorite contains giant crystals of potassium feldspar, similar to the Cathedral Peak Granodiorite of the Tuolumne Meadows.

Mist Falls - *The Mist Falls trail leaves from the Roads End permit station; 8 mi. RT; moderately strenuous.*
This trail follows the glaciated valley of the South Fork of the Kings River. At Mist Falls, the river washes down a 300-foot steep ledge of polished granite and then plummets 45 feet to form the falls. The granite is part of the Paradise Granodiorite, and is hard with few joints. The granite was polished by glaciers during Pleistocene glaciation.

→North Dome as seen from Roads End. The top of North Dome lies back from the canyon rim.

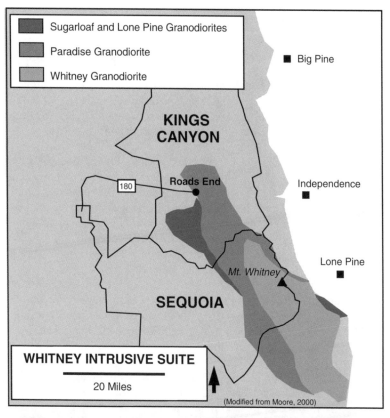

Legend:
- Sugarloaf and Lone Pine Granodiorites
- Paradise Granodiorite
- Whitney Granodiorite

Big Pine

KINGS CANYON

180 Roads End

Independence

Lone Pine

Mt. Whitney

SEQUOIA

WHITNEY INTRUSIVE SUITE

20 Miles

(Modified from Moore, 2000)

❹ *Lodgepole Village*

Lodgepole Village is in the valley of the Marble Fork of the Kaweah River at an elevation of 6,720 feet. The highest and least accessible part of the Sierra Nevada lies in Sequoia National Park to the east of Lodgepole Village. Although the direct distance from Lodgepole Village to Mt. Whitney is only 23 miles, the trail distance is at least 50 miles, and the trail would involve crossing the Great Western Divide, the deep Kern River Valley, and several other major passes and valleys.

During the Pleistocene glacial episodes, glaciers flowed down Marble Fork from the High Sierra and left a number of lateral and recessional moraines in and around Lodgepole Village. Glacial deposits of Tioga age, deposited during the last glacial episode, now cover the central part of the valley. Older moraines of Tahoe age lie at higher elevations along the flanks of the valley for a mile or so west of Lodgepole Village. The road to Wolverton crosses the Tahoe moraine.

The glacial deposits in the Lodgepole area mark the western extent of the glaciers that flowed down the Marble Fork. Further west, the Marble Fork enters a steep V-shaped river valley and descends rapidly to join the Middle Fork of the Kaweah River at the Potwisha Campground, over 4,000 feet below Lodgepole Village.

East of Lodgepole Village, the Marble Fork flows through a typical U-shaped glacial valley with steep walls of granite. The floor of this valley rises gently to the east for two miles and then ends abruptly in a steep granite slope that leads to the Sierra High Country. Tokopah Falls tumbles nearly 1,000 feet down this steep granite slope.

Tokopah Falls – *The trail to Tokopah Falls begins at the Lodgepole Campground; 3.5 mi. RT; moderate.*
The trail to Tokopah Falls goes east along the glaciated valley of the Marble Fork of the Kaweah River. The granite along the valley walls has been grooved and polished by the glaciers. Tokopah Falls lies at the end of the valley. The slope down which the falls tumble is made up of a number of ledges and cliffs that were formed by vertical and sub-horizontal joints in the hard granite. The glaciers that flowed down the valley plucked and quarried the granite along these joints.

The Lodgepole Visitor Center at Lodgepole Village has excellent exhibits on the history, geology and forest life of Sequoia.

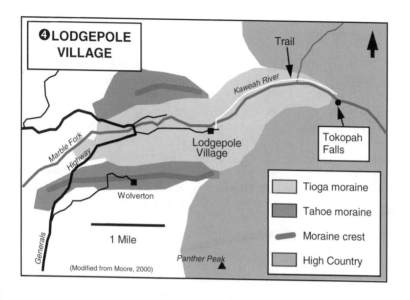

Tokopah Falls cascade down the steep slope that lies at the head of the Marble Fork of the Kaweah River.

❺ *Moro Rock*

From Lodgepole Village to Moro Rock, Generals Highway traverses a heavily forested, rugged, upland plateau that lies at an elevation of about 6,500 feet. To the southwest, this plateau is being rapidly dissected by the Kaweah River and its tributaries. The drop from the edge of the plateau to the Kaweah River valley at the base of the plateau is about 3,000 to 4,000 feet. One of the most spectacular places to see this drop is from the top of Moro Rock, which is situated at the southwest edge of the plateau. From Moro Rock to Hospital Rock, which is at the base of the plateau, there is a drop of 4,000 feet. In a straight line, this distance is two miles. The Generals Highway takes a more leisurely ten miles as it winds its way down the grade from Moro Rock to Hospital Rock.

The steep grade on Generals Highway from the upland plateau to Hospital Rock lies along the contact between two vastly different types of basement rock. Moro Rock and the plateau on the east side of the contact are underlain by granitic rocks of the Sierra Nevada batholith. In contrast, the rocks on the west side of the contact are metamorphic rocks that are part of the large Sequoia Roof Pendant of the Kings Terrane. These rocks are mainly slate, schist, quartzite, and marble. As Generals Highway twists and turns down the grade, it is sometimes in the granitic rocks on the east side of the contact and sometimes in the metamorphic rocks on the west side of the contact. You will see the granite during the trip to Moro Rock. The metamorphic rocks are well exposed at Amphitheater Point and at Buckeye Flat near Hospital Rock.

Forests cover much of the western part of Sequoia National Park. Most of the upland area from Lodgepole Village to Moro Rock was never glaciated, so the deep soil cover was preserved and the area was able to support large trees. Giant Forest, immediately north of Moro Rock, has some of the largest trees on the face of the earth.

Moro Rock - From Lodgepole Village drive S on Generals Highway 4 mi. to Giant Forest Village; turn left on Crescent Meadow Rd.; drive 1.5 mi. to the parking area.

Moro Rock is an imposing granitic dome at the southern edge of Giant Forest. The top of the dome is easily accessible by a 400-step stairway. Because of its sensitive design and the craftsmanship of its construction, this stairway was entered into the National Register of Historic Places in 1978. Moro Rock was formed from a hard sparsely-jointed granitic rock called the Giant Forest Granodiorite. This rock is the oldest unit of the Sequoia Intrusive Suite, and is characterized by its dark color and high content of hornblende and sphene. The sphene occurs as wedge-shaped honey-brown crystals.

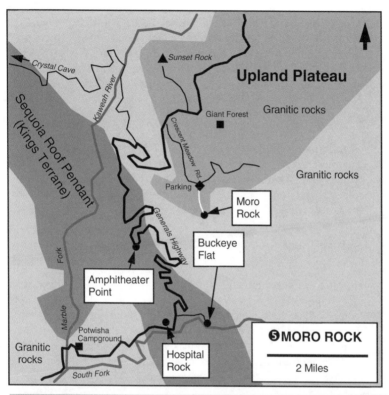

The summit of Moro Rock is easily accessible by a 400-step stairway and path.
The large blocks are slabs of granite that are exfoliating from Moro Rock.

Moro Rock got its rounded shape from exfoliating shells of granodiorite. Like Sentinel Dome in Yosemite, Moro Rock was never covered by glaciers. From the top of Moro Rock, looking east, you can see the Middle Fork of the Kaweah River leading up to the Great Western Divide in the High Country of the Sierra Nevada. To the south are Castle Rocks, and to the southwest the main valley of the Kaweah River.

Amphitheater Point - *On Generals Highway, 5 mi. S of Crescent Meadow Rd.*
There are good exposures of the schist of the Kings Terrane in the roadcuts at Amphitheater Point. The schist is medium brown, foliated, and stands in near-vertical beds. Prior to metamorphism, these beds were sandstone and shale.

Hospital Rock - *On Generals Highway 5 mi. S of Amphitheater Pt.; park at the picnic area; follow the signs to Hospital•Rock, across the Highway from the picnic area.*
Hospital Rock is a large granite boulder that has a flat surface with pictographs painted by Native Americans. The flat surface was formed when the boulder cracked along a joint surface. However, there is one additional problem. The bedrock in the vicinity of Hospital Rock is not granite, but consists of the metamorphic rocks of the Sequoia Roof Pendant. This large granite boulder is therefore not in place, but came here from somewhere else.

Hospital Rock was once part of an exfoliation slab on Moro Rock. When the slab broke loose, it shattered into a number of pieces and the pieces tumbled down the steep slope of the Kaweah River valley as an avalanche. The avalanche left Hospital Rock at this locality. Other granitic boulders from this and other avalanches occur in the Hospital Rock area and clog several of the gulches along Generals Highway from Deer Ridge to Hospital Rock.

Buckeye Flat - *Take the gravel road that goes E from Hospital Rock; drive 2 mi. to the campground; take the trail to the river between campsites 23 and 25.*
At Buckeye Flat, the metamorphic rocks of the Sequoia Roof Pendant are exposed along the Middle Fork of the Kaweah River. These rocks are mainly dark gray slate, phyllite and schist. The rocks are highly deformed, so that the rock layers dip steeply and some are twisted into tight folds. Prior to metamorphism, these rocks were mud and shale. A number of granodiorite boulders are scattered around Buckeye Flat. These boulders arrived here as avalanches from Moro Rock, similar to Hospital Rock.

This photo, from Hospital Rock, shows Moro Rock on the horizon. The large rock at the far end of the parking lot is one of many pieces of granite in this area that have broken from Moro Rock and rolled into this area in large avalanches.

Hospital Rock is a part of an exfoliated slab of granite that tumbled down the steep slope from Moro Rock. Pictographs drawn by Native Americans can be seen on the flat overhanging surface of the broken rock.

❻ *Crystal Cave*

There are approximately 100 caves in Sequoia and Kings Canyon National Parks. Of these, Crystal Cave is the most popular, and the only one that is open to the public. All of these caves occur in beds of marble that lie within roof pendants of the Kings Terrane. The marble is usually interbedded with quartzite and schist. No one knows where the roof pendants of the Kings Terrane came from nor how they got to the southern Sierra. However, we do have some clues as to how and when the rocks in the roof pendants were formed. The marble of the Kings Terrane began its life as limestone in a shallow warm-water sea. Fossils indicate that the limestone was deposited during late Triassic to early Jurassic time. The sea was near a continent that shed sandstones into the sea from time to time. These sandstones now form the beds of quartzite that are interbedded with the marble. The rocks of the Kings Terrane could not have been in the foothills of the southern Sierra when they were formed, since great thickness of volcanic and volcaniclastic rocks were being deposited in the Sierra at that time. It appears likely that the rocks of the Kings Terrane were brought into this area by large transform faults during late Mesozoic or early Tertiary time, probably from the south.

Crystal Cave - *From the Crescent Meadow Rd. turnoff to Moro Rock, go S on Generals Highway 2 mi. to the turnoff to Crystal Cave; turn right and drive 7 mi. on the twisting access road to the parking area; hike 0.5 mi. to the cave entrance. Visit is by guided tour only; seasonal; tickets for tours must be purchased in advance at the Lodgepole or Foothills Visitor Center.*

The bed of marble that is the host for Crystal Cave forms a 700-foot wide ridge between Yucca Creek and Cascade Creek. The cave was formed by water that flowed from Yucca Creek into a pit in the floor of the creek. From the pit, the water flowed through a series of sub-horizontal joints in the marble until it emerged on the other side of the ridge and flowed into Cascade Creek. As the water followed these joints, the weak acid in the water dissolved the marble along the joints to form sub-horizontal passages. From time to time, the water level would drop, and a new set of passages would form at a lower level. When this happened, surface water seeping through the joints in the marble would begin decorating the higher passages with the many limestone forms typical of caves. As a result of this process, Crystal Cave has several large sub-horizontal rooms at different levels, and these rooms have a variety of cave forms, including stalactites, stalagmites, pillars, draperies, flowstone, and shields. The different forms were created by the many ways that water moves across the irregular surfaces of the cave passages.

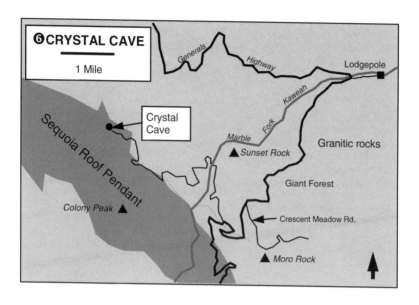

The entrance to Crystal Cave is just above Cascade Creek, which lies at the lower left. This cave is open to the public and is the most popular cave in Sequoia National Park.

GLOSSARY

adit: a horizontal passage from the surface into a mine.

agglomerate: a volcanic rock consisting mainly of rounded volcanic fragments.

air-fall ash: volcanic ash deposited from clouds of ash thrown into the air during a volcanic eruption.

alaskite: a light-colored plutonic rock consisting of feldspar and quartz with few or no mafic minerals.

alluvial fan: a fan-shaped deposit of alluvium bordering the base of a steep slope at the mouth of a canyon.

alluvium: sediment deposited by streams, mainly sand, silt, gravel, and clay.

andesite: a volcanic rock intermediate in composition between basalt and rhyolite.

aplite: a fine-grained light-colored dike rock consisting mainly of quartz and feldspar.

ash: particles of solid volcanic rock thrown into the air from a volcano.

ash flow: a swiftly flowing turbulent gassy cloud of volcanic ash erupted from a volcano; contains ash and pyroclastics in the lower part; travels down the flanks of a volcano like an avalanche.

asthenosphere: the plastic-like layer of the earth below the lithosphere in which isostatic adjustments take place.

basalt: a dark gray or greenish gray fine-grained volcanic rock; forms the upper part of the earth's crust under most of the world's oceans.

batholith: a large mass of granitic rocks, with an outcrop area greater than 40 square miles.

bed: smallest layer of sedimentary rock, usually formed during one depositional event.

biotite: black mica.

boulder: a large rounded piece of rock, usually larger than 10" in diameter.

calcite: a mineral composed of calcium carbonate ($CaCO_3$).

caldera: a large circular or oval basin formed by collapse following a voluminous volcanic eruption.

chemical weathering: the process by which minerals are chemically altered by conditions near the earth's surface.

chert: a fine-grained, hard, silica-rich rock that usually occurs as thin layers or concretions; may be colored white, black, gray, red, green, brown, or yellow.

cinder cone: a cone-shaped accumulation of volcanic cinders erupted from a central vent.

cirque: a bowl-shaped basin at the head of a glacial valley.

clastic: a rock composed mainly of fragments of pre-existing rocks.

clay: very small rock or mineral particles; also refers to a family of hydrous aluminum silicate minerals with sheetlike structure.

claystone: a sedimentary rock consisting of clay minerals, but without the partings of shale.

cleavage: the tendency of a mineral to break along a smooth flat surface.

cobble: a rock fragment, usually rounded, between 2.5 and 10" in diameter.

columnar jointing: prismatic columns in basaltic flows formed as a result of cooling of the lava flow.

conglomerate: a sedimentary rock consisting of boulders, cobbles, and pebbles in a sand matrix.

convection currents: currents within the heavy viscous rocks of the earth's mantle that move the continental and oceanic plates that cover the surface of the earth.

coulée: a flow of viscous lava with a steep front.

crater: a steep-sided, circular depression commonly produced by an explosion.

crust: the outer layer of the earth. *Oceanic crust* is mainly basalt and about five miles thick. *Continental crust* is typically granitic, and about 25 miles thick.

crystal: a homogeneous solid body composed of elements in an orderly arrangement.

deposition: the process of laying down sedimentary rocks.

devitrification: conversion of volcanic glass to a crystalline state.

diabase: a fine-grained igneous rock that has the same chemical composition as gabbro and basalt; differs from basalt in that it was not extruded onto the earth's surface and is finer-grained than gabbro.

dike: a tabular, igneous, intrusive body, discordant with the structure of the country rock.

diorite: a plutonic rock intermediate in composition between granite and gabbro.

dip: the inclination or tilting of beds from the horizontal; the direction that water would flow down a tilted surface.

dolomite: similar to limestone, but contains magnesium in addition to calcium.

dome (lava): a dome-shaped mountain formed by extrusion of lava.

drift mine: a mine opened by a horizontal passage.

earthquake: shaking of the earth due to movement along a fault.

element: a substance that cannot be decomposed into other substances except by radioactive decay.

erosion: the wearing away of the earth's landscape by natural forces of water, waves, ice, or wind.

erratic (glacial): a large rock transported from a distant source by glacial ice.

exfoliation: the process by which concentric shells or plates of a rock are spalled from the surface of the rock.

extrusion: emission of relatively viscous material, commonly lava, onto the ground surface.

extrusive: an igneous rock that has erupted on the surface of the earth.

fault: a fracture in the earth's crust along which the opposite sides have been offset.

fault scarp: a cliff formed by a fault that reaches the earth's surface.

feldspar: a common group of rock-forming minerals found in many igneous, sedimentary and metamorphic rocks. Feldspars are colorless, white, or pink, and consist of aluminum silicates with various quantities of potassium, sodium or calcium. Feldspars rich in potassium are commonly referred to as *orthoclase* or *potassium feldspar* and those rich in sodium and/or calcium are referred to as *plagioclase feldspar*.

fissure: an extensive crack in rock.

formation: a body of rock of large areal extent that has consistent characteristics that allow it to be mapped.

fracture: a break in a rock caused by mechanical failure under stress; includes joints and faults.

fumarole: a small volcanic vent that emits hot vapors.

gabbro: a coarse-grained igneous rock similar in composition to basalt.

geothermal: involving heat from within the earth.

glacier: a large body of natural ice that flows.

glacial, interglacial: a glacial period is a climatic episode in which very large glaciers develop. Glaciers recede during *interglacial* periods. There have been at least four major glacial periods during the last three million years.

glacial polish: a smooth surface on bedrock caused by movement of abrasive-laden glacial ice.

glacial staircase: a glaciated valley whose floor rises in a series of steps.

gneiss: a strongly metamorphosed rock composed of alternating bands of coarse crystals and darker platy or prismatic minerals; indicates a high degree of metamorphism.

granite: a coarse-grained light-colored igneous rock rich in quartz and feldspar, usually contains minor amounts of biotite and hornblende.

granodiorite: similar to granite, but contains less potassium feldspar and more plagioclase feldspar.

gravel: rounded rock fragments, mainly the size of pebbles.

greenstone: a dark green volcanic rock. The green color is due mainly to chlorite and other minerals that were formed by low-grade metamorphism of the volcanic rock.

hanging valley: a tributary glacial valley whose mouth is high above the floor of the main valley.

hornblende: a shiny black mineral common to many igneous and metamorphic rocks; commonly occurs in the rock as columns or elongated blades with striations.

hornfels: a fine-grained metamorphic rock typically formed by heating along the contact of an intrusive body of magma.

hydraulic mining: washing of gold-bearing gravel into sluices by strong jets of water to extract the gold.

ice age: the time during the Pleistocene when large sheets of ice covered many continental areas.

icefield: a glacier of considerable thickness; over 50,000 sq. km in area; forms a continuous cover of ice and snow over a land surface; spreads outward in all directions; not confined by underlying topography.

igneous rocks: rocks that have solidified from molten rock. Includes both volcanic and plutonic rocks. *Volcanic* igneous rocks solidified on or near the earth's surface. *Plutonic* igneous rocks solidified deep in the earth.

interbedded: alternating beds.

intrusive: a rock formed by intrusion of magma into a pre-existing rock.

intrusive suite: a grouping of plutonic rock units that have significant common features and formed from the same parent magma.

isostatic: a condition of equilibrium, similar to floating, of the lithosphere above the mantle.

joint: planar fracture in a rock without displacement; often in parallel sets.

karst: an irregular topography formed on limestone, mainly by solution of the limestone; characterized by pots and sinkholes.
kettles: a depression in glacial drift formed by melting of a block of ice buried in the drift.

lahar: the rocks deposited from a mudflow of pyroclastic material on the flank of a volcano.
lateral moraine: see moraine.
latite: an extrusive igneous rock intermediate in composition between andesite and rhyolite; usually has phenocrysts of plagioclase and potassium feldspar and little or no quartz.
lava: magma that has solidified on the surface.
limestone: sedimentary rock composed largely of the mineral calcite.
lithosphere: the outer rigid part of the earth; usually about 60 miles thick; continental and oceanic crust represent the upper part of the lithosphere.
lode: a mineral deposit consisting of a zone of veins.

M: the Richter scale measurement of the intensity of an earthquake. The scale is logarithmic and ranges from M1 for small earthquakes not generally felt to M8 for "great" earthquakes that cause tremendous damage.
magma: molten rock within the earth; formed by heating of rocks below the earth's surface.
mantle: the part of the earth between the base of the lithosphere and the earth's core at a depth of 1800 miles. The mantle is composed of ultramafic rocks, mainly pyroxene and olivine.
marble: metamorphosed limestone or dolomite, usually recrystallized.
marine sediment: a sedimentary rock deposited in the sea.
mariposite (mineral): a green chrome-bearing mica that contains chromium.
mariposite (rock): a green rock that contains mariposite and veins of fine-grained white quartz.
matrix: fine-grained rock or mineral particles that fill the spaces between the larger grains in sedimentary, igneous, or metamorphic rocks.
medial moraine: see moraine.
melange: a mixture of angular blocks in a clay matrix formed by intense shearing action in a subduction zone.
metamorphic rock: a rock that has been formed from an earlier igneous or sedimentary rock by the action of heat, pressure, or hot water solutions, usually deep within the earth's crust.
metasedimentary: metamorphosed sedimentary rock.
metavolcanic: metamorphosed volcanic rock.
mica: a common potassium-containing mineral found as small shiny flakes in many granitic and metamorphic rocks. *Muscovite* is white mica and *biotite* is black mica.
mineral: a naturally occurring inorganic substance composed of crystalline chemical elements or compounds. Common minerals include quartz, feldspar, hornblende, and pyroxene.

moat: the gullylike depression in a volcanic cone that lies between the dome and the explosion rim.

moraine: a mound of poorly sorted rock debris deposited by a glacier; the debris deposited at the end of a glacier is a *terminal moraine*; the debris deposited along the sides of a glacier is a *lateral moraine*; the debris deposited in the center of a glacier is a *medial moraine*; debris deposited during recession of a glacier is a *recessional moraine*.

moulin: a vertical hole or shaft in a glacier down which water flows.

mudflow: a mass movement of highly fluid muddy debris.

mudstone: indurated mud; lacks the fissility of shale.

MYA: million years ago.

nunatak: an isolated peak of bedrock surrounded by glacial ice.

obsidian: black volcanic glass that formed when lava cooled too quickly to form crystals.

ophiolite: a slab of oceanic crust now on land; typically consists of basalt, pillow basalt, sheeted dikes, gabbro, and serpentine.

orogeny: the process of forming mountains; typically includes folding, faulting, metamorphism, uplift, and erosion.

orthoclase: see feldspar.

outwash: glacial rock debris washed out and deposited beyond the margin of a glacier by its meltwater.

pebbles: small stones, usually rounded.

peridotite: a coarse-grained igneous rock composed mainly of olivine; may also contain other mafic minerals.

petroglyphs: carvings on a rock by early Native Americans.

phenocryst: a large crystal in an igneous rock that is embedded in a finer matrix.

phreatic: a volcanic eruption of steam caused by heating of groundwater.

phyllite: a metamorphic rock intermediate between slate and schist; typically has a milky sheen and crinkly cleavage surfaces.

pillow basalt: basalt that has formed under water; characterized by the formation of pillows.

pinnacles: towers of tufa formed in saline lakes; usually form at spring outlets.

placer gold: gold that occurs in stream and river deposits.

plagioclase: see feldspar.

plate: a discrete segment of the earth's lithosphere that moves as a unit as if it were rigid.

plate tectonics: the concept that the outer part of the earth is composed of a number of plates that move horizontally over geologic time. The plates are moved by convection currents in the earth's mantle. Major geologic features of the earth's crust are formed along plate margins.

plug: relatively small, cylindrical, intrusive body filling a volcanic vent.

pluton: a body of intrusive igneous rock of deep-seated origin.

plutonic rock: see igneous rocks.

porphyritic: an igneous rock with a texture of larger crystals scattered in a finer matrix.

potassium feldspar: see feldspar.

pothole: cylindrical hole drilled into the rock bed of a high-velocity stream by a fixed vortex armed with sand and gravel.

pumice: light colored, light weight volcanic rock of rhyolitic composition; floats on water.

pyroclastic: clastic rock material formed by volcanic explosion.

quartz: a very common mineral composed of silicon dioxide; occurs in igneous, sedimentary, and metamorphic rocks, and also as veins in all of these rocks; typically translucent or glassy; extremely hard and resistant to weathering; a major component of most sandstone.

quartzite: metamorphosed sandstone.

quartz monzonite: similar to granite, but less quartz.

recessional moraine: see moraine.

rhyolite: a volcanic rock with the same composition as granite; commonly light colored or reddish; rich in silicon and poor in iron, magnesium, and calcium.

roche moutonnée: a protruding knob of bedrock glacially eroded to have a gently inclined, striated upstream slope and a steep and rough downstream side.

rock: a hard naturally occurring material composed of one or more minerals. The major rock categories are igneous, sedimentary and metamorphic.

roof pendant: a downward projection of country rock into an igneous intrusion.

sandstone: a sedimentary rock composed of sand-sized particles.

scarp: a steep linear face from a few feet to a few thousand feet high; usually formed by faulting or erosion.

schist: a foliated coarse-grained metamorphic rock that tends to break into platy fragments.

sedimentary basin: a low area of the earth's crust where sediments accumulate.

sedimentary rock: a layered rock composed of consolidated sediments. Common sedimentary rocks include conglomerate, sandstone, siltstone and shale. May also include rocks precipitated from solutions, like salt, and rocks composed of organic remains, like limestone.

sediments: rock fragments transported and deposited mainly by wind or water to form layers of loose rock, such as mud, silt, and sand.

serpentine: a dense, dark-green rock formed by the alteration of ultramafic rocks in the earth's mantle by hot water solutions.

shale: a sedimentary rock consisting largely of clay minerals; finely laminated structure which gives a fissility along which the rock tends to split.

silicate: a mineral containing silica and oxygen along with other elements. Most of the earth's crust consists of minerals that are silicates.

siliceous: consisting largely of silica (SiO_2), especially non-crystalline silica, such as opal.

silt, siltstone: sediment or sedimentary rock composed of grains smaller than sand and bigger than clay.

slate: a fine-grained dark metamorphic rock easily split into thin plates; mainly formed from shale.

sphene: a brown accessory mineral common in granitic rocks ($CaTiSiO_5$).

spreading center: the zone along which plates are pulled apart by upwelling convection currents in the earth's mantle.

stalactite: a conical deposit of calcite hanging from the roof of a cave; formed by dripping water.

stalagmite: a conical deposit of calcite formed on the floor of a cave by water dripping from above.

subduction zone: the zone along which an oceanic plate descends into the earth's mantle.
subsidence: lowering of the earth's crust by tectonic forces within the earth. Sedimentary basins tend to form in these areas.

talus: rock fragments at the base of a steep slope from which they were derived.
terminal moraine: see moraine.
terrace: a flat or gently sloping bench that is the remnant of an old coastline.
terrane: a large rock unit brought to its present location by plate movement; may have traveled thousands of miles; may differ considerably from adjacent terranes; place of origin may be unknown.
thrust fault: a nearly horizontal fault in which the upper plate has been placed over the lower plate.
till: unsorted clay, sand, and boulders deposited by a glacier without reworking by meltwater.
transform fault: a fault that offsets spreading centers.
travertine: calcium carbonate precipitated from water; forms around the mouths of springs, also forms stalactites and stalagmites in limestone caves.
tufa: rock composed mainly of calcium carbonate or silica deposited from water and found at spring sites or along strandlines of saline lakes.
tuff: a general term for all consolidated pyroclasitc rocks.

ultramafic: a rock that contains a superabundance of heavy dark minerals that are rich in magnesium and iron silicates, such as olivine and pyroxene.
unconformity: an erosional surface that separates younger rocks from older rocks; represents a time period without a rock record.
uplift: upward movement of the earth's crust. If the uplifted area is above sea level, the uplifted area will be subjected to erosion and will supply sediments to sedimentary basins.

vein: sheetlike deposit of a mineral or minerals within a fracture in rock.
vent (volcanic): near-vertical, roughly cylindrical opening through which volcanic material is extruded.
vesicle: a small cavity in lava formed by escaping gas.
viscous: state of a fluid with a cohesive, sticky consistency. A viscous fluid flows sluggishly; a nonviscous fluid flows easily.
volcanic: igneous rocks that solidified near the earth's surface, usually fine-grained.
volcaniclastic: a clastic rock composed of volcanic material of any origin.

weathering: the alteration of a rock as a result of conditions at the earth's surface, usually involving reaction with water, atmospheric gasses, and organic products. In humid areas weathering normally results in the formation of soil.
welded tuff: glass-rich, coherent, fragmented volcanic rock, indurated by melting of hot constituents.
winze: a steeply inclined passageway from one mine level to another.

xenolith: an inclusion of foreign rock in granitic rock; often consists of pieces of the intruded rock.

INFORMATION SOURCES

The geologic information in this book comes from many different places, including books, pamphlets, maps, scientific periodicals, guidebooks, and magazine articles. Without these sources, the present book would not have been possible. Some of the sources that I found particularly helpful are described below and are also listed in the section on References Cited. If you wish to delve further into the geology of the Sierra Nevada, you may want to take a look at some of these references.

The California Division of Mines and Geology has a number of publications of special interest. These include bulletins, special reports, maps, and *California Geology*, a bimonthly magazine that has articles about earth sciences in California. The magazine also serves as a guide to the many publications of the California Division of Mines. Bateman and Wahrhaftig (1966) in Bulletin 190 provide a classic technical description of the geology of the Sierra Nevada. In Bulletin 193, Clark (1970) describes the geology, production, and history of gold mining in California. Bulletin 141 (Jenkins, 1948) is a guidebook along Highway 49 and the Mother Lode. This bulletin is no longer available, but an updated version is available in five issues of *California Geology*. Special Report 150, edited by Sherburne (1980), has a number of articles about the earthquakes of the Mammoth Lake area, with emphasis on the earthquake of May 1980. Special Publication 122 (Brooks and Dida, 2000) is a field guide to the metamorphic rocks in the northern Sierra. The *Geologic Map of California* (scale 1:250,000) has a number of different sheets that cover parts of the Sierra. Of particular interest is the Mariposa sheet that covers Yosemite, Mono Lake, and the Long Valley Caldera. Many other detailed geologic quadrangle maps are also available from the Division of Mines and Geology, such as the map of the Fallen Leaf Lake area by Loomis (1983).

The U.S. Geological Survey also has a number of publications and maps dealing with the Sierra Nevada. The early U.S.G.S. report by Russell *Quaternary History of the Mono Valley, California* (1889) is still the classic for the Mono Lake area. Although the original report is no longer available, it was reprinted in 1984 by Artemisia Press, so you can still get a copy. Another classic is Professional Paper 160 by Matthes (1930), which describes the geology of Yosemite Valley. Although this professional paper is no longer available, another book by Matthes, *The*

Incomparable Valley (1950), is available and is a must-read for anyone interested in the geology of Yosemite Valley. Two U.S.G.S. maps worth a good look include the bathymetric map of Lake Tahoe (Gardner et al., 1999), which reveals much about the geology of the Lake Tahoe basin, and the map of Yosemite National Park by Alpha, Wahrhaftig, and Huber (1987), which shows the extent of the Tioga-age glaciers. A great souce of information about the volcanic and earthquake activity in the Mammoth area is the U.S.G.S. website on the Long Valley Caldera (http://quake.wr.usgs.gov/VOLCANOES/LongValley). This website also has links to other information sources within the U.S.G.S.

There are also a number of books dealing with the geology of the Sierra Nevada. For an excellent summary of the geology of the Sierra Nevada, see *Geology of the Sierra Nevada* by Hill (1975). An update of this book is currently in progress by Mary Hill. The books on California Geology by Norris and Webb (1990) and Hardin (1998) both have sections that describe the geology of the Sierra Nevada. Huber (1989) describes the rocks, glaciers, and evolution of the landscape of Yosemite National Park in a well-illustrated book published by the Yosemite Association, *The Geologic Story of Yosemite National Park.* Moore (2000), in *Exploring the Highest Sierra*, gives an account of the history of exploration and mapping in the Sequoia and Kings Canyon National Parks as well as an in-depth review of the rocks and geology of this region. In *Crystal Cave, A Guidebook to the Underground World of Sequoia National Park*, Despain (1994) gives an excellent description of Crystal Cave and its geologic evolution as well as the development of limestone caves in general. Guyton (1998), in *Glaciers of California*, describes many of the glaciers of the Sierra Nevada and includes several geologic field trips. In *Gold, The California Story,* Hill (1999) gives a very readable account of the history of gold in California. Koeppel (1996), in *The California Gold Country,* describes the gold rush history of many of the towns along the Mother Lode. This is a great book to take with you while investigating the geology of the Mother Lode.

A number of geologic field trip guides are available for different parts of the Sierra Nevada. In *Roadside Geology of Northern and Central California*, Alt and Hyndman (2000) describe the geology along the highways of the northern Sierra. In *Geology Underfoot in Death Valley and Owens Valley*, Sharp and Glazner (1997) cover much of the eastern Sierra from Lone Pine to the Mammoth Lakes area. In *The Long Valley Caldera, Mammoth Lakes and Owens Valley Region, Mono County, California*, Baldwin et al. (1999) have compiled a number of papers concerning the Long Valley Caldera along with a field guide to the caldera. In *Geology of the Mono Basin*, Tierney (2000) provides a field guide for Mono Lake and the surrounding area. In *Roadside Geology of the Eastern Sierra Region*, Wilcox (2000) provides a field guide along Highway 395 from Bridgeport to Big Pine, with many interesting side trips. In Y*osemite and the Mother Lode Gold Belt...*, Landefeld and Snow (1990) provide a field guide for Yosemite Valley and for Highway 49 from Mariposa to Coloma. The book also includes a number of technical papers concerning gold mines along the Mother Lode. For a field guide to Yosemite Valley, see *Domes, Cliffs, and Waterfalls* by Jones (1990).

Many local books are also available that cover much of the history and background of specific parts of the the Sierra. *Gold Giants of Grass Valley* by Lescohier (1995) gives the history of the Empire and North Star Mines. *Hydraulicking North Bloomfield and the Malakoff Diggins State Historic Park* by Wyckoff (1999) goes into the fascinating history of hydraulic mining in the North Bloomfield area. *Spanish Hill, Placerville's Mountain of Gold* by Wilson, Blanchard and Lindstrom (1994) gives a detailed historic account of hydraulic mining in the Placerville area.

Many more excellent articles, books, and maps are available, but these should give you a running start.

REFERENCES CITED

Alpha, R.T., Wahrhaftig, C., and Huber, N.K., 1987, *Oblique Map Showing Maximum Extent of 20,000-Year-Old (Tioga) Glaciers, Yosemite National Park, Central Sierra Nevada, California*, U.S. Geological Survey Map I-1885.

Alt, D. and Hyndman, D.W., 2000, *Roadside Geology of Northern and Central California*, Mountain Press Publishing Co., Missoula, Montana, 369 p.

Anonymous, 1957, *Basic Placer Mining*, California Division of Mines and Geology Special Publication 41, 16 p.

Bailey, E.H., 1966, editor, *Geology of Northern California*, California Division of Mines and Geology Bulletin 190, 508 p.

Bailey, R.A., Dalrymple, G.B., and Lanphere, M.A., 1976, *Volcanism, Structure, and Geochronology of the Long Valley Caldera, Mono County, California*, Journal of Geophysical Research, vol. 81, p. 725-743.

Baldwin, J., Hughes, K., Sharp, G.M., Steiner, E., and West, M.D., 1999, editors, *The Long Valley Caldera, Mammoth Lakes and Owens Valley Region, Mono County, California*, South Coast Geological Society Annual Field Trip Guidebook, 374 p.

Bateman, P.C. and Wahrhaftig, C. 1966, *Geology of the Sierra Nevada, in Geology of Northern California*, California Division of Mines and Geology Bulletin 190, p. 107-172. Edited by E.H. Bailey.

Bateman, P.C., 1992, *Pre-Tertiary Bedrock Map of the Mariposa 1^0 by 2^0 Quadrangle, Sierra Nevada, California*, U.S. Geologic Survey Map I-1960, 1:25,000.

Brooks, E.R., 2000, *Geology of a Late Paleozoic Island Arc in the Northern Sierra Terrane, in Field Guide to the Geology and Tectonics of the Northern Sierra Nevada*, California Division of Mines and Geology Special Publication 122, p. 53-110. Edited by E.R. Brooks and L.T. Dida.

Brooks, E.R. and Dida, L.T., 2000, editors, *Field Guide to the Geology and Tectonics of the Northern Sierra Nevada,* California Division of Mines and Geology Special Publication 122, 212 p.

Burnett, J.L., 1993, *The Gold Bug Mine,* California Geology, May/June, p 68-73.

Calkins, F.C. and Roller, J.A., 1985, *Bedrock Geologic Map of Yosemite Valley, Yosemite National Park, California,* U.S. Geological Survey Map I-1639, 1:24,000.

Clark, W.B., 1966, *Economic Mineral Deposits of the Sierra Nevada,* in *Geology of Northern California,* California Division of Mines and Geology Bulletin 190, p. 209-216. Edited by E.H. Bailey.

Clark, W.B., 1970, *Gold Districts of California,* California Division of Mines and Geology Bulletin 193, 186 p.

Clark, W.B., 1987, *Mother Lode Gold Mines, Jackson-Plymouth District, Amador County,* California Geology, March, p. 51-58.

Cleveland, G.B., 1961, *Economic Geology of the Long Valley Diatomaceous Earth Deposit, Mono County, California,* California Division of Mines and Geology Map Sheet 1.

Collum, K.R., 1990, *The Geology of the Carson Hill Gold Mine, Calaveras County, California,* Pacific Section, American Association of Petroleum Geologists Book GB68, p. 157-164. Edited by L.A. Landefeld and G.G. Snow.

Curtis, G.H., 1954, *Mode of Origin of Pyroclastic Debris in the Mehrten Formation of the Sierra Nevada,* University of California Publications in Geological Sciences, V. 29, no. 9, p. 453-502.

Despain, J., 1994, *Crystal Cave, A Guidebook to the Underground World of Sequoia National Park,* Sequoia Natural History Association, Three Rivers, California, 49 p.

Fink, J.H., 1985, *Geometry of Silicic Dikes Beneath the Inyo Domes, California,* Journal of Geophysical Research, v. 90, no. B13, p. 11,127-11,133.

Fiske, R.S. and Tobisch, O.T., 1994, *Middle Cretaceous Ash-flow Tuff and Caldera-collapse Deposit in the Minarets Caldera, East-central Sierra Nevada, California,* Geological Society of America Bulletin, v., 106, p. 582-593.

Gardner, J.V., Dartnell, P., Mayer, L.A., Hughes Clark, J.E., 1999, *Bathymetry and Selected Perspective Views of Lake Tahoe, California and Nevada,* U.S. Geological Survey Water-Resources Investigation Report 99-4043, 2 sheets.

Geologic Map of California, Mariposa Sheet, 1967, California Division of Mines and Geology, 1:250,000.

Guyton, B., 1998, *Glaciers of California,* California Natural History Guides, 59, University of California Press, Berkeley, 197 p.

Hardin, D.R., 1998, *California Geology,* Prentice Hall, Inc., New Jersey, 479 p.

Hill, M., 1975, *Geology of the Sierra Nevada,* University of California Press, Berkeley, 232 p.

Hill, M., 1999, *Gold, The California Story,* University of California Press, Berkeley, 306 p.

Huber, N.K. and Rinehart, C.D., 1965, *Geologic Map of the Devils Postpile Quadrangle, Sierra Nevada, California,* U.S. Geological Survey Map GQ-437, 1:62,500.

Huber, N.K., 1989, *The Geologic Story of Yosemite National Park,* Yosemite Association, Yosemite National Park, California, 64 p. Previously published as U.S. Geological Survey Bulletin 1595.

Huber, N.K., Bateman, P.C., and Wahrhaftig, C., 1989, *Geologic Map of Yosemite National Park and Vicinity, California,* U.S. Geological Survey Map I-1874, 1:125,000.

Jenkins, O.P., 1948, editor, *Geologic Guidebook along Highway 49 - Sierran Gold Belt; the Mother Lode Country,* California Division of Mines and Geology Bulletin 141, 164 p. Updated in five issues of California Geology, 1997: March/April, May/June, July/August, September/October, November/December.

Jenkins, O.P., 1964, *Geology of Placer Deposits,* California Division of Mines and Geology Special Publication 34, 27 p.

Jennings, C.W., 1977, *Geologic Map of California,* California Division of Mines and Geology Geologic Data Map No. 2, 1:750,000.

Jones, W.R., 1990, *Domes, Cliffs, and Waterfalls: A Brief Geology of Yosemite Valley,* Yosemite Association, 18 p.

Kistler, R.W., 1966, *Geologic Map of the Mono Craters Quadrangle, Mono and Tuolumne Counties, California,* U.S. Geological Survey Map GQ-492, 1:62,500.

Knopf, 1929, *The Mother Lode System of California,* U.S. Geological Survey Professional Paper 157, 88 p.

Koeppel, E.H., 1996, *The California Gold Country,* Malakoff & Co. Publishing, California, 235 p.

Kortick, B., Raper, J., Wolfman, M., and Yarbrough, N., 1985, *The Foothills Counties Mining Handbook,* California Division of Mines and Geology Special Publication 86, 106 p.

Landefeld, L.A. and Snow, G.G., 1990, editors, *Yosemite and the Mother Lode Gold Belt: Geology, Tectonics, and the Evolution of Hydrothermal Fluids in the Sierra Nevada of California,* Pacific Section of the American Association of Petroleum Geologists GB 68, 200 p.

Landefeld, L.A., 1990, *The Geology of the Mother Lode Gold Belt, Foothills Metamorphic Belt, Sierra Nevada, California,* in *Yosemite and the Mother Lode Gold Belt: Geology, Tectonics, and the Evolution of Hydrothermal Fluids in the Sierra Nevada of California,* Pacific Section of the American Association of Petroleum Geologists GB 68, p. 117-124. Edited by Landefeld, L.A. and Snow, G.G.

Lescohier, R., 1995, *Gold Giants of Grass Valley, History of the Empire and Grass Valley Mines,* Empire Mine Park Association, Grass Valley.

Lindgren, W., 1911, *The Tertiary Gravels of the Sierra Nevada,* U.S. Geological Survey Professional Paper 73, 226 p.

Loomis, A., 1983, *Geology of the Fallen Leaf Lake 15-Minute Quadrangle, El Dorado County, California,* California Division of Mines and Geology Map Sheet 32, 1:62,500.

Matthes, F.E., 1930, *Geologic History of the Yosemite Valley,* U.S. Geological Survey Professional Paper 160, 137 p.

Matthes, F.E., 1950, *The Incomparable Valley,* University of California Press, Berkeley, 160 p.

Mayfield, J.D. and Day, H.W., 2000, *Ultramafic Rocks in the Feather River Belt, Northern Sierra Nevada,* in *Field Guide to the Geology and Tectonics of the Northern Sierra Nevada, California,* California Division of Mines and Geology Special Publication 122, p. 1-15. Edited by E.R. Brooks and L.T. Dida.

Miller, C.D., Mullineaux, D.R., Crandell, D.R., and Bailey, R.A., 1982, *Potential Hazards from Future Volcanic Eruptions in the Long Valley-Mono Lake Area, East-Central California and Southwest Nevada - A Preliminary Assessment,* U.S. Geologic Survey Circular 877.

Moore, J.G., 2000, *Exploring the Highest Sierra,* Stanford University Press, Stanford, California, 427 p.

Norris, R.M. and Webb, R.W., 1990, *Geology of California,* John Wiley & Sons, Inc., New York, 541 p.

Peck, D.L., Wahrhaftig, C., and Clark, L.D., 1966, *Field Trip, Yosemite Valley and Sierra Nevada Batholith, California* in *Geology of Northern California,* California Division of Mines and Geology Bulletin 190, p. 487-502. Edited by E.H. Bailey.

Russell, I.C., 1889, *Quaternary History of the Mono Valley, California,* U.S. Geological Survey Eighth Annual Report, p. 267-394. Reprinted in 1984 by Artemisia Press, Lee Vining, California.

Schaffer, J.P., 1998, *The Tahoe Sierra, A Natural History Guide to 112 Hikes in the Northern Sierra,* Wilderness Press, Berkeley, 402 p.

Schiffman, P. and Wagner, D.L., 1992, *Field Guide to the Geology and Metamorphism of the Franciscan Complex and Western Metamorphic Belt of Northern California,* California Division of Mines and Geology Special Publication 114, 78 p.

Schlappi, J., 1987, *Placerville, A Walk Through the Gold Rush,* Gold Rush California Publications, Placerville, 16 p.

Sharp, R.P., 1968, *Sherwin Till-Bishop Tuff Geological Relationships, Sierra Nevada, California,* Geological Society of America Bulletin, v. 79, p. 351-364.

Sharp, R.P., 1976, *Southern California, Field Guide,* Kendall/Hunt Publishing Company, Dubuque, Iowa, 208 p.

Sharp, R.P. and Glazner, A.F., 1997, *Geology Underfoot in Death Valley and Owens Valley,* Mountain Press Publishing Co., Missoula, Montana, 321 p.

Sharp, G.M., West, M.D. and Steiner, E., 1999, *Long Valley Caldera, Mammoth Lakes, and Northern Owens Valley Field Trip Road Log,* in *The Long Valley Caldera, Mammoth Lakes and Owens Valley Region, Mono County, California,* South Coast Geological Society Annual Field Trip Guidebook, p 1-53. Edited by J. Baldwin, K. Hughes, G.M. Sharp, E. Steiner, and M.D. West.

Sherburne, R.W., 1980, *Mammoth Lakes, California, Earthquakes of May 1980,* California Division of Mines and Geology Special Report 150, 141 p.

Silva, M., 1986, *Placer Gold Recovery Methods,* California Division of Mines and Geology Special Publication 87, 32 p.

Slemmons, D.B., 1966, *Cenozoic Volcanism of the Central Sierra Nevada, California,* in *Geology of Northern California,* California Division of Mines and Geology Bulletin 190, p. 199-208. Edited by E.H. Bailey.

Sloan, D. and Wagner, D.L., editors, 1991, *Geologic Excursions in Northern California: San Francisco to the Sierra Nevada,* California Division of Mines and Geology Special Publication 109, 130 p.

Sorey, M., Evans, B., Kennedy, M, Rogie, J., and Cook, A., 1999, *Magmatic Gas Emissions from Mammoth Mountain,* California Geology, September/October, p 4-16.

Sorey, M, Hill, D, and McConnell, V.S., 2000, *Scientific Drilling in Long Valley Caldera, California - An Update,* California Geology, January/February, p 4-11.

Tierney, T., 2000, *Geology of the Mono Basin,* Mono Lake Committee Field Guide Series, Kutsavi Press, Lee Vining, California, 73 p.

Wahrhaftig, C. and Birman, J.H., 1965, *The Quaternary of the Pacific Mountain System in California,* in *The Quaternary of the United States – A Review Volume for the VII Congress of the International Association for Quaternary Research,* Princeton University Press, p. 299-340. Edited by H.E. Wright Jr. and D.G. Frey.

Wakabayashi, J. and Sawyer, T.L., 2000, *Neotectonics of the Sierra Nevada and the Sierra Nevada-Basin and Range Transition, California, with Field Trip Stop Descriptions for the Northeastern Sierra Nevada,* in *Field Guide to the Geology and Tectonic of the Northern Sierra Nevada,* California Division of Mines and Geology Special Publication 122, p. 173-212. Edited by E.R. Brooks and L.T. Dida.

Whitney, S., 1979, *A Sierra Club Naturalist's Guide to the Sierra Nevada,* Sierra Club Books, San Francisco, 526 p.

Wilcox, L.A., 2000, *Roadside Geology of the Eastern Sierra Region,* Kutsavi Press, Lee Vining, California, 42 p.

Wilson, N., Blanchard, C., and Lindstrom, S., 1994, *Spanish Hill, Placerville's Mountain of Gold,* Susan Lindstrom, Truckee, 29 p.

Wyckoff, R.M. 1999, *Hydraulicking North Bloomfield and the Malakoff Diggins State Historic Park,* Wyckoff, Nevada City, 52 p.

Yeend, W.E., 1974, *Gold Bearing Gravel of the Ancestral Yuba River, Sierra Nevada, California,* U.S. Geological Survey Professional Paper 772, 44p.

ACKNOWLEDGMENTS

This book is based on the work of hundreds of geologists that have studied and written about the many different aspects of the geology of the Sierra Nevada for over one hundred years. I would like to acknowledge all of these geologists at this time. However, the list would be impossibly long, and would still be incomplete. Several of the books and reports that I found particularly helpful are described under Information Sources.

Thanks to the many people that were involved in the completion of this book. I wish to especially thank Doris Sloan, with the University of California, Berkeley, for her detailed review of the manuscript and James Moore with the U.S. Geological Survey for his review and comments concerning the trip to Sequoia and Kings Canyon National Parks. Also, thanks to Lucie Marshall for editing of the manuscript, to Wendy Blakeway for her help in the design and printing, and to Bob Lorentzen of Bored Feet Press for his interest, consultation, and encouragement during all phases of the preparation of the book.

INDEX

The author in the Sierra, 1949. If you have been on the geologic trips you will know where the photo was taken, what the ledge is made of, and how the ledge was formed. Thanks to the good sense of the Park Service, this ringside seat to Yosemite Valley is no longer accessible. (Photo by Stan Kahan.)

ABOUT THE AUTHOR

Ted Konigsmark is a native Californian and a geologist. He is now retired and living with his wife, Marilyn, in northern California on the eastern edge of the Pacific plate. During his school years in Los Angeles, he spent as much time as possible hiking, climbing, caving, prospecting, and working in the Sierra Nevada. After graduating from U.C.L.A. and receiving a Ph.D. degree in geology from Princeton, he spent most of his career with Exxon, where his primary interest was in geologic evaluation of frontier exploration areas worldwide. Within Exxon, he held various supervisory and management positions, including manager of geologic research and Chief Geologist for Exxon's international oil exploration activities. Since retiring, Ted has taken many different groups on geologic walks and field trips in northern California and has written geologic field guides for the non-geologist.

Other books by the author include:
Geologic Trips, Sea Ranch, GeoPress, 1994
Geologic Trips, San Francisco and the Bay Area, GeoPress, 1998